Christianity, Climate Change, and Sustainab
engagement with the issue of climate change a
production. Spencer, White, and Vroblesky
cal, economic, and theological thinking that
imperative and distinctive. Their practical conclusions explore what can be
done at the personal, community, national, and international levels to ensure
that future generations will have the resources necessary for life. Firmly rooted
in the good news of the Christian faith, this is, above all, a constructive and
hopeful book that offers a realistic vision of what the future could and should
look like.

Endorsements of *Christianity, Climate Change, and Sustainable Living*

"This is the book I have been waiting for. It tackles some of the biggest challenges of our time—environmental and social sustainability—as integrated
parts of the same whole, and convincingly demonstrates what my generation
is rediscovering—that our individual and collective well-being is an inherently
relational issue. Accurate, accessible, thoughtful, practical, and thoroughly
hopeful, here is a guide for understanding these confusing times and living
faithfully together as part of God's inbreaking kingdom. When students and
peers ask me to recommend a resource on climate change and the Christian
faith, this will be it."

—**Ben Lowe,** author of *Green Revolution* and Co-Coordinator of Renewal:
Students Caring for Creation

"Are we on the brink of a global climate calamity that will require significant
social and economic change to avert disaster, or is climate change merely a
mirage? How can Christians find clear, honest and reliable scientific answers
to these questions, plus the biblical insight to respond faithfully, authentically and creatively to the challenge of our time? Delve into Spencer, White,
and Vroblesky's *Christianity, Climate Change, and Sustainable Living* and you
will find they are trustworthy guides on an intellectual and spiritual journey,
pointing us to a destination of solutions and soul-formation.

—**Dr. Chris Elisara,** Founder and Executive Director of the Creation Care
Study Program (CCSP), Belize, New Zealand/Samoa, and the United States

"Few works on the religion and ecology nexus cover the territory so compre-
hensively as *Christianity, Climate Change, and Sustainable Living* does. The
book is thoroughly researched and clearly written, and it speaks with equal
authority on the scientific and theological dimensions of the modern ecological crisis. I highly recommend it to anyone curious about a Christian perspective on ecological issues."

—**Gary Gardner,** Senior Researcher, Worldwatch Institute

"*Christianity, Climate Change, and Sustainable Living,* which tackles the complexity and breadth of issues related to climate change, is extremely well written. The authors present the issue of climate change for the Christian community in a way that has great theological depth and reflects a biblical hope. The authors also present an extremely careful and nuanced case in terms of the science of climate change. And, finally, they are unusually evenhanded in their portrayal of the international discussions and policy options that are now before the world. It is rare to find a book that can cover this breadth with such high levels of understanding across the topic, and still be clear and honest, yet hopeful!"

—**Dr. Janel Curry,** Dean for Research and Scholarship, Gary and Henrietta Byker Chair in Christian Perspectives on Political, Social, and Economic Thought, Calvin College, and coauthor of *Community on Land: Community, Ecology, and the Public Interest*

"What Spencer, White, and Vroblesky have crafted in *Christianity, Climate Change, and Sustainable Living* is not only what has been sorely missed in the Christian community, but it also represents a magnificent, balanced, and comprehensive overview from which all of society should benefit. The authors have done a masterful job weaving scientific evidence, socio-economics, stewardship, and practicalities together, presenting a winsome perspective (even a 'vision'!) that should assuage much of the skepticism and concern that has often held many back from doing anything at all. Their balanced approach should help nurture in us a desire to understand that we not only can, but must work together to ensure that we enjoy our planet with sustainable living and ecosystems for the century ahead of us—'creation care'!"

—**Dr. Alan E. Strong,** Consultant-Senior Scientist, National Oceanic Atmospheric Administration's Coral Reef Watch, Silver Spring, Maryland

"This book was a pleasure and delight to read. If you only read one book on climate change and sustainability, then make it this one! Spencer, White, and Vroblesky have succeeded in making this difficult and sometimes arcane scientific subject understandable. In plain language they carry the reader through a web of technical and theoretical detail. They are always sure-footed, explaining the relevant facts in everyday terms.

But the most singular feature of this book is not just that it clearly explains climate change. There are many works that will do that for you. It is its biblical focus on sustainable living. In eight concise chapters, the authors cover the nature of the problem of sustainability from a biblical perspective. They go beyond a brief introduction to an in-depth analysis of the biblical rationale for caring for the earth. Humans, they emphasize, aren't just a part of the environment; we function in our uniquely moral role within it. If we care for people, then we must also care for God's good earth.

Here is a vision for sustainable living for today, as well as for tomorrow. And here is clear guide to the practice of sustainable living today. The authors identify the key needs in a Christian response to the pressing needs around us. There is a need for social, economic, and environmental solutions to the complex problems we face. The authors have brought together both the theological and scientific resources necessary to explore these complex and interlinked problems. This book will make an excellent study guide for any group or individual."

—**Dr. John Wood,** Professor of Biology and Environmental Studies, The King's University College, Alberta, Canada, and Academic Dean, Au Sable Institute of Environmental Studies

"Jesus warned against discerning signs in the sky while neglecting to understand the signs of the times. Today, we have reversed the process and must recover an understanding of where our climate is heading. *Christianity, Climate Change, and Sustainable Living* provides a salutary warning accompanied by a healthy redirection. This book is a necessary tool to enable those living today to be ready for life tomorrow."

—**Rev. Dr. Clive Calver,** Senior Pastor, Walnut Hill Community Church, former President of World Relief, and signatory to "Climate Change: An Evangelical Call to Action"

This book is endorsed by:

The Au Sable Institute of Environmental Studies,
A Rocha: Christians in Conservation,
The Jubilee Centre,
Creation Care Study Program,
Plant With Purpose (an initiative of Floresta),
The Faraday Institute for Science and Religion.

Dedicated to our children:
Ellen, Jonathan, Sarah, Mark, and Sarah,
who will inherit the consequences of our actions.

Nick Spencer and Bob White

Dedicated to a shopkeeper in Croatia and others like
him who remind us that we share a common home.

Ginny Vroblesky

CHRISTIANITY, CLIMATE CHANGE, and SUSTAINABLE LIVING

NICK SPENCER, ROBERT WHITE, AND VIRGINIA VROBLESKY

Christianity, Climate Change, and Sustainable Living
by Nick Spencer, Robert White, and Virginia Vroblesky
North American Edition published by Hendrickson Publishers Marketing, LLC
P.O. Box 3473
Peabody, Massachusetts 01961-3473

This North American edition is a revision of *Christianity, Climate Change and Sustainable Living*, by Nick Spencer and Robert White. First published in Great Britain in 2007. Society for Promoting Christian Knowledge, 36 Causton Street, London SW1P 4ST. Copyright © the Jubilee Centre and the Faraday Institute 2007.

ISBN 978-1-59856-229-3

Printed in the United States of America

First Printing — November 2009

Cover Photo Credit: Keith Davis Young, 2008. Used with permission.

This book was printed with a FSC (Forest Stewardship Council) chain-of-custody certified printer. Highest environmental and social standards are applied to forest conservation, responsible management, and community level benefits for people near the forests that provide this paper and in the printing facilities that turned the paper into this book. The cover is 100% PCW recycled stock, and the text is printed on 30% post consumer waste paper, using only soy or vegetable content inks.

Library of Congress Cataloging-in-Publication Data

Spencer, Nick, 1973–
    Christianity, climate change, and sustainable living / Nick Spencer, Robert White, and Virginia Vroblesky.
      p. cm.
    Originally published: London : SPCK, 2007.
    Includes bibliographical references and indexes.
    ISBN 978-1-59856-229-3 (alk. paper)
    1. Nature—Religious aspects—Christianity. 2. Environmental protection—Religious aspects—Christianity. 3. Sustainable development—Religious aspects—Christianity. I. White, Robert. II. Vrobleski, Ginny, 1946– III. Title.
    BR115.N3S64 2009
    261.8′8—dc22
                    2009019492

CONTENTS

LIST OF ILLUSTRATIONS

Figures

Table

Boxes

FOREWORD

CLIMATE CHANGE HAS BECOME a topic of immense interest and concern; information about it pervades the media for much of the time. How damaging is it likely to be? In an article I wrote for the *Guardian* newspaper I described it as a "weapon of mass destruction." I was accused at the time of abandoning scientific accuracy for "hype" and exaggeration. But since then, many political leaders and others have accepted that the scale of damage due to climate change warrants such a description. Sir David King, the UK government's chief scientist, has described it as worse than terrorism. In fact, it is now generally recognized as probably the *biggest and most challenging issue* that the world faces this century.

Climate change is a *global issue* because nearly everybody in the world is contributing to it and everybody will be affected by it. But more than that, it is not only humans that will suffer. The rate of change will be such that much of the world's flora and fauna will be unable to adapt. All ecosystems will be affected, and millions of species will be lost for ever. There is, therefore, an inescapable requirement that all governments, institutions, industries, and individuals address the problem and contribute to its solution.

Climate change began in the 1970s and 1980s as a *scientific issue,* then only of interest to the scientific community. In 1988, at an international ministerial meeting in Canada, it began to be recognized as a serious *political issue;* in that year also the Intergovernmental Panel on Climate Change (IPCC) began its work. International interest and concern was consolidated in 1992 with the signing of the Climate Convention by all the world's nations at the Earth Summit in Rio de Janeiro.

Since then, as the ramifications of climate change have been understood, the realization has come home that its implications intrude into all parts of our lives and behaviour. That is a difficult message to get over. We all prefer to compartmentalize the problem or look for a single silver bullet from new technology or imaginative economics to provide the solution. But there are no silver bullets. All disciplines within natural and social sciences must be brought to bear upon it. But more than that, choices have to be made by individuals and societies, choices that need to be influenced by new attitudes and paradigm shifts—changes in hearts and minds. At its core, therefore, climate change is also a *spiritual and religious issue*.

With regard to action to combat climate change, Christians have a particular contribution to make. Of all the world's religions, Christianity emphasizes most strongly the connections between the material and the spiritual. Caring for creation was the first task given to Adam and Eve in the Genesis creation story. God could not have demonstrated more forcibly his commitment to his creation than to send his son, Jesus, to become part of it. In our stewardship of creation, we are called to follow Jesus especially in his concern for the poor and disadvantaged who will be the most adversely affected by climate change.

There are books about the science of climate change, books about the theology of climate change, and books about what can be done about it. The value of this book is that it covers all three—science, theology, and praxis—working through the fundamentals of each and the connections between them. The excitement of putting all three together is evident as the realization emerges of a whole that adds up to a great deal more than the sum of its parts. A total vision is presented that goes far beyond the boundaries of the problem of climate change, to a future in which sustainability in all its aspects is paramount and where the whole global human community no longer rapes the Earth and its resources, but lives harmoniously and comfortably with it. To begin to realize this vision is a matter of great urgency. Don't read this book if you are not prepared for its challenge!

Sir John Houghton, FRS

PREFACE TO THE NORTH AMERICAN EDITION

A FRIEND AND I WANDERED into a tiny shop on a back street in Dubrovnik, Croatia on a rainy day. Surprisingly, the shopkeeper began the conversation with a comment about climate change. He seemed to think that as an American I had a responsibility towards his country thousands of miles from my home. "What am I supposed to do? You tell me," he said. At the time, the best I could offer was "plant some trees." He was adamant that this would not be enough. So, I promised that I would do what I could with no idea what that might be. A few months later, the Jubilee Centre provided the opportunity to fulfill that promise by asking me to help "North Americanize" their book, *Christianity, Climate Change, and Sustainable Living,* published in England.

Originally, we planned to substitute North American examples, from both the United States and Canada, for British ones, find comparable statistics, and revise word spellings. However, it soon became clear that not only were the countries different culturally but they also had different starting points in relationship to climate change. Simple statements from the British edition such as "we have more free time than any other generation" proved false for the United States, one of the most overworked nations in the world. Thus, while the outline of the two versions is the same, there is quite a bit of difference in the details, especially in chapters 2 and 7, which examine how we use energy, the connections with our lifestyles and well-being, and steps we can take to bring a vision of sustainable living into reality.

The United Kingdom has been studying ways to meet its obligations under the Kyoto Protocol and other international agreements for years. "Sustainability" is a goal already included in government reports and incorporated into proposed actions. The British edition built upon these studies. Chapter 7 examined specific national policy proposals to determine which might reflect the principles of sustainability established in chapter 6.

At the beginning of this project, the US government had resisted serious engagement on climate change at a national level. As a result, there were no studies similar to those in the United Kingdom. "Sustainability" did not have the same meaning in the two countries. Canada, one of the first nations to participate in the Kyoto Protocol, was backing away from its agreements. From outside North America it appeared that we were taking no positive action on climate change. But in truth there are positive things happening, as the examples in Chapter 7 demonstrate.

It is our hope that readers of the North American edition will grasp the power they have to make a difference. We change from the "bottom up" rather than "top down," meaning that leadership, especially on environmental issues, begins with citizen groups and local and state governments, and grows until the federal government finally acts. This "fermenting" has been happening across North America fed by the unprecedented melting of Artic summer sea ice in 2007, the series of reports issued by the Intergovernmental Panel on Climate Change, and rising energy costs.

The election of Barack Obama as President in 2008 set the stage for a new emphasis on climate change and renewable energy. The President's early agenda included weaning the United States off of its dependence on foreign oil, limiting greenhouse gas emissions, and becoming an international leader on climate change. In 2009 efforts to resolve the economic crisis were tied to creating a new economy based on renewable energy and efficiency. The determination to confront climate change was also reflected in the appointment of America's first special envoy on Climate Change (Department of State) and the filling of key posts within the administration with scientists and energy and climate experts. Internationally, the growing concern for climate change created opportunities for cooperation that were not possible when the UK version of this book was published.

While these recent political changes bring a renewed sense of hope and opportunity, transferring a vision of a sustainable world into reality may be harder than we realize. It certainly will continue to require our active participation and engagement. The details of our lives, as people or nations, may change, but principles such as those highlighted in chapters 3–5 are firm and provide solid guidelines for evaluating actions, technological opportunities, and national and international policies. May we become like the men of Issachar in the Old Testament who "understood the times" with knowledge of what we as people should do.[1]

Ginny Vroblesky
Annapolis, Maryland 2009

PREFACE

THOSE WHO HAVE FOLLOWED the work of the Jubilee Centre will not be surprised to see this book. Since 1983 the Centre has conducted research into a biblical vision for society and how that vision might inform our response to a wide range of contemporary concerns. This has taken us into Sunday trading, credit and debt, international peace-building, criminal justice, care for the elderly, asylum and immigration, and numerous other fields. Our goal has always been the big picture—a rival to the "isms" of our age. Two years ago we drew together the conclusions of our work to date in *Jubilee Manifesto: A Framework, Agenda and Strategy for Christian Social Reform*, edited by Michael Schluter and John Ashcroft (Inter-Varsity Press UK).

Our contention is that our well-being, both individually and collectively, is an essentially relational issue. Relationships is the big idea.

Applied to the problem of climate change, we have sought in the research culminating in this book to explore the relational roots of this well known problem. If perfect love of God and neighbor is the pinnacle of the good life (Matt 22:34–40), disordered relationship—both with God and others—is the root of every evil. Our failure to love God means we fail to care for the things God cares about, including the Earth (e.g., Ps 65). As physical creatures, we possess an intimate solidarity with the Earth; our well-being is tied to its. Failure to care for creation, therefore, is also symptomatic of a breakdown of neighbor-love, whether he or she be near or far, in space or in time.

But ours is a message of hope: the cross and empty tomb announce that we *can* live a rich relational life.

As we think relationally, some things begin to matter more and others less. Family-time, local community life, and a shared day off, for example, assume a new urgency, and our former habits of gratuitous consumption start to look rather shallow. In short, our argument is that relational priorities and environmental priorities are pulling in the same direction. Societies that actively pursue relational well-being will tread more lightly upon the Earth.

The social vision in which this book is rooted possesses an elegant unity, which we at the Jubilee Centre have come to expect of biblical wisdom. We commend this book to Christians and non-Christians alike as a uniquely holistic response to the problem of climate change.

J. W. Fletcher
Director
Jubilee Centre

Acknowledgements

W ARE GRATEFUL TO Shirley Decker-Lucke of Hendrickson Publishers for catching the vision for a North American version and to Doug Brown (World Vision Canada) for his challenge to include Canada. This added greatly to the richness of this version. Ben Lowe and Dr. John Wood provided valuable insights into student and congregational climate actions. Kim Schaefer kindly reviewed and prioritized home energy actions and green building techniques. A host of friends graciously endured debates about key issues: Jim and Doreen Skillen (Center for Public Justice), Bill and Gail Herald, Dan Smith, Barbara Mearns, Ann Donaldson, Mary Connell, Susan Beall, Elliot Abhau, Carole Alexander, Nina Martin, Marilyn Clemes, and Trish Wynkoop. A special thank you to Tom Rowley, A Rocha USA, for his encouragement to tackle this project, and to Ben Campbell, Conservation International, for his challenge to include biodiversity, willingness to read and comment on drafts, and valuable assistance in finding good sources of data. Of course, while we hope they are pleased with the product, any errors remain solely our responsibility.

Ginny Vroblesky

THIS BOOK IS A work of diverse hands, and the authors would like to register their debt of thanks to many people.

The Jubilee Centre and the John Ray Initiative conceived and nurtured both this book and the project to increase awareness of and to promote an appropriate Christian response to global climate change, of which it is but the first phase. Mike Schluter and John Ashcroft provided helpful comments on many drafts, as did Jason Fletcher. Jason deserves our particular thanks for the way in which he managed the project, organized meetings, kept minutes, and dealt with administrative issues with his customary diligence and thoughtfulness. The book benefited from regular meetings with a climatologists, meteorologists, geologists, biogeochemists, ocean-ographers, and others responsible for collating and analyzing the data over the last thirty years leaves no serious reason for doubt: warming of the climate system is unequivocal.[3] No assessment of any other scientific topic has been so thoroughly researched and reviewed.[4] Climate change is real, serious and potentially "apocalyptic."

In one respect, however, apocalypse is a misleading word to use of climate change. Although the term is now used as shorthand for "(a vision of) massive and traumatic devastation," it originally meant a "revelation" or "uncovering" of what was always there. An apocalypse was an exposing of reality, a literal and metaphorical opening of eyes to what had always been standing before us.

Whatever else climate change is, it is not this kind of apocalypse. As we discuss in chapter 1, the Earth's temperature has fluctuated significantly over its history but the changes of the last 50 years have been unprecedented. Scientists have not been revealing an age-old phenomenon for the first time, but rather detecting a new and unparalleled change in the Earth's atmospheric composition, which is being driven by an equally unparalleled change in human behavior.

This link—between a global temperature rise and meteorological extremes on the one hand and everyday human behavior on the other—is now well understood and is slowly becoming public knowledge. Melting glaciers, rising sea levels, and extreme weather patterns can be traced back to our massive, growing, and unsustainable use of fossil fuels. This, in turn, is driven in large part by the way we travel, use energy at home, and consume goods and services.

What is less widely recognized is that two of those same human activities are damaging our lives in the West in subtle but insidious ways. Life is good for most people living in high-income countries. Longer lives, better health, more money, more goods, longer holidays: most of us have never had it so good.

Except that we don't think so. Social studies consistently show that, in spite of the genuine and inspiring material progress of recent years, we are no happier than our parents' or grandparents' generations, and in some instances rather less happy. Levels of well-being have flatlined, and we are only just beginning to understand why.

There are, of course, numerous reasons for such a complex and far-reaching trend, but, as we discuss in chapter 2, the way we travel and consume are foremost among them. Our long commutes and overstretched families; our "clone" towns, ghost villages, and yearning after "community"; our consumer culture and searching after meaning and purpose: these may seem to have little to do with climate change, but, in reality, they are the other side of the same coin. Environmental and social sustainability cannot be understood or addressed separately.

Environmental issues, however, tend to be more newsworthy. Every now and then some disaster grabs the headlines and our attention for a few days. Oil spills are the classic example. We remember the *Torrey Canyon* pouring 38 million gallons of oil into the sea near Land's End in 1967, or the *Exxon Valdez,* running aground in the Prince William Sound in Alaska in 1989, releasing nearly 11 million gallons of crude oil, or the Iraqi leadership deliberately releasing an estimated 240 to 460 million gallons of crude oil from tankers into the Persian Gulf during the Gulf War, and our response is instant and visceral.

We applaud the selfless work of volunteers scraping oil off bedraggled sea birds. We make a donation, "doing our bit" to help out. We hold forth about how "they" ought to do something to regulate oil companies or shipping owners. And then, unaware of any connection, we telephone our local takeaway, order a meal, drive round to collect it, and flick through the latest travel brochure, while planning our vacation break as we wait for our food.

Oil spills are headline-catchers and rightly provoke indignation. But it is our ordinary, everyday lifestyle that will, in the long term, do more to damage the environment. Counter-intuitive as it may at first seem, our lifestyles are likely to lead, albeit indirectly, to far more suffering than all the oil spills of the last 50 years put together. As we outline in Part 1, by driving, flying, consuming goods, and using energy in the way we do, we pump carbon dioxide into the atmosphere, which is causing the rapid climate changes that threaten not only to desecrate landscapes more severely than the oil spills we bemoan but also to kill many more human beings and other species than even the worst tanker disaster.

How long we can continue living in this way is a moot question. It is misleading to treat the apocalyptic language that surrounds the climate change debate as literal. The world will not end, burn, be destroyed, or laid waste if we do not stop what we are doing. It

Overall, Part 2 seeks first to convince Christians that they have
a duty to respond to the situation outlined in Part 1, second to
expose them to a vision that will guide and inspire their response,
and third to detail a series of biblically-rooted measures that should
inform and shape that response.

Part 3 goes on to explore what form that response should take
today. Chapter 6 sketches out what sustainable living might look
like in the light of the material discussed in Part 2. It outlines eight
principles derived from that material and then paints a picture of
a modern Western society that takes those principles seriously. In
the fashion of Isaiah, it is a picture intended to guide and inspire
our response.

Chapter 7 then explains how that vision might be realized. It
details five levels of response: personal, communal, governmental, technological, and international. The first and second are
self-explanatory: how should we, as individual Christians and as
congregations, live our lives according to the responsibilities and
principles outlined in earlier chapters. The third looks at the challenges and opportunities of policies at various levels of government,
specifically those which might best fulfill the criteria implicit in
those principles.

The fourth remains in the area of policies, looking not at those
intended to change public behavior but at those intended to shape
our technological response. Should we "go nuclear"? Are renewables an option? Is energy efficiency the answer? In doing so it
addresses the question that so often lies just beneath the surface of
this debate: is there a techno-fix to all this?

The fifth, on international responses, returns to the truly global
nature of the problem, acknowledging that the only genuine solution will be international and exploring the best options currently
available. It emphasizes, however, that for something to happen
everywhere, it needs first to happen somewhere, and thus refocuses
the question on the reader. However long a journey, it always starts
with a single step. Are we, as Christians, prepared to *do* something
about this?

Chapter 8 draws together these strands and returns, from the
details of chapter 7, to the big picture. In doing so, it seeks to remind us that while personal and political action is critical, if we lose
sight of the big story of God making "all things new" in Christ, we

are liable to lose direction, impetus, and, ultimately, hope. "What counts," as Paul reminded the church in Galatia, "is a new creation" (Gal 6:15).

For those interested in further study, a study guide to this book is available as an additional resource. Our five-part Bible study focuses on the relational roots for a holistic response to the questions, "why and how should we care about the environment?" This guide can be found in *.pdf format at the Hendrickson Publishers website (www.hendrickson.com) on the *Christianity, Climate Change, and Sustainable Living* book detail page and may be downloaded without further cost.

Climate change consciousness has never been higher. Former US Vice-President Al Gore won an Oscar and the Nobel Peace Prize for his film *An Inconvenient Truth,* which deals solely with global climate change. Hardly a day passes without some climate-related story making the headlines. Often they are tales of gloom: the Arctic ice is melting, rainforests disappearing, the world's coral reefs dying. Opinion formers, like the environmentalist James Lovelock, proclaim that we are fast approaching or have passed a "tipping point." The damage is done. There is no way back.[8]

Yet the Christian response should not be one of despair but of hope. Hope because God has created a world that he judges to be "very good" (Gen 1:31). Hope because, in spite of repeated human failings, he has promised never to give up on his creation (Gen 8:21). Hope because he has proclaimed how "I am doing a new thing!" (Isa 43:19). Hope because he came himself, in human form, to "make all things new" (Rev 21:5). And hope because it is not yet too late for us to participate in that new thing; that today's looming environmental crisis may yet prove to be the call that summons us back towards a recognition that "the earth is the Lord's, and everything in it" (Ps 24:1).

Ten years ago Bartholomew I, Ecumenical Patriarch of Constantinople, said: "for humans to cause species to become extinct and to destroy the biological diversity of God's creation . . . to degrade the integrity of the Earth by causing changes in its climate . . . those are sins." More recently, Richard Chartres, the Bishop of London, captured headlines with the same point: "making selfish choices such as flying on holiday or buying a large car are a symptom of sin."[9]

Such sentiments sound strange, even old-fashioned to many today. Nevertheless, we need to be alert to the far-reaching consequences of sin if we wish to address them. If Christians are serious about participating in God's new creation and responding to the challenges of climate change and sustainable living, we need to be realistic about the sinful desires and actions that have gotten the world into the mess it is in today.

But God's new creation and his invitation to participate in it is *good* news. Realism about the reality and pervasiveness of sin must be balanced by properly rooted Christian hope: the hope that Jesus' life, death, and resurrection inaugurate the kingdom of God that marks the end of sin, that his kingdom is breaking into our lives even today, and that it will be fully realized when Jesus returns.

It is our hope that this book will encourage people to understand the problem, to envision the solution, and to take their responsibilities seriously. We hope that it will equip them to re-examine their values, shape their lives and communities accordingly, and to influence their leaders and policy makers as appropriate. And we hope that it will convince readers that responding to the challenges of climate change and sustainable living are not optional extras, still less distractions from the gospel, but are an integral part of the call to love God with all our heart and soul and mind, and to love our neighbors as ourselves.

Ultimately, it is our individual *choices* that collectively will determine the future of this planet. In the words of Sir Martin Rees, President of The Royal Society: "Even in a cosmic or a geological time-perspective, there's something unique about our century: for the first time in its history, our entire planet's fate depends on human actions and human choices."[10]

Part 1

THE NATURE OF THE PROBLEM

1

GLOBAL WARMING, LOCAL CAUSES

THE WORLD IS GETTING warmer. Eleven of the 12 warmest years on record in the whole world have occurred in the past 12 years.[1] Sea levels are rising, ice sheets and glaciers are melting, and between 15 and 37 percent of all species that live on land could be committed to extinction in the next 50 years as a result of climate change.[2]

What is causing this? Is it due to human activity or just natural variability in the Earth's climate? And does it matter anyway? In this chapter we explore the facts about global warming and its causes. We show that unsustainable consumption of the Earth's resources lie at its root. Finally, we discuss why global climate change and sustainable lifestyles are so important to a world facing other major problems such as water quality, sanitation, famine, and flood.

The Greenhouse Effect

The temperature at the surface of the Earth, averaged across the entire globe over a long period such as a decade, is about 14°C. It is this equable temperature that makes human life possible: if it were less than 0°C the entire surface would be an icy waste; if more than 100°C all the water would have boiled off. The surface temperature is dependent on the balance between incoming energy from the Sun, which acts to warm the surface of the Earth and the atmosphere, and the outgoing loss into space of infrared radiation from the Earth and atmosphere, which acts to cool the Earth. There must be a long-term balance between the incoming and outgoing radiation, otherwise the Earth would inexorably heat up or cool down.

The amount of energy reaching the Earth from the Sun is huge. At the equator, when the Sun is directly overhead, every square meter receives 1370 watts. At higher latitudes the Earth's surface is oblique to the Sun, so the average input from the Sun across the whole globe is rather less, averaging 342 watts for every square meter (this is equivalent to the heat output from nearly 4,000 electric fires in an area the size of a soccer field). It would rapidly get extremely hot if this energy were not reradiated back to space. However, there is one important change when the energy is reradiated. The incoming energy from the Sun is largely in the form of visible sunlight. But energy emitted from the soil and plants at the surface of the Earth is in the form of invisible infrared radiation. Infrared radiation carries just as much heat, as anyone who has used an infrared electric cook top will know, but is invisible to the human eye.

The significance of the change in the form of energy (technically known as the wavelength) between incoming and outgoing radiation is that it allows the greenhouse effect to operate. The gases in the atmosphere that envelops the Earth act as a blanket to keep the surface of the Earth warmer than it would otherwise be because they absorb infrared radiation but are transparent to the Sun's incoming radiation. The glass in a greenhouse has similar properties, which is why this phenomenon is known as the greenhouse effect (Figure 1.1). The glass in a greenhouse transmits almost unimpeded the incoming Sun's radiation in the visible spectrum, which warms up the soil and plants inside. The soil and vegetation then emit that energy in the infrared spectrum. Since the glass absorbs infrared radiation and re-emits some of it back into the greenhouse, the inside of the greenhouse warms up.[3]

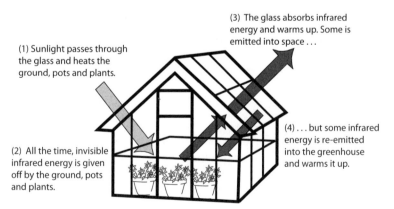

(1) Sunlight passes through the glass and heats the ground, pots and plants.

(2) All the time, invisible infrared energy is given off by the ground, pots and plants.

(3) The glass absorbs infrared energy and warms up. Some is emitted into space . . .

(4) . . . but some infrared energy is re-emitted into the greenhouse and warms it up.

Figure 1.1 Illustration of the greenhouse effect

This effect was first recognized by the French scientist Jean-Baptiste Fourier in 1827. Around 1860 a British scientist, John Tyndall, measured the absorption of infrared radiation by water vapor and carbon dioxide and suggested that a decrease in the greenhouse effect of carbon dioxide might be a cause of the ice ages. In 1896 a Swedish scientist, Svante Arrhenius, calculated the effect on the global temperature of increasing the concentration of carbon dioxide: he estimated that doubling the atmospheric concentration would increase the global average temperature from 5 to 6°C. That value is not so far from our present estimates using complex computer simulations.[4] So the basic mechanism of the greenhouse effect has been understood for over a century, and it was worked out, appropriately enough, by international scientists.

The atmospheric gases that cause the greenhouse effect are not static like the glass in a greenhouse, so a more rigorous explanation is required to show why an increase in the concentration of greenhouse gases causes an increase in global temperature. As more greenhouse gases are pumped into the atmosphere, they thicken the layer of the blanketing gases. So just as adding an extra blanket or duvet on your bed increases the temperature in it, so too does thickening the layer of greenhouse gases cause an increase in the temperature at the surface of the Earth.

The bulk of the atmosphere is made up of oxygen and nitrogen which neither absorb nor emit thermal radiation. So if they were the only constituents of the atmosphere, there would be no greenhouse effect and the average temperature at the Earth's surface would be about 30°C lower, or -16°C, well below the freezing point of water, and the Earth would be uninhabitable. Fortunately, the atmosphere contains several natural greenhouse gases, including water vapor (which condenses to form clouds), carbon dioxide, ozone, methane, and nitrous oxide. Of these, the largest greenhouse effect comes from water vapor, which accounts for about two-thirds of the greenhouse warming. Carbon dioxide is the next most important greenhouse gas. Human activity is not directly increasing the water vapor content of the atmosphere, but, as we shall see later in this chapter, humankind is dramatically and very rapidly increasing the carbon dioxide content: carbon dioxide has already increased by about 38 percent (equivalent to 600,000 million tons of carbon) in the last two centuries. It is this that is beginning to cause a major change in the global climate systems, with an overall increase in surface temperature—global warming.

Greenhouse Gases

Which greenhouse gases should we worry about most? Since the concentration of water vapor in the atmosphere is mainly controlled by the temperature of the sea, in the long term human activity will affect the amount of water vapor indirectly, via global warming. This may amplify the global temperature increase by as much as 40 to 50 percent. However, over the last 200 years it is the increase in carbon dioxide which has contributed most to enhancing the greenhouse warming effect of the atmosphere, accounting for about 70 percent of the warming since pre-industrial times.

Most of the increases in greenhouse gases have been caused by burning fossil fuels (coal, oil, and gas). A smaller, but significant component is due to the destruction of forests, particularly in tropical areas. A surprisingly large percentage of the effect of global greenhouse gases—18 percent, which is more than the entire transport sector—comes from the 1.7 billion cows in the world: each animal releases about 500 liters of methane per day, which accounts for more than one-third of all methane caused ultimately by human activity.[5]

The long-term impact of a greenhouse gas on climate depends on two main factors: how long it stays in the atmosphere (the longer it stays, the more time it has to exert a warming influence), and its potency in absorbing outgoing infrared radiation. If the extra gases emitted by human activity into the atmosphere were all absorbed back immediately into the oceans, or into vegetation (which are the two main repositories of carbon on Earth), then there would be little long-term effect. But unfortunately the Earth reacts on a much longer timescale. Carbon dioxide stays in the atmosphere for up to 100 years, while some gases, like nitrous oxide, remain in the atmosphere for much longer than that.

In order to compare the capacity of different greenhouse gases to cause global warming, a useful measure is to calculate the future warming effect of the gas emitted today over the next 100 years, compared to the effect of the same amount of carbon dioxide. This is known as its Global Warming Potential (GWP). Current estimates are listed in Table 1.1: they vary from 1 for carbon dioxide (by definition) to more than 22,000 for sulphur hexafluoride. What this means is that even tiny amounts of sulphur hexafluoride would have enormous long-term effects on the climate. Fortunately, concentrations of sulphur hexafluoride are extremely low, so we do not have to worry about it as much as we do about carbon dioxide.

Gas	Main sources	Effective lifetime in atmosphere	Global Warming Potential
Carbon dioxide	Fossil-fuel burning, land-use changes	Approx. 100 years	1
Methane	Natural gas extraction, agriculture	12 years	23
Nitrous oxide	Fossil-fuel burning, fertilizer use	114 years	296
Chlorofluorocarbons	Refrigerators, aerosol sprays	100–200 years	7,300
Sulphur hexafluoride	Industrial processes	>1,000 years	22,200

Table 1.1 Global warming potentials of 1 kg of a range of greenhouse gases relative to 1 kg of carbon dioxide for a time horizon of 100 years

Source: Data from IPCC 2001: Climate Change 2001: The Scientific Basis, Contribution of Working Group 1 to the Third Assessment Report of the Intergovernmental Panel on Climate Change, J. T. Houghton et al., eds. (Cambridge University Press, 2001).

Although carbon dioxide is the least potent of the greenhouse gases, it is the most important one produced by human activity. This is because such huge quantities are being pumped into the atmosphere. Burning fossil fuels accounts for three-quarters of the total carbon dioxide production by humans, while land-use change (mainly deforestation) accounts for most of the remainder.

The main contributor to global warming over the next 100 years, accounting for nearly two-thirds of the effect, will be carbon dioxide (Figure 1.2, see next page). Methane, although much smaller in quantity, makes up for that with its greater global warming potential, producing about one-quarter of the total warming. Nitrous oxide accounts for about 10 percent, with all other greenhouse gases adding up to only a minor contribution. In order to provide a simple measure of the effect of all greenhouse gases in the atmosphere, sometimes they are lumped together into a single measure known as the carbon dioxide equivalent. When targets for concentrations in the atmosphere of greenhouse gases are set, for example by governments, it is important to be clear as to whether they refer to carbon dioxide alone or to carbon dioxide equivalent. If the target is set as a carbon dioxide equivalent, then of course the actual carbon dioxide concentration target will be lower.

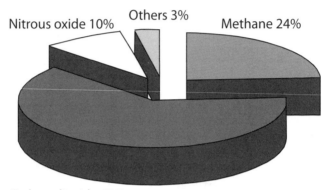

Nitrous oxide 10%   Others 3%   Methane 24%

Carbon dioxide 63%

Figure 1.2 Effect of current greenhouse gas emissions as contributors to global warming over the next 100 years

Source: Data from IPCC 2001: *Climate Change 2001: The Scientific Basis,* Contribution of Working Group 1 to the Third Assessment Report of the Intergovernmental Panel on Climate Change, J. T. Houghton et al., eds. (Cambridge University Press, 2001).

Before we move to contemporary issues, it is relevant to see how the Earth's temperature has changed in the past, and how this might compare with what we are likely to face in the coming decades.

Climate on Earth: The Geological Perspective

One of the most striking features of the Earth is that it has maintained a surface temperature favorable to life throughout almost all its history. This certainly requires temperatures to remain above the freezing point of water, 0°C, and lower than its boiling point of 100°C, although for life as we know it to thrive the temperatures need to remain in a rather narrower band toward the bottom end of this range.

Scientists date the Earth at 4,566 million years old, a figure considered accurate to within a few million years.[6] Scientists find evidence from carbon isotopes indicate forms of life existing on Earth around 3,850 million years ago. Life was present on Earth almost as soon as the environmental conditions made it possible. Microbial fossils have been found from 3,500 million years ago. The Earth has maintained a temperature suitable for life ever since then, despite the solar output of the Sun having risen by about 30 percent over the same period. No other planet has fared this well. For example, our nearest planetary neighbor, Venus, has an atmosphere with a massive amount of carbon dioxide as its main constituent. This results in a surface temperature of about 500°C—red hot. Venus is much nearer the Sun than is the Earth, and the huge greenhouse effect of the carbon dioxide caused all the water vapor to boil off into space.

On a longer timescale there are well-documented cyclic changes in the global temperature of the Earth of about 9°C. The primary cause of these temperature changes is regular variations in the orbit of the Earth about the Sun, coupled with precession of the tilted axis of rotation of the Earth relative to the plane of its orbit around the Sun. Regular climatic cycles have been identified ranging from 19,000 years to 413,000 years in duration. The effects of these cyclic global temperature changes can be recognized from sediments dating back more than 30 million years.[7]

Global temperature changes of up to 9°C through the last eight ice ages have been estimated by sampling the isotopic composition of bubbles of air trapped in ice recovered from cores drilled through thick ice accumulations in continental interiors such as the Greenland and the Antarctic ice caps. In Greenland an ice core has penetrated back to 123,000-years-old ice, while in the Antarctic a core has reached ice some 740,000 years old.[8]

Average temperature changes of about 5°C are sufficient to switch between an ice age and an interglacial temperate period such as we now enjoy. The last ice age, which ended some 12,000 years ago, was about 9°C colder than at present. In the absence of any human influence, the next ice age resulting from orbital changes would not be expected for some 50,000 years. So we certainly cannot rely on these long-term changes either to explain the current rapid global temperature change or to counteract the effects of human-induced temperature increases. Another striking feature of the climate changes found between ice ages is that they are much greater than those caused by solar radiation changes resulting from variations in the Earth's orbit around the Sun. They also require enhancement of the temperature changes, possibly by interactions between the concentration of carbon dioxide and biological processes.

All of these changes are on far longer timescales than that of human civilization. Scientists find evidence of communities of humans existing since 8000–9000 BC. But the large temperature variations evidenced, for example, by the ice ages and intervening temperate periods serve to demonstrate that the Earth can, and

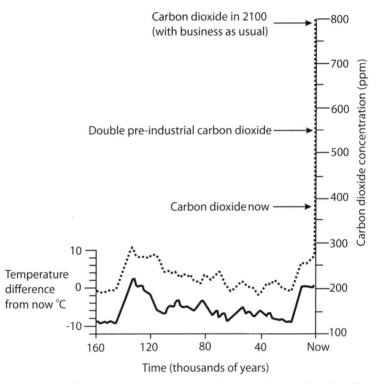

Figure 1.3 Variations of polar temperature and atmospheric carbon dioxide concentrations

Continuous line: variations of polar temperature. Broken line: atmospheric carbon dioxide concentrations.

Source: From D. Raynaud et al., "The Ice Core Record of Greenhouse Gases," Science 259 (1993), pp. 926–34.

frequently has, experienced major changes in temperature and climate. We should expect the same to happen again if we dramatically change the volume of greenhouse gases in the atmosphere. The only difference now is that humans are causing climatic change at a speed unmatched in the history of humankind on Earth—and it is that very rapidity which is the crux of the problem, since we now live on an extremely densely settled Earth with limited room for maneuver without megascale human disruption. And we are starting our experiment in global warming from an interglacial warm period where the Earth's climate is already far warmer than the average over the past 600,000 years.

Climate on Earth: The Historical Perspective

The last ice age began about 120,000 years ago and ended some 12,000 years ago. Analysis of air trapped in bubbles in an ice core from the Antarctic over the past 160,000 years shows a close correlation between carbon dioxide concentrations and surface temperatures inferred from the concentration of deuterium, a heavy form of hydrogen (Figure 1.3). Perhaps the most striking point to be made from Figure 1.3 is the unprecedented rapid rise of carbon dioxide in the last two centuries: on the timescale of the graph they appear to be rising almost vertically, just as is the global population shown in Figure 1.4 (see next page). Already carbon dioxide concentrations are 38 percent higher than in pre-industrial times and are higher than at any time in the past 650,000 years. Yet they are certain to rise much higher in the future, as we discuss later.

Carbon dioxide content in the atmosphere was constant at about 280 ppm (parts per million) for 800 years (and probably more) prior to 1800. The carbon dioxide level in 2007 was 384 ppm and is currently increasing at nearly 2 ppm every year.[9] Other greenhouse gases show similar increases since pre-industrial times: methane has more than doubled; nitrous oxide up by 15 percent; and ozone in the lower atmosphere up by about 3 percent.

If we zoom in on the last century and a half, the period of most intense industrial activity by humankind, sufficient direct measurements of surface temperatures are available to make meaningful

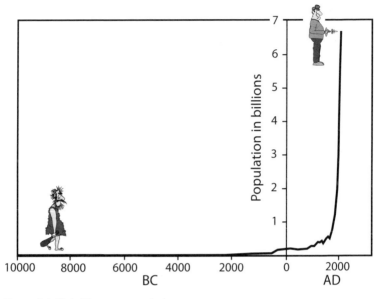

Figure 1.4 Global human population

Source: Values from United Nations Population Division.

global averages (Figure 1.5). Although there is considerable year-to-year variability in the annual-mean global temperature, a clear upward trend can be seen. Some of the variability is natural within the complex climatic system of the Earth; other is due to additional consequences of human activity. For example, atmospheric pollution caused by sulphates and particles, either from burning fossil fuels or from biomass burning, actually causes global cooling because the particles reflect some of the incoming solar radiation before it reaches the surface of the Earth. Similarly, the destruction of natural vegetation and of forests causes the land surface to be more reflective, again leading to a small overall cooling effect. But the addition of greenhouse gases far outweighs any cooling effects. Ironically, as industry in the high-income nations is quite properly required to clean up its emissions, the overall warming trend becomes still more dominant. Pollution from the expansion of heavy industry in the decades following 1940 probably caused the dip in temperatures shown in Figure 1.5. The resumption of an upward trend in temperature from 1970 accompanied the implementation of clean air legislation.

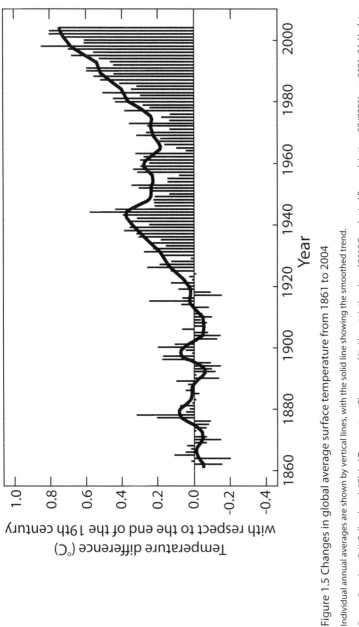

Figure 1.5 Changes in global average surface temperature from 1861 to 2004

Individual annual averages are shown by vertical lines, with the solid line showing the smoothed trend.

Source: Based on C. K. Folland et al., "Global Temperature Change and Its Uncertainties since 1861," *Geophysical Research Letters*, 28 (2001), pp. 2621–24. Updates available from the Meteorological Office Hadley Centre Web site at www.metoffice.gov.uk/climatechange/.

The take-home message is that global warming is real and unequivocal, and is caused by humans.[10] Not only was 1998 the hottest year on record globally, but strikingly, each of the first eight months set temperature records for that month. Successive years, such as 2006 and 2007 have vied for the record. Although the average mean temperature increase so far is less than 1ºC, it is sufficient to be noticeable in North America by changes in flowering times for plants and the earlier arrival of spring migratory birds.[11] In our polar regions, such as Alaska and northern Canada, the effects are more dramatic. Over the past 50 years, temperatures have risen by twice the global average. Arctic sea ice has been melting inexorably over the last 30 years, losing about 1 million square kilometers, or 2.5 percent of its area per decade. Summer sea ice was predicted to disappear by the end of this century,[12] but this may occur much faster as seen by the unprecedented melting during 2007.

Effects have reached far beyond retreating glaciers, polar bears, and walrus to disturbing human lives, ecosystems, and the economy. For example, approximately 184 native Alaskan communities are at risk from flooding and erosion due to melting sea ice. Some villages that have been settled for hundreds of years will have to relocate or slip into the sea. Forty-five percent of Yukon River salmon have become infected by a parasite not known prior to 1985, a result of 10ºF warming of the river. Four million acres of mature forest were destroyed by the world's largest outbreak of the spruce bark beetle. Warmer temperatures allowed the beetle to mature faster, survive the winter, and devastate trees already stressed by heat and drought.[13] Canada's forests, which cover almost half of the landmass and are a crucial part of their economy, are expected to be the most vulnerable in the world. It is estimated that 80 percent of the mature pine forest of British Columbia is predicted to be destroyed by the mountain pine beetle over the next decade, again the result of warmer winters.[14]

Can we be sure about the scientific story presented above? The answer is that we can be very sure: it is based on work by many thousands of scientists from numerous different disciplines and over 100 different countries. No assessments on any other scientific topic have been so thoroughly researched and reviewed as has the question of global climate, through the Intergovernmental Panel on Climate Change (IPCC). In June 2005, 11 leading academies of science from around the world (the G8 plus India, China, and Brazil) issued a statement unequivocally endorsing the IPCC's conclusions.[15] The IPCC was set up in 1989, and since then has issued four authoritative assessments of climate change, in 1990, 1995, 2001, and 2007,[16] together with many other specialist reports. As each report has been issued the evidence for climate change has become stronger, and the models for expected future changes better constrained with reduced uncertainty.

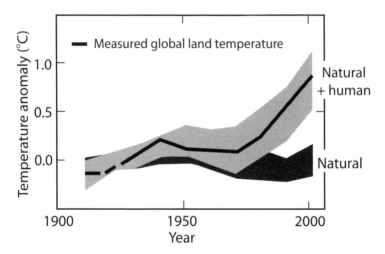

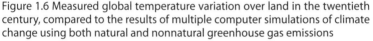

Figure 1.6 Measured global temperature variation over land in the twentieth century, compared to the results of multiple computer simulations of climate change using both natural and nonnatural greenhouse gas emissions

Dark-shaded band: results of multiple computer simulations of climate change using only natural factors. Light-shaded band: simulations using both natural and nonnatural greenhouse gas emissions.

Source: Redrawn from IPCC, *Climate Change 2007: The Physical Science Basis, Summary for Policymakers* (2007).

Could the observed climate change be due to natural variations rather than human causes? Figure 1.6 shows the observed global temperature variation over land in the twentieth century (solid black line), compared to the results of numerous computer simulations of climate change using only natural factors (dark-shaded band). It is clear that although the natural factors produce small variations in global temperature, they do not begin to match the observed temperature increase. However, once the effects of greenhouse gas emissions by humans are included (light-shaded band) the predictions match the observations well.

Unfortunately, there are strong vested interests that have spent tens of millions of dollars on spreading misinformation about the climate change issue.[17] They first denied the scientific evidence and have argued more recently that its impacts will not be large, that we can "wait and see" and that in any case we can always "fix" the problem if it turns out to be substantial. The scientific evidence cannot support such arguments.

Future Projections

The response of the surface temperature of the Earth to a sudden injection of greenhouse gases into the atmosphere is complex and generally sluggish. This means that even if humans completely stopped emitting any more greenhouse gases with immediate effect, we have already committed the Earth system to wide-ranging changes in climatic patterns, to overall global warming and to sea level rises, which will take centuries to work through. This is partly due to the long periods over which greenhouse gases remain in the atmosphere before being removed into the oceans or the vegetation and soils of the land (Table 1.1 [see p. 15]), and partly due to the huge thermal inertia of the ocean systems. It takes several decades to transfer heat from a warmed atmosphere to the surface waters of the oceans, and then many centuries to spread that heat through the deep ocean circulation system. To add to this complexity there are likely to be a wide variety of biological, chemical, and physical feedback systems that may dampen, or more likely amplify, the global warming effect of the greenhouse gases. For example, once large regions of snow-covered areas or glaciers decrease as a result of melting caused by global warming, the highly reflective snow cover is replaced by less reflective land, so less energy is reflected directly back to space. This leads to yet further global warming.

More difficult to predict are changes to the oceanic circulation system that might be caused by the global warming. For example, the Gulf Stream (or, as it is more properly called, the North Atlantic Drift), carries a huge amount of heat northwards, keeping the British Isles much warmer than, for example, those parts of western Canada at the same latitudes. If it were not for this ocean circulation, the average temperatures in the UK would be from 3 to 5°C cooler. Could global warming cause the North Atlantic Drift to switch off, as has happened more than once in the past? In principle it certainly could because several mechanisms associated with global warming could cause a decrease in density of the surface waters in the northern North Atlantic, which could then reduce and eventually switch off the ocean circulation system.[18] Fortunately for those in the United Kingdom, current models for realistic future scenarios suggest that although the Atlantic Ocean circulation is likely to decrease in strength from 15 to 25 percent by 2100, the decrease in heat carried by the Gulf Stream would be more than offset by direct greenhouse warming.

Despite the complexities of climate models, and the range of uncertainty in some of the feedback mechanisms, continuing improvements in the power of computers used for modeling, plus continual improvements in the long-term measurements relevant to global warming collected worldwide is leading to improved confidence in the predictions. More difficult to quantify is the likely future behavior of humanity. At one extreme is the "business as usual" response, which ignores any possible damaging effects of our behavior on others; at the other extreme would be the unrealistic scenario of a complete stop in the production of greenhouse gases. In the middle lie a range of realistic responses, such as attempting to stabilize global atmospheric carbon dioxide equivalent between 450 to 550 ppm; this represents a range of 400 to 490 ppm in terms of carbon dioxide alone, the lower limit of which will be reached within a decade. The upper limit would cause an estimated average temperature increase of about 3 °C,[19] although the uncertainties in predictions of the future and of feedback mechanisms that might operate mean that the temperature might still rise much more, even in this optimistic case. But at least there would be a limit to it, and appropriate adaptation procedures for the worst effects could be put in place.

The IPCC spent a considerable amount of effort outlining a range of realistic scenarios,[20] and in the following sections we will use their results to outline likely consequences of our behavior. What emerges is that our behavior thus far has already led to irrevocable effects on the Earth's climate.

Fossil Fuel Supply

There are still enormous quantities of fossil fuels available underground, and unless concerted action is taken to reduce or mitigate the effects of their consumption the likelihood is that we will keep extracting them. To date we have used about half the easily available oil. Although experts disagree whether or not we have already passed "peak oil," the year with the highest rate of oil extraction, they are all agreed that, even if we haven't done so already, we shall do so within a decade or thereabouts.[21] After that the rate of oil production will decrease. We have used less than half of the natural gas and there are massive amounts of coal still available (see Figure 1.7). On present rates of usage, oil would last another 40 years, gas well into the latter third of the twenty-first century and coal for another 150 to 250 years.[22] This is without even considering unconventional sources of oil such as oil sands and oil shales, or the production of coal bed methane gas. These latter are all much "dirtier" than oil and would have a much greater greenhouse effect on the Earth than burning oil. Coal already accounts for 40 percent of all electricity generated worldwide, and is the biggest single source. In China, in 2008, a new 1 Gwatt low-technology coal-fired power station was commissioned every five days, so it is likely that coal will remain a widely used fuel through the twenty-first century.

It is not only the consumption of fossil fuels, but the extraction process as well, that contributes to climate change, both through the destruction of natural carbon sinks and direct greenhouse gas emissions. Alberta Canada's oil sands contain the second largest source of petroleum in the world, behind those of Saudi Arabia. The open pit mining technique required to extract this resource destroys the boreal forest and natural muskeg of the area. While oil companies are required to restore the land after mining, they are not required to restore it as forest, so much has been converted to pasture. It is estimated that for every barrel of oil produced from the oil sands, 80 kg of greenhouse gases are emitted into the atmosphere, three times the amount resulting from the production of oil by conventional methods. Yet this resource has the potential to satisfy the world's oil needs for several hundred years. Alberta's oil sand production has become Canada's fastest growing source of carbon dioxide emissions.[23]

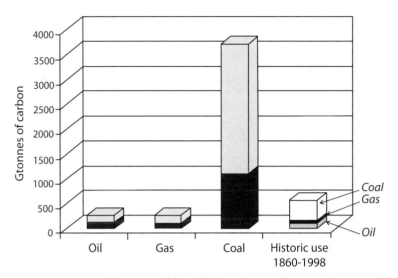

Figure 1.7 Estimated reserves of fossil fuels with upper limits and amount of fossil fuel burnt to date

Estimated reserves of fossil fuels with upper limits (light shading). Right-most column shows amount of fossil fuel burnt to date.

Note: Figures are from www.ipcc.ch and do not include unconventional sources of oil such as oil sands and oil shales or unconventional gas resources such as coal bed methane, which would treble the total oil and gas resources that could potentially be extracted. For approximate conversion from tonnes of carbon to tonnes of carbon dioxide, multiply these figures by 3.2.

There is little doubt that if humanity chose to do so, it could readily burn all this fossil fuel and overheat the planet. It does not make much difference whether we slow the rate of usage or use it as fast as possible: the end result would be much the same because the main greenhouse gases remain in the atmosphere for around a century. The problem is not one of insufficient supply of fuel: rather it is whether we choose to use it at all, or at least whether we choose to allow the carbon dioxide that results from burning it for energy to enter the atmosphere.

Figure 1.8 (see next page) shows three representative scenarios for the future projection of carbon dioxide emissions from burning fossil fuels.

- A—continuing much as at present, with high carbon dioxide emissions resulting from rapid economic growth and use of fossil fuels, and continued growth in world population which peaks in the mid twenty-first century;

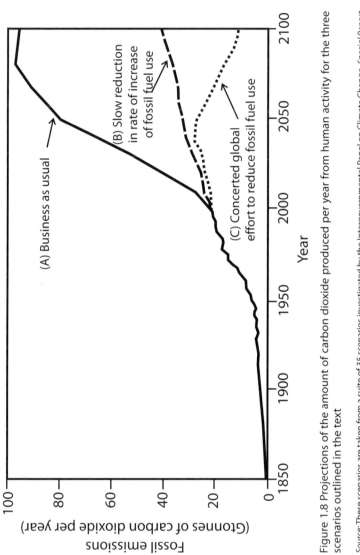

Figure 1.8 Projections of the amount of carbon dioxide produced per year from human activity for the three scenarios outlined in the text

Source: These scenarios are taken from a suite of 35 scenarios investigated by the Intergovernmental Panel on Climate Change, *Special Report on Emissions Scenarios: A Special Report of Working Group III of the IPCC*, N. Nakicenovic et al., eds. (Cambridge University Press, 2000).

- B—medium to low carbon dioxide emissions by lowering the rate of increase of usage of fossil fuels and emphasizing local solutions to social, economic, and environmental sustainability;

- C—low carbon dioxide emissions, with the same population growth as in A, but with a rapid and concerted effort to reduce carbon dioxide pollution through the introduction of sustainable energy.

It is the latter two scenarios with the assumption of a move toward sustainable consumption that we hope will be attainable. However, even the best attainable scenario is likely to lead to considerable global temperature increase.

The worst case (A), where little serious attempt is made at carbon dioxide reduction, causes a fivefold increase in the rate of production of carbon dioxide over present levels during the twenty-first century, and by the end of the century the total amount of carbon dioxide in the atmosphere would reach over 900 ppm, more than three times its pre-industrial level. The two cases that move towards manageable long-term stability of the global climate require either slowly lowering the annual rate of increase of carbon dioxide production below the rate of increase in the latter half of the twentieth century (case B) or, in the best outcome, a decrease in the amount of carbon dioxide generated worldwide back to 1970 levels (case C). Even in the best-envisaged case, the atmospheric concentration of carbon dioxide continues rising long after the rate of increase has been cut back, due to the long period it stays in the atmosphere (as shown in Table 1.1; see p. 15). If we make the most aggressive measures for cutting back carbon dioxide production, we could aim for a global concentration of carbon dioxide in the atmosphere that eventually flattens out at something less than twice its pre-industrial level. And this, like the other even less palatable scenarios, would have multiple effects.

Temperature Increases

The consequences of the carbon dioxide increase for global warming are shown in Figure 1.9 (see next page). All the scenarios, including the most optimistic, predict continuing and large

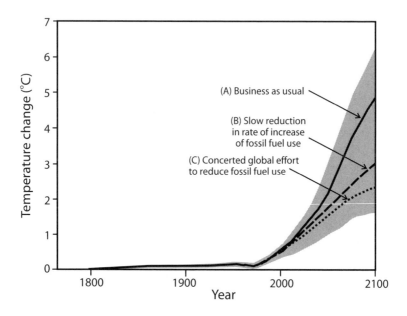

Figure 1.9 Predicted change in global average temperature for the three scenarios shown in Figure 1.8

Shading shows the range of predictions for these models with realistic estimates of the uncertainties.

temperature increases. By the year 2100 we should expect increases of at least 2°C above "normal" pre-industrial temperatures even if humanity cooperates to achieve the best of the modeled scenarios. If they don't, then increases of up to 5°C are very likely. Although these may sound relatively small temperature increases, we need to bear in mind that the most extreme global average temperature changes sustained by the Earth over the past million years are of a similar size—and they occurred between the depth of an ice age and the warmest interglacial period. Since our baseline pre-industrial temperature is already that of a warm interglacial period, these projected global temperature increases will take the Earth well above anything it has experienced in its recent geological history, and at a rate of change far greater than that imposed by "natural" processes.

Human activity has already committed the Earth to considerable long-term temperature change. Figure 1.10 shows predicted global average temperatures if we were able to stabilize greenhouse

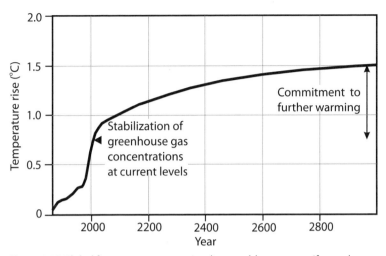

Figure 1.10 Global future temperature rise that would occur even if greenhouse gases were stabilized at today's levels

This shows that even if greenhouse gases could be stabilized immediately at today's levels, the global temperature would keep rising and eventually warm the Earth a further 1°C, or almost twice the global warming already produced.

Source: Diagram from Hadley Centre, *Climate Change and the Greenhouse Effect* (December 2005).

gases at today's levels—in practice, an almost impossible task. As can be seen, the consequences of human behavior to date will persist for hundreds of years to come and in the long term will cause temperature increases almost double those that have already been produced. The larger the temperature increases and the further into the future we try to look, the more uncertainty there is. This is because there is nothing with which to compare such massive changes to the Earth's climate and we cannot be certain of all the consequences of global warming on the climate system. To take but one biological example, an increase in atmospheric carbon dioxide may speed up the growth of some land plants, and thus in the short term remove more carbon than expected from the atmosphere, while the same increase may acidify the surface water of the oceans and inhibit carbon take-up by marine organisms. There may be other sudden and dramatic changes when a particular threshold of temperature increase is crossed such as switching off the North Atlantic Drift, as discussed earlier, which could cause extremely abrupt climate changes.

Irrespective of these uncertainties, the overall message is clear: what humankind does now will have serious long-term consequences on the global atmospheric temperature.

Climatic Patterns and Extreme Weather Events

So far we have only discussed global average temperatures. But what affects individuals most is the day-to-day climate in the region where they live. Two main conclusions have emerged from climate modeling. First, there will be regional variations that are very different from the average. For example, in North America the greatest temperature increases are projected to be in Alaska and northwestern Canada, with substantial warming in the interior of the continent, more modest changes in the southeastern United States and slight cooling in eastern Canada. Globally rainfall is likely to increase in mid to high latitudes, while droughts will become more common in lower ones. Africa is likely to fare particularly badly. This pattern can also be seen across the United States with decreased precipitation in the already arid southwest, but increases over the rest of the country.[24] Second, it is likely that extreme weather events—typhoons, hurricanes and storms causing floods and landslides, and extreme temperatures causing heat waves—will become on average more intense.

Because the land surface heats up and cools down much more rapidly than ocean areas, the surface temperature just above the land is likely to experience 40 percent greater warming than ocean areas. Model projections suggest that there will be a large increase in the number and severity of extremely hot summer days, coupled with a decrease in the daily variability of winter temperatures. By late in the century Chicago will experience 25 percent more heat waves annually, and heat wave days will increase in Los Angeles from 12 to between 44 and 95.[25] Heat waves are particularly hard in large cities and on vulnerable populations where heat stress can double or triple the normal death rate. In 2006, record heat persisted across most of the United States and Canada for over a month, resulting in hundreds of heat-related deaths.[26] Record high temperatures that in many places rose above 40ºC during a heat wave in Europe in summer 2003 caused over 20,000 additional deaths.[27] The warm summers also caused great losses in agricultural productivity in southern Europe.[28]

In the absence of any human modification of climate, the European heat wave of 2003 could have been as rare as a one-in-a-million year event.[29] But human-produced greenhouse gases have already doubled the probability of another such event. And as the prediction of the increase in summer temperatures in Europe over the twenty-first century shows (Figure 1.11), by the 2040s a 2003-type summer will be about average, and by the 2060s it would typically be the coldest summer of the decade.

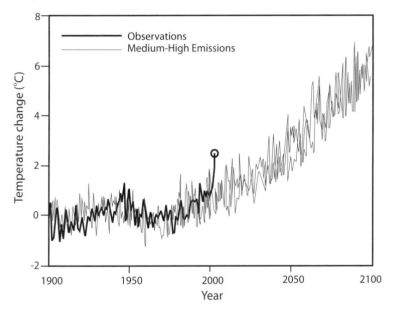

Figure 1.11 Measured average summer temperatures in southern Europe up to 2003, compared to predictions of past and future temperatures from several computer models

Several different model predictions (in fine lines) to show the range of likely increases in summer temperatures over southern Europe from an increase in carbon dioxide similar to case (A) of Figure 1.8. Heavy line shows actual temperatures. The models reproduce well the observations from 1900 to 2003 except for the summer of 2003 which was much hotter than either the model simulation or the normal climate. By the mid twenty-first century, the heat wave of 2003 will become the norm.

Source: Modelling by Hadley Centre, reported in Climate Change and the Greenhouse Effect (December 2005).

However, the greatest impact of global warming is likely to be a large increase in the intensity of rainfall from storms. Although there is no evidence that the number of storms will increase, there is both observational data and scientific reasons for a marked increase in the *intensity* of storms as a result of global warming.[30] For example, the total power dissipated by tropical storms has nearly doubled over the past 30 years.[31] The reason for this is that the volume of moisture drawn into a storm's circulation rises as the sea temperature rises, and the energy released as the water vapor condenses in clouds increases the wind speed. Computer simulations suggest that doubling the carbon dioxide in the atmosphere leads to an increase of between 5 to 10 percent in the peak wind intensities and an increase of about 30 percent in the peak rainfall. In 1998, Hurricane Mitch stalled over Central America as a relatively weak storm, but nevertheless, killed over 11,000 people from rainfall alone.[32] 2007 marked the first year that two hurricanes, Dean and Felix, made landfall as Category 5 storms during the same season, both striking Central America.

Deaths as a result of flooding and cyclones are humankind's worst natural disasters, accounting for two-thirds of deaths from all forms of natural disaster including earthquakes and volcanic eruptions. This is partly because settlements are usually in river valleys near a source of water. The worst known flooding disaster was on the Huang He (Yellow) River in China in 1931, when it was estimated that from 1,000,000 to 3,700,000 people died. Nor was this an isolated incident: in 1887 from 900,000 to 2,000,000 people died in floods of the same river. The worst death toll caused by a hurricane was on 13 November 1970 in Bangladesh when more than 500,000 people living in low-lying areas perished in a single day. In the last part of the twentieth century, floods affected 100 million people per year. The United Nations estimates that by 2025 half the world's population will be living in areas at risk from storms and other weather extremes.

Accompanying the human misery associated with deaths from floods are huge economic losses that add to the long-term suffering caused by the flood events. Moreover, the disease and famine that follow floods often cause more deaths than the floods themselves. So the increase of extreme storms are a real and frightening by-product of global warming, particularly since they will increase in intensity over coming decades and centuries.

Ironically, some areas with naturally low rainfall will become drier still. This is because the more intense cycling of water between the sea and the atmosphere as a result of climate change will cause a bigger proportion of the rain to fall in the more intense events. So although more water will be carried further upward into the atmosphere where air is rising, the areas where air is sinking will become drier. In the naturally dry areas of the world, the total rainfall will become less, and the number of rainy days will become substantially fewer, with more chance of prolonged periods with no rainfall at all—in other words, much more chance of drought. Adding to these woes, the higher temperatures will cause increased evaporation, thus reducing still further the amount of moisture available at the surface and deepening the drought conditions. Sub-Saharan Africa, already struggling with famines caused by drought, will suffer particularly badly. It is estimated that today 2 percent of the world's land area is suffering extreme drought, a doubling since 20 years ago. By 2050 this is expected to rise to between 10 to 12 percent of the land area.

Sea-Level Rise

As the global temperature rises, so the oceans will warm up. In doing so the water expands slightly, thus resulting in global sea-level rise. An additional, though smaller contribution to sea-level rise comes from melting of continental ice and snow masses—if the entire Greenland ice cap were to melt, for example, the extra water released into the oceans would raise sea level globally by about 7 meters, although this is predicted to take several centuries. Over the twenty-first century, melting of glaciers and part of the Greenland ice sheet are expected to contribute to about one-third of the total sea-level rise, but most will come from thermal expansion of the oceans.

We have already seen that the full effect of global warming lags behind the release of greenhouse gases into the atmosphere: translation of increased surface temperatures into sea-level rise takes even longer, due to the relatively slow circulation patterns of the ocean currents. But it is inexorable. By our actions to date we have already committed the world to steady sea-level rise for hundreds of years into the future. So at any time, the human-produced greenhouse effect carries with it a commitment to an additional, inescapable rise in sea level many times larger than at present. Generations following us will suffer the effects of what we are doing now.

The average global sea-level rises over the twenty-first century from the range of likely greenhouse gas scenarios vary from 0.1 meter to 0.9 meter. The central value is about 0.5 meter. This expected sea-level rise is about three times that which occurred in the twentieth century. As with global average temperature rises this may not at first sound like a huge problem, until one remembers that 15 million people live within one meter of sea level in Bangladesh or that many Pacific islands have only a few meters of freeboard. So for those people their homes will become literally uninhabitable. But, more importantly, there are likely to be regional variations in the size of the sea-level rise by a factor of two or so, depending on local ocean heat uptake and changes in atmospheric pressure and currents. Such regional variations are hard to predict which makes them even more problematic.

Almost half of the United States, twenty-four states, face the Atlantic or Pacific Oceans, the Gulf of Mexico, or are along tidal rivers. Eighty percent of the nation's shoreline is formed by bays or estuaries. While the potential flooding of New York City is dramatic, sea level rise has more subtle consequences. Marshes and wetlands along these shallow waters purify water, buffer and protect shorelines, and are nurseries for numerous species of fish and shellfish. Low-lying off-shore islands protect the coast from storms. As development has increased along the coasts, space for marshes and wetlands to migrate with the rising water has disappeared or declined.[33]

Some areas such as Maryland and the delta of the Mississippi are at greater risk from sea level rise because the land itself is subsiding. Between 2000 and 2100 up to 21 percent of the remaining wetlands in the Mid-Atlantic will likely be flooded. In low lying areas, such as the Chesapeake Bay, farmland has been lost as sea water has gradually infiltrated inland making the soils too salty for agriculture.[34] Fifty percent of the US population lives within 50 miles of the coast. For every 1-foot rise in sea level, 100 to 200 feet of shoreline is likely to erode. In a state like California where 85 percent of the population lives in coastal counties, the effects can be profound. By 2050, California expects a 1-foot rise in sea level; by 2100 the increase could be 3 feet. Not only will this change the shoreline and inundate homes close to the sea, but each rise in sea level increases the energy from wave actions by the square of the wave height. For instance, a 2-foot wave has four times the power of a 1-foot one.[35]

On top of the average sea-level rise, the biggest problem local populations face will be an increase in extreme high-water levels resulting from the increased intensity of storm surges. Much of Hurricane Katrina's devastation along the US Mississippi coast was a result of the record 27-foot storm surge. New Orleans was not on the coast, and Katrina had weakened to a Category 3 storm by the time it passed the city. But years of flood control practices that had stopped the river sediments from rebuilding the delta, the loss of vast areas of wetlands as the Gulf of Mexico crept further inland, and the building of navigation channels through the marshes allowed the force of the storm surge to reach further inland. Water broke through a weakened levee system, and large parts of the city were destroyed and are unlikely to ever be rebuilt. Some regions of the world have begun adapting to projected increased sea level rise and storm surges. For example, it is predicted that by the 2080s, with a medium to high greenhouse gas scenario generating a 0.3 meter average global sea-level rise, the average high-water levels in the southern North Sea and Thames Estuary are likely to be more than a meter above present levels, three or four times higher than the average. They will also happen more frequently: extreme high-water events that currently occur on average once every 100 years will instead occur as often as once every seven years in the 2080s. London already has a protective Thames Barrage which is raised when high tides threaten: it is likely that this defense will have to be substantially enhanced to protect against extreme future events caused by human-created global warming.

Food, Water, and Health

Social consequences of global climate change are more difficult to predict than is the physical response of the Earth's environment to temperature changes because they are dependent on the complexities of human and societal response as well as on the changes in the physical environment. But in general it is clear that high-income countries will have more freedom to respond and to adapt to changing circumstances, for example, by building higher sea barriers in response to sea level rise, than will low-income countries. So the deleterious effects will have a greater impact on the populations that are already marginalized or with low incomes, such as those in sub-Saharan Africa. As a general rule, human communities have adapted their lives over long periods to existing normal climate patterns, and most rapid climate changes are likely to produce adverse effects. Since settled human societies jealously guard their territory, and indeed most wars are fought over territorial rights, it is likely that large numbers of environmental refugees could in the future lead to widespread unrest or even war.

It is estimated that already, by the beginning of the twenty-first century, the approximately 20 million environmental refugees forced to leave their homes because of deteriorating environmental conditions exceed all other refugees from war and political repression combined. By 2050 there could be from 150 to 200 million refugees as a result of global warming.[36] In a world where the population has quadrupled in the twentieth century, land is increasingly at a premium. So huge numbers of stateless people will provide both a humanitarian and a political challenge.

The *global* capacity of agriculture to feed the world's population may not initially change greatly as a result of climate change. The mid to high latitudes will in general initially become slightly more favorable for agriculture, with a longer growing season and warmer temperatures, although further global warming would remove this advantage. The low latitudes, where there are already stresses on the food supply due partly to drought and partly to inept political management, will probably become still more stressed. Climate change is likely to produce more extreme events than at present, droughts that last several years, or floods that are more ferocious, and this is likely to be a bigger problem for agriculture than is the average temperature change. The problem is made more acute by environmental degradation already produced by human activity—loss of soil through poor agricultural practice, overextraction of groundwater and damage due to acid rain will only be made worse by the impact of global warming. But the problem is more than physical: already many millions of people die of famine in one part of the world while elsewhere there is an overabundance of food to the extent that large percentages of the population are clinically obese with all the attendant health problems that go with that. This is a significant issue of justice and sharing of resources, to which Christianity speaks powerfully. And as with many of the effects consequent on climate change, it is the poor and the marginalized who will suffer most, indeed who are already suffering, and who have the least resources to enable them to adapt to the changes forced on them.

Sustainable fresh-water supplies are crucial for human life to flourish, both for direct use and for agriculture. It is estimated that by 2050 some 100 million people will be living in areas with extreme water stress caused by climate change alone.[37] Much of the American and Canadian west is dependent on water supplied by snow melt fed river systems such as the Columbia or Colorado, or drawn from underground aquifers which are recharged by rainfall. Intense competition for water use between agriculture, energy production, industry, human consumption, and even care for endangered species has characterized this region and may become more intense over the next decades. By 2020, 41 percent of southern California's water supply will be affected by the decline in the snow pack in the Sierra Nevada and Colorado watersheds.[38] Glacier National Park, which drains into the Columbia River, has lost approximately 80 percent of its glaciers since 1850 with the rest expected to disappear by 2030.[39] Loss of glaciers, diminished snowfall, and earlier snow melt affect the timing and availability of water, especially for the summer months when demand increases. A 2.5°C warming is predicted to decrease the recharge ability of the Ogallala aquifer by 20 percent. This vast underground aquifer underlies eight of the most agriculturally productive states in the United States, from North Dakota to Texas.[40]

The impact of global warming on human health is more uncertain since health is so strongly tied to living conditions and is dependent on the income available to provide medical care to counter poor living conditions. Again it is the poor people and the low-income countries that are likely to suffer most. Even today, lack of clean drinking water can be linked to roughly 250 million cases annually of water-related diseases and between 5 and 10 million deaths worldwide. Increased spread of insect-borne diseases, such as malaria, is also likely in a warmer world. We have already discussed the increased incidence of deaths due to extreme high temperatures that will become more frequent and more widespread, especially in urban populations. Although highly uncertain, one estimate suggests that human-produced climate change over the past 30 years already claims over 150,000 lives annually and that the excess risk of climate-induced health problems may more than double by 2030.[41]

Global Population

At the beginning of the nineteenth century there were only one billion people on this planet; the six billion mark was passed before the end of the twentieth century. Population studies show that as life expectancy and individual wealth increase, the birth rate drops. The United Nations predicts that on present evidence the world population will not continue rising indefinitely, as it has hitherto (Figure 1.4, see p. 20), but will stabilize at between 9 and 11 billion by the middle of this century. That is still nearly double the present population; but it is not beyond the capacity of this Earth to provide sufficient food, water, and energy for everyone, provided it can be equitably distributed. It does, however, mean that we can no longer treat our local environment, including the atmosphere, as an inexhaustible sink for our waste products. Rather we will have to manage both our use of finite supplies and our disposal of waste products, including greenhouse gases, in a way which can be sustained in the long term.

The importance of global population to climate change is that as the number of people increases so do the greenhouse gas emissions. Perhaps even more pertinently, the largest rates of population increases are in Asia. India passed one billion inhabitants early this century, and China is already well over that size. Asia contains more than half the world's population, yet its current production of carbon dioxide per person is among the lowest on Earth (Figure 1.12). It is the high-income societies, who have built their wealth and their lifestyles on the back of technology, who are by far the worst polluters. So as the prosperity of Asian countries increases, as it is doing now, the generation of greenhouse gases globally will increase massively, far faster even than the rate of population increase.

Are Other Issues More Urgent than Global Warming?

The long-term consequences of climate change are serious and potentially disastrous. Notwithstanding the complexity of the systems involved and resultant level of uncertainty over the consequences, it is beyond serious doubt that the lives, health, security, and happiness of millions of people are threatened.

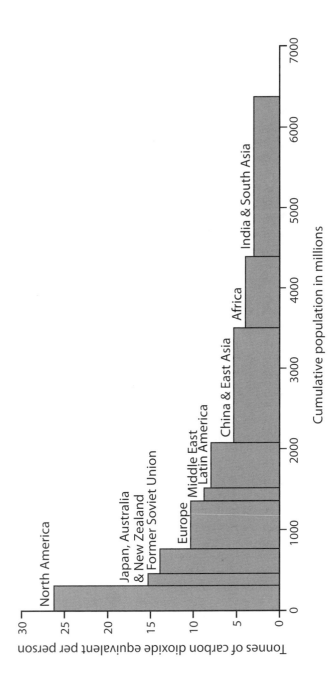

Figure 1.12 Carbon dioxide emissions in 2000 from different countries expressed per person plotted against their population

Source: From M. Grubb, "The Economics of the Kyoto Protocol," *World Economics* 4 (2003), p. 145.

But the lives, health, security, and happiness of millions are also threatened by many other factors, such as HIV/AIDS or a lack of clean drinking water. Should we invest money and energy in trying to reduce long-term global warming when there are many seemingly more pressing issues for the Christian commanded to love his or her neighbor? What of more traditionally Christian priorities, such as the breakdown of family life? And more obviously spiritual ones, such as the importance of proclaiming the gospel and seeking to bring unbelievers to a salvation faith?

The answer, of course, is that the Christian has to be concerned about, and responsive in an appropriate way, to all these issues. A lack of access to clean water and sanitation, for example, is a daily crisis for millions of people. Dirty water claims more lives through disease than any war claims through guns. Some 1.8 million children die each year as a result of diarrhea caused by unclean water and poor sanitation. The United Nations estimate that 1.1 billion people live without access to adequate clean water. The majority of those use only 5 liters (1.1 gallons) per day, about one-tenth of the average daily amount used in rich countries to flush toilets.[42] One part of the world sustains a designer bottled-water market that generates no tangible health benefits while another part suffers acute health risks because people have to drink from contaminated drains or lakes and rivers.

As the United Nations Development Programme reports, there is more than enough water in the world for domestic purposes, for agriculture, and for industry. The problem is that the poorest people tend to be systematically excluded from access to clean water by their poverty, by their limited legal rights, or by public policies that restrict access to the infrastructures that provide water. In other words, the solution lies primarily in the social and political structures in the countries where they live. Water governance must improve if poor people's health and livelihoods are also to improve, and therefore responses that push for structural change as well as improved service delivery are vital. Given the current scale of the problem, it is a sobering thought that, as our climate changes, the situation is actually likely to get worse.

Global climate change has a major impact on the hydrological cycles that determine the availability of water. It is clear from modeling that the consequences of climate change at the local level are complex and depend on local microclimates. But one thing seems certain: there is likely to be an increase in local variability and extreme events, of temperature, droughts, and floods. Many of the world's water-stressed areas will get less water, and water flows will become less predictable and more subject to extreme events. It is these aspects that make tackling global climate change, and damping the rate of climate change, such a crucial objective. All countries also need to improve their water governance and ensure that fair and open processes are put in place to decide who is entitled to use existing resources so that, if water scarcity increases, the poor are not marginalized further.

Then there are the problems of famine and disease that often accompany issues of water. Global communications mean that images of emaciated and starving people are beamed by TV direct into our living rooms. They cannot be ignored. Surely we need to respond to such desperate need?

Provision of emergency medical, food, and relief supplies are a crucial immediate response to famine and disease, as too is helping to create a sustainable infrastructure for agriculture and rural development. But beyond this short-term response, many of the factors governing stable food supply in an area are dependent on the consistency of the climate. So just as with the provision of adequate water, one of the main threats to agriculture, particularly in areas of subsistence farming, is rapid climate change and the associated increased variability and occurrence of extreme events. It is crucial to address climate change and to attempt to reduce rapid changes in it in order to guarantee the long-term stability of the food supply and to reduce the malnutrition that provides a fertile breeding ground for disease.

Though the high-income countries, such as those in North America and the European Union, comprise only one-sixth of the world's population, they produce 55 percent of the greenhouse gases responsible for global warming. In contrast, the poorest sixth of the world's population produce less than 3 percent of the global carbon dioxide. And yet it is this poorest segment of the world's population that does not have the economic or technical resources to counter the effects of global warming such as changes in rainfall and temperature, or rising sea levels. So they will pay for it by increased death rates from famine or disease, or by displacement from their homelands. Since we all live on one small globe and the circulating atmosphere carries the pollution that causes global climate change around the whole world in a matter of days, then no one can avoid responsibility for the effects their actions will have on others.

People in high-income countries who have benefited historically from the burning of fossil fuels have a particular responsibility to deal with the results of their actions. And they can hardly claim to love their (global) neighbor when the consequences of their lifestyles may lead to suffering and an increased probability of an early death by people elsewhere. To refuse to consider the physical and social welfare of others when the consequences of our actions are already clear is not only reckless but at root selfish. And selfishness is nothing less than sinfulness, of putting oneself first. If our daily actions are at root an expression of sinfulness then we need not only to repent of that but also to change our behavior.

Summary: Global Warming, Local Causes

Global warming caused by human activity is real, and we now understand the main causes of it. Most prominent is the injection of massive amounts of carbon dioxide into the atmosphere from the indiscriminate burning of fossil fuels—oil, gas, and coal. The Earth has seen temperature swings of up to 10ºC in the geological past, and there is no doubt that, by continuing our present behavior, humans would cause exactly the same sort of temperature changes again. The significant difference is that the present rates of change forced on the planet by human activity are at least 30 times faster than anything the Earth has suffered before. The consequences of this are likely to include massive ecological disturbance and loss as natural ecosystems fail to respond sufficiently quickly to the rapidly changing environment.

But more significant still are the likely consequences on a planet crowded by more humans than it has ever supported before and where one-quarter of the population live in poverty, with a marginal lifestyle that is extremely vulnerable to changes caused by drought or flooding, by the failure of agricultural crops, or by rising sea levels. To continue our present reckless experiment with the Earth's future climate would be a morally gross failure both towards those who are less fortunate than ourselves in their material resources and towards future generations.

There are many other issues that press equally hard for attention, and Christians need to be able to respond to all of them as appropriate. However, the sheer scale and impact of climate change makes it a priority. Global temperature increases, extreme weather patterns, rising sea levels, desertification, drought, flooding, water crises, and health scares will affect billions of people. Global warming demands a response.

That sheer scale also, however, makes the issue appear rather daunting to us, leaving individuals feeling distinctly powerless, unable to do anything meaningful by way of response. That feeling is misleading however, as climate change may be a global problem but it has distinctly local and human causes. It is to these we now turn.

2

SUSTAINABILITY AND WELL-BEING

THE PROBLEM WITH CLIMATE change is that it is global. The phrase invokes images such as those of the previous chapter: melting ice caps, vanishing atolls, ruinous hurricanes, inexorably rising tides, droughts, and heat waves. Yet, in spite of this impression—of an incalculable, insurmountable, inevitable catastrophe, bearing down on us with the destructive violence of a tsunami—climate change is not one vast, impersonal challenge, but rather billions of tiny, personal ones. It is our coffee pot in the morning, our daily drive to work, our weekly supermarket shop, and our annual holiday. It is a thousand things we do without thinking: everyday behavior that we assume, quite wrongly, is a normal part of life and therefore sustainable.

Sustainability

Sustainability is not a new idea. For many centuries, agricultural societies rotated crops, pruned plants, coppiced trees, and left fields fallow in order to maintain productivity and secure the long-term future of the natural resources on which they depended. Although rarely put in such terms, sustainability was part of the natural order of things.[1]

The modern interest in sustainability can be traced back to the early twentieth century.[2] It was only in the period after the Second World War, however, that sustainable thinking began to emerge as a significant force, as it became increasingly evident that human activity was having a serious, long-term, detrimental affect on the environment. The World Commission on the Environment and Development, set up by the United Nations in 1983, put the term "sustainability" on the map, and its report, *Our Common Future* (more popularly known as the Brundtland Report after its chairwoman), published in 1987, offered what remains the most widely quoted definition of sustainable development: "development that meets the needs of the present without compromising the ability of future generations to meet their own needs."[3] In 1992, chapter 4 of Agenda 21 of the Rio Earth Summit focused the blame for the continued deterioration of the global environment on: "the unsustainable pattern of consumption and production, particularly in industrialized countries, which is a matter of grave concern, aggravating poverty and imbalances."[4]

"Sustainability," "sustainable development," "sustainable consumption and production," and "sustainable prosperity" are often used interchangeably, despite subtle differences. Sustainability is, properly speaking, the goal to which we aspire, the "capacity for continuance into the long-term future . . . [the] point at which we can genuinely claim to be living within biophysical parameters."[5] "Sustainable consumption and production" and "sustainable prosperity" share this ambition but place a greater emphasis on continued economic growth within these limits. A US Environmental Protection Agency panel noted that "sustainability requires the simultaneous promotion of equitable economic growth, environmental protection, and social well being."[6] Sustainable development according to Jonathan Porritt, Chairman of the UK's Sustainability Development Commission, is the "process or journey which we must undertake in order to get to that destination [of sustainability]."[7]

In practice, the terms are used almost interchangeably because they are almost interchangeable. The path of sustainable development requires adopting practices that are essential to the destination of sustainability. The very process of sustainable development blends seamlessly into sustainability—at least in theory.

North America's impact on climate change is primarily the result of unsustainable energy consumption through burning of fossil fuels, though our consumer lifestyles also promote other causes, such as deforestation and land use changes in various parts of the world. The effect of unsustainable fishing or forestry is relatively clear: it leaves future generations unable to consume fish or wood at anything like our current rate, and perhaps at all. Energy is different. Few think future generations will be short of energy, in the way they may be short of fish or wood. Even after fossil fuels have been exhausted the tides, winds, and waves will remain, the Sun will still shine, and nuclear energy will still be available. Were we able magically to transform our current energy mix into an inexhaustible, carbon-neutral supply, we would obviate most—though not all—of the problems associated with our present levels of energy consumption.

The fact is, however, that no magic wand exists and our present level and mix of energy consumption is unsustainable because of the effect it is having on the atmosphere (and thereby on everything and everyone else). It is unsustainable because, as observed in chapter 1, it is directly or indirectly resulting in desertification, flooding, species extinctions, and extreme weather events. It is unsustainable because millions of people, most of who already live in poverty, stand to lose the little they do have, and possibly their lives. And it is unsustainable because, as we shall note in the second part of this chapter, it has, in a number of forms, a serious, negative impact on well-being for all of us.

This chapter initially explores our unsustainable energy consumption in greater detail, explaining precisely what it is we are doing that is warming up the world and threatening the lives and livelihoods of so many. It then shifts focus slightly, remaining with our unsustainable energy consumption, but examining the often-overlooked impact it is having on our own well-being. In doing so, it links social and environmental concerns, pointing to a theme that will be explored in greater detail in Part 2.

Global and National Energy Use

Total global primary energy consumption (see below) has nearly doubled since 1970. The bulk of this increase has been driven by economic growth in Asia, although Asian economies remain a long way behind Western ones, and African ones further still. The United States, as the world's largest and most diverse economy, accounts for 23 percent of the world's total primary energy consumption, China for around 11 percent, Russia for 7, Canada 3, and the UK for about 2.5 percent.[8] As fast industrializing economies, such as China and India, grow their proportion of global total primary energy consumption is expected to increase.

"Primary energy" may be derived from fossil fuels, nuclear power, or renewable resources and refers to all the energy consumed, including that which is lost in the production process and through transmission across national electricity grids. Because of this loss, a better guide to the relationship between *human activity* and energy consumption is "total energy," a figure that measures the energy actually used by the final consumer.[9] Total energy consumption in the United States has increased by 47 percent since 1970, driven by both population and economic growth. Total energy is allocated across four economic sectors—transportation, residential, commercial, and industrial—a pattern that is broadly similar in other industrialized nations, although measured in slightly different categories.[10] Changes in the type of fuel used across sectors influences not only total energy consumption but also the quantity and nature of greenhouse gas emissions.

For example, electrification has been a key factor in the total energy use and emissions of the United States. The electric power industry is both the largest consumer of primary energy as well as the largest source of greenhouse gas emissions. Early in our history, coal had been a major fuel source for home heating and transportation, but petroleum and natural gas gradually took over these tasks. Between 1949 and 2000, however, residential, industrial, and commercial use of electricity for other purposes rose by 1,315 percent, with the surge in electricity generation bringing a renewed emphasis on coal, a tenfold increase in the amount needed as fuel. In fact, by 2005, the electric power sector was responsible for 92 percent of all coal consumption in the United States.[11] Of the three fossil fuels, coal, as the most carbon intensive, produces proportionally more greenhouse gas emissions. Petroleum holds second place, followed by the relatively carbon-clean natural gas. In 2005, coal supplied 52 percent of the electricity generation sector's fuel needs but produced 85 percent of its greenhouse gas emissions.

The amount of fuel consumed is also a factor in emissions. Petroleum use, primarily for transportation, has tripled in the United States since the late 1940s. While less carbon intensive than coal, the sheer volume of petroleum used is impressive, 40 percent of the total primary energy consumption. Overall, the United States depends on fossil fuels for 85 percent of its energy needs. Nuclear energy contributes about 8 percent; renewables 7 percent, mainly from hydroelectric power.

Energy consumption is a *rough* guide to levels of carbon dioxide emission. Differences in energy sources, both between sectors and between countries, can have a significant impact. Norway and Sweden, for example, have similar climates and economies but emit rather different levels of carbon dioxide, largely because Norway has historically been dependent on its extensive oil industries, while nearly half of Sweden's energy comes from renewable sources. France emits proportionately little carbon dioxide, in part because it derives nearly three-quarters of its electricity from nuclear power, whereas Australia is one of the world's biggest carbon dioxide producers because much of its electricity comes from cheap, opencast coal, one of the most carbon intensive of fossil fuels. Although around 80 percent of the UK's energy comes from fossil fuels, the decline of coal and the rise of gas over recent decades have made the United Kingdom a "cleaner" country.

Calculating national carbon dioxide emission levels is, therefore, a complex business, integrating energy consumption, source, and efficiency, and necessitating numerous assumptions and estimations. Notwithstanding those complications, however, calculations show that US energy use is a reasonably good guide to US carbon dioxide emission levels. For example, greenhouse gas emissions rose by 25 percent between 1980 and 2005. During this same time, total energy use rose by 28 percent.

The production of electricity, by itself, consumes 39 percent of the US's primary energy and produces 39 percent of carbon dioxide emissions. Electricity is used as a fuel source for the residential, industrial, and commercial sectors, so both the energy used to create electricity and the resulting greenhouse gas emissions are factored into each sector's totals based on their respective electrical demands. The residential sector is the largest consumer of electricity. Therefore, how we utilize electricity in our homes becomes closely connected with the amount of greenhouse gases emitted by power plants. Following electricity generation, the transportation sector is the nation's largest producer of greenhouse gases, consuming 28 percent of energy but emitting 33 percent of the carbon dioxide.

Canada's greatest challenge is the industrial sector, particularly energy producing industries, such as oil and natural gas, which are also intense energy consumers. The oil sands have become increasingly important to Canada's fossil fuel production, but they are much more energy intensive and produce greater greenhouse gases than conventional methods of oil extraction and refining.[12]

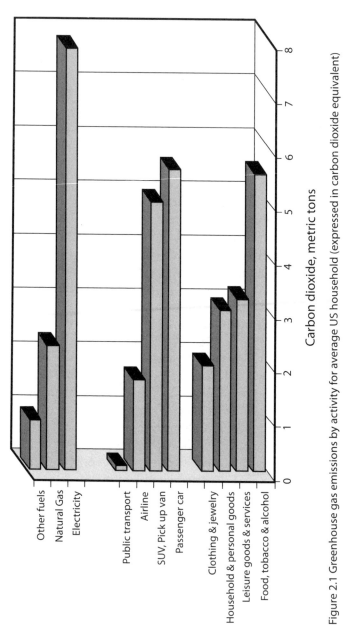

Figure 2.1 Greenhouse gas emissions by activity for average US household (expressed in carbon dioxide equivalent)

Source: Energy Information Agency Annual Energy Review 2006; US Environmental Protection Agency. Inventory of Greenhouse Gas Emissions and Sinks: 1990-2005; www.epa.gov/climatechange/emissions; US Census Bureau: Table 2.5.5 Personal Consumption Expenditures by Type of Expenditure. http://www.census.gov/compendia/statab/

Between 1990 and 2005, exports of oil and gas products increased by 156 percent and greenhouse gas emissions from the fossil fuel industries almost doubled.[13] Canada's national greenhouse gas emissions grew by 25 percent over the same period. The United States and Canada are interconnected through the energy sector. Each nation both imports and exports electricity to the other, depending on the section of the continent. Pipelines currently connect oil production facilities in Canada to such US locations as Oklahoma City, Chicago, and Casper, Wyoming. Canada is proposing a pipeline from Edmonton, Alberta to deep water Pacific ports in British Columbia making it easier to ship oil to the western United States and to new markets in China and India. In 2005, 80 percent of US imports of natural gas came from Canada, traveling by pipelines to such places as Oregon, California, Massachusetts, and Long Island.[14]

Because of the difficulty of relating national emissions or energy consumption figures to our own lives, the clearest way of illustrating how our behavior or lifestyle promotes unsustainable energy use is to calculate those figures per person or per household (see Figure 2.1).

The US's and Canada's per capita figures differ from each other markedly. They have similar lifestyles and cultures, but in 2005, Canadians consumed 25 percent more energy per capita (although the United States used seven times the amount of total energy as Canada). While climate may play a part, the primary difference was the impact of Canada's energy intensive fossil fuel industries. In order to understand the steps we must take towards sustainability, we need to see that it is not only total primary energy use that matters, or the amount each individual uses, but also how our industry, manufacturing, and other sectors of the economy function and the ways we are connected to our global neighbors.[15] Using this concept, per capita figures show that the average US household emits about 53 tons of carbon dioxide equivalent each year.[16]

This total household figure has three components: life at home (direct use of oil, gas, and electricity to heat, light, etc. homes); travel (both domestic and international); and consumption (of goods and services, such as food, drink, tobacco, clothing, household durables, etc.) the production, packaging, and transportation of which consumes considerable energy.

This chapter examines these three areas in greater detail, exploring precisely what we do in each area that is environmentally unsustainable, before going on to examine how at least two of these areas are also socially problematic.

Life at Home

The total amount of residential energy used in the United States has risen by nearly 52 percent since 1970. This is partly because the population has grown, but mostly because we choose to live in smaller household units, thus increasing the total number of houses we occupy. While the population has increased by around 45 percent since 1970, the national housing stock has risen by almost twice that amount. Not only have the number of homes increased but the square footage of the average home has as well. We have, in other words, much more space to heat and more rooms to light.

Broadly speaking, we use energy at home for four different functions: space heating, utilizing appliances, water heating, and air conditioning or cooling (see Figure 2.2).

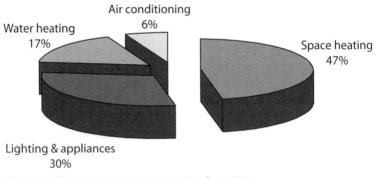

Figure 2.2 Domestic energy consumption by activity

Source: US Energy Information Agency Annual Energy Review 2006. www.eia.doe.gov

On a positive note, although there has been an increase in households and a corresponding rise in total energy consumption, the actual amount used per household has remained relatively stable since the late 1970s. This has partly been the result of a shift in population from the colder northeastern states to the south and west in the United States with a decline in space heating energy use. In addition, new homes, especially those built after 1980 use much less energy than older homes due to better quality insulation and more efficient windows and doors. Nevertheless, over 40 percent of the money an average US household spends in utility bills goes to heat or cool their home. In Canada, 60 percent of energy used in homes is devoted to space heating. These costs, as well as greenhouse gas emissions, are influenced not only by the age and style of our heating and cooling systems, but also by our choice of thermostat settings.

Water heating consumes nearly 17 percent of all domestic energy. Energy use for water heating has risen by 10 percent since 1978, caused by more people, in many more but better-insulated dwellings, heating more water at a comparatively lower cost, by more efficient means. More power showers and more dishwashers have demanded more energy. More efficient water heaters, and better-insulated water tanks and hot-water pipes have demanded less.

Lights and appliances represent the area of greatest growth in residential energy use. Not only has this area increased by 67 percent since 1978, but three quarters of this growth was in the form of electricity, so convenient but environmentally costly. A power plant draws on three units of primary energy to generate and transfer one unit of electricity to the end consumer.

Lighting is the least efficient use of electricity in the home. An incandescent bulb converts only 10 percent of the energy it consumes into light; the rest is lost as heat. This inefficiency, combined with the length of time such bulbs as kitchen ceiling lights, family and living room lamps and outdoor porch lights are used, makes lighting a significant contributor to unsustainable energy use and greenhouse gas emissions. In fact, incandescent bulbs will be legally phased out in the United Statesby 2014. Compact florescent lights (CFL's), the main focus of energy efficiency improvements for domestic lighting, consume one-fifth of the energy of an equivalent incandescent bulb but present other challenges, such as finding convenient and safe ways to dispose of the mercury containing bulbs.

The story of appliance usage is similar but more serious. The doubling of personal income since the early 1970s has enabled ever more people to own ever more domestic appliances. Increased efficiency levels have helped offset the impact of many more goods per households—but only marginally. Rapid growth in the consumer electronics sector (where the trend is towards higher rather than lower energy use) have mitigated against improvements in energy efficiency. Even when switched off, many appliances, including kitchen appliances, computers, and home entertainment devices, continue to draw a small amount of electricity known as "standby power." The US Department of Energy estimates that 75 percent of the electricity an average home uses to power home electronics is consumed when the products are "turned off." This translates into approximately 5 percent of total residential energy use or around $4 billion in energy costs annually, powering products such as TVs, VCRs, and CD players while they are "sleeping at their posts."[17]

The only area of domestic activity that has witnessed a *reduction* in energy usage over recent decades is cooking. The growth of the convenience food market, increased use of microwaves (which use less energy than conventional ovens), and the steady increase in the number and frequency of people eating out have all meant that we spend less time and use less energy cooking at home. What this actually means, though, is that we have transferred the energy use and emissions to another sector—to the commercial realm, or have added to the emissions from transport by traveling to the restaurant or fast food eatery. Between 1990 and 2004, sales of food consumed away from home almost doubled growing by $226 billion.[18] Our eating habits are not only affecting our waistline, but the environment as well.

Overall, the average American household emits eleven tons of carbon dioxide every year from direct energy use, and while that figure would be considerably greater were it not for improvements in energy and appliance efficiency, it is still unsustainable and, frustratingly, needlessly high. Even if one accepts that we need all the gadgets and gizmos that we have, the manner in which we use them (e.g., use of the standby facility), our lack of interest in energy efficient equivalents (e.g., the slow growth of CFLs), and our generally casual attitude to domestic energy use (e.g., the "power's cheap so we'll leave all the lights/heating on" attitude) mean that we could reduce our domestic carbon dioxide production easily without much effort—and save money in the process.

Travel

If what we do at home poses a threat to our environment, what we do when we close the front door behind us is even more of one. Around the world, the transportation sector is the fastest growing consumer of energy, mostly in the form of petroleum. This trend is predicted to continue, not only in industrialized countries but also in low-income countries. For some nations, such as the UK, the greatest challenge to any attempt towards environmental sustainability has been the rapid growth of airline transport and the increasing volume of personal vehicles. In the United States, petroleum consumption is predicted to grow by 48 percent by 2025.

The increasing hunger for petroleum not only affects greenhouse gas emissions, but impacts all aspects of a nation's economy, threatens its national security and illustrates the interdependence (and vulnerability) of countries in the modern world. Some industrialized nations, such as Japan and Germany, import over 90 percent of their petroleum. In some instances, 90 percent of these imports come from unstable regions of the world.[19] The United States is the world's largest consumer of petroleum, importing 25 percent of global production and meeting 60 percent of its petroleum needs through imports.[20]

Between 1970 and 2005, total energy consumption from transport in the United States grew by 75 percent. Three factors affect total energy consumption—the number and type of vehicles, vehicle miles traveled and fuel economy or miles per gallon. During this time, the number of registered highway vehicles grew faster than the population. Not only were there greater numbers of personal vehicles on the road, but the increasing demand for consumer goods drove the freight industry to rely more heavily on trucking, less fuel efficient than rail transport. In 1970, an average freight truck traveled about 14,000 miles per year. By 2005, this had almost doubled, to 26,000 miles per year.[21] Fuel economy for heavy duty trucks has improved somewhat, to almost seven miles per gallon. Between 1990 and 2005, carbon dioxide emissions from freight trucks increased by 69 percent, representing the largest emissions rate increase of any transport mode. Nevertheless, 61 percent of carbon dioxide emissions in the transport sector in 2005 came from passenger vehicles. In 2005, the transportation sector produced one third of all carbon emissions in the United States (see Figure 2.3 for a breakdown).

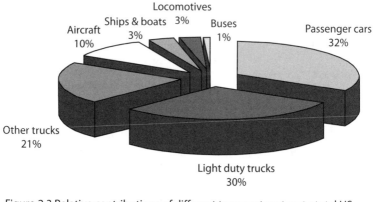

Figure 2.3 Relative contributions of different transport sectors to total US carbon dioxide emissions from transport

Source: Inventory of US Greenhouse Gas Emissions and Sinks: 1990–2005. www.epa.gov/climatechange

It is worth looking at each of the transportation modes most connected with household use in more detail, to get a better idea of how our behavior in this critical area is unsustainable.[22]

Public Transport

In the early part of the last century the United States had one of the best public transportation systems in the world, with city trolleys, buses, and trains. After World War II, the government invested in the interstate highway system, opening the nation not only to easier transport of goods, but also to the lure of the "open road," family adventures to see the country. The public transport sector declined both in infrastructure and in ridership. This has begun to change, especially in urban areas. Between 1982 and 2005, public transportation miles traveled grew by 34 percent. That said, public transportation only constitutes about 2 percent of ridership in the United States, 7 percent in Canada, and 10 percent in Western Europe—despite the fact that for every mile traveled by public transport, emissions are two to three times lower than they would have been otherwise.[23]

Aviation

Approximately 744 million Americans traveled by plane in 2005. For many, planes may have seemed more crowded, but this greater percentage of occupied seats per plane actually helped aviation to be the one mode of transportation in the United States that experienced a moderating rise in greenhouse emissions. Increased fuel efficiency also helped. Between 1990 and 2005 passenger miles increased by 69 percent, while emissions rose only by 15 percent. Aviation currently represents about 3 percent of the total United States greenhouse gas emissions and 10 percent of emissions from all forms of transportation. Airplanes have a longer lifespan than land based vehicles, and finding alternative fuel technologies also presents a greater challenge. As air travel, whether for passengers or freight, increases over the next decades, aviation's contribution to greenhouse gas emissions is also expected to rise (by as much as 60 percent by 2025).[24]

Personal Transport

In the United States, the greatest challenge in the transport sector is our love affair with the car. For many families, having a personal vehicle is seen as a necessity rather than the luxury it once was. This is especially true outside of urban areas where travel to work, shopping, or taking children to sports practice is not easily accomplished by public transport. In fact, 92 percent of US households have at least one personal vehicle. The greatest growth in car ownership occurred during the late 1960s through the 1990s as many women entered the workforce. By 2003, there were more vehicles in US households than drivers.

Not only is the sheer number of vehicles important but so is the type. In the United States, in 2001, half of personal vehicles were passenger cars, the rest were vans (22%), SUVs (17%), and pick-up trucks (11%). This shift in style has affected not only fuel efficiency but also emissions. The increases in fuel economy for passenger cars over recent years have been the result of retiring older models of cars rather than genuine new technology. But even these gains have been offset by the increasing numbers of less fuel efficient light-duty trucks such as SUVs and small pick-ups. In fact, fuel efficiency for these light duty trucks has actually *declined* since 2001. While greenhouse gas emissions from passenger cars remained essentially the same between 1990 and 2005, emissions from vans, SUVs, and pick-ups rose by 75 percent over the same period.

By 2001, the average American household spent as much on personal transport as on energy use in household services (such as water heating, lighting, refrigeration, and cooking). The US Energy Information Agency reported: "what America drives on its roadways has become as important energy wise as what heating equipment it places in its basements and appliances in its electrical sockets."[25]

Consumption

The third aspect of our everyday lives that is using energy unsustainably is our overall consumption, how *much* we consume and the *way* we consume it. This affects not only our personal lives, but is intertwined with our economy. Seventy percent of the US's Gross Domestic Product (GDP)[26] is based on personal consumption. In other words, a large part of the economy is focused on supplying those things we need to live or want to have. It is for this reason that "consumer confidence" is often given as a measure of the health of the economy.

This drive to consume is fed by both the industrial and commercial sectors. The latter includes such diverse enterprises as retail stores, restaurants, and medical care. These two economic sectors use approximately half of the US energy and produce 46 percent of the greenhouse gas emissions. But this is not the total story. The rise in international trade over the past decade has allowed both business and industry to move a portion of their energy costs and emissions to other countries. A phone call to the customer service department of a business may be answered by a representative in India. A glance at the label inside our clothing may read: Made in Guatemala, Panama, Indonesia, Bangladesh, or China. Our consumption affects not only energy use and emissions in our own country but around the world.

Consumption Levels

The United States is wealthier today than at any time in the past. GDP has risen almost constantly over the last 35 years, doubling since the early 1970s. Over the same period, real household disposable income—the amount of money a household has to spend or save—has also doubled, though at a slightly slower rate.

Having more money to save is not the same as having more savings, however. The last few years have seen the household savings ratio (i.e., household saving expressed as a proportion of total resources)[27] fall to its lowest recorded level. In fact, by 2005 the personal savings rate had dropped to zero. For the first time since the Great Depression, American families spent more than they earned and were $1.2 trillion in debt. This is partly a result of stagnant wages and increased costs for housing, health care, and education. But a large portion of income is still invested in the accumulation of "stuff."

International trade has brought the world to our door and we have benefited by lower prices on consumer goods without bearing the social and environmental costs of their manufacture. For instance, in 2001, the average family spent 4.4 percent of its budget on clothing, down from 14 percent in the 1920s.[28] However, the number of garments purchased per year has actually gone up—by 70 percent just between 1996 and 2001. Estimates show that the average family buys 48 new pieces of clothing a year. Computers are a similar story. Prices have fallen with the advent of more powerful chips, low wages, and the off-shoring of environmental costs. In 2001, nearly 23 million new computers were purchased in the United States.

Another way to look at this is the amount of waste we generate as a result, some of which we recycle and some of which winds up in landfills. In 2005, an estimated 63 million computers were retired in the United States. Over the 1990s, people donated 10 percent more goods than the previous decade to Goodwill Industries for resale. Every year, about 1,130 pounds of waste per person arrives at a landfill. Each of these pounds emits .94 pounds of carbon dioxide equivalent in the form of methane. In other words, every person in the United States contributes 1060 pounds of carbon dioxide equivalent to the atmosphere just by what we throw away.[29]

Consumption Patterns

The stuff in our homes today has traveled much further than stuff did thirty, or even ten, years ago. International trade, rightly seen as the most effective way of delivering millions from poverty, also contributes to climate change.[30]

The problem is not simply international, however. Patterns of consumption have been changing at a national level as well. As car ownership has increased, town centers, with their restricted parking facilities and traffic congestion, have became less attractive to retailers and shoppers, leading to the development of out-of-town supermarkets and shopping malls.

These new shopping venues have necessitated not only higher levels of car use but also have driven an unprecedented growth in commercial centralization. This has had an important if indirect impact on levels of well-being nationally, which are explored below, and has also affected the climate. Market centralization, particularly in the grocery sector, has resulted in food and drink traveling thousands of miles before it reaches our kitchens. In Great Britain, it has been estimated that around 1 percent of the nation's *total* carbon emissions is due to car-based food shopping—that is, the distance shoppers drive for groceries—and a further 3.5 percent due to the distance food travels on UK roads before it reaches the store.[31] Within the UK alone, supermarket trucks travel around 670 million miles per year and the food system accounts for around 40 percent of all UK road freight.[32]

Impacts in the United States are even greater due to the sheer size of the country. In 1998, fresh produce destined for the Chicago Terminal Market traveled an average 1,518 miles by truck one way, and then was distributed to surrounding markets. An apple, in a supermarket in Iowa, may have journeyed 1,700 miles to get there. An increasing portion of food we eat is produced in other countries. In the United States, in 2001, this accounted for an estimated 12 percent of vegetables, 39 percent of fruit, 40 percent of lamb, and 78 percent of shellfish and fish. A normal American prepared meal may consist of ingredients from at least five countries outside the United States.[33] Overall, the length of the modern food chain means that we actually put more energy, in the form of non-renewable fossil fuels, into our food than we get out in the form of food calories. We are eating oil.

Sustainability: A Summary

Climate change is not one big, intractable problem but billions of tiny, tractable ones. The heart of the issue is not that there is too much carbon dioxide in the atmosphere, end of story. It is that so many of the things that we do, everyday, without thinking, put more carbon dioxide there. We are careless in the way we use energy at home. We love the freedom that our personal mobility affords us. We are trapped on a "hedonistic treadmill" of stuff and convenience that is polluting the planet and, as we shall observe below, ourselves.

What is the best way to motivate ourselves and our fellow citizens for long-term change? It would be easy to compare the energy consumption rates and greenhouse gas emissions in the United States, Canada, or Great Britain with those in other countries and feel a measure of guilt. But however justifiable guilt is, it is not the best motivator for change in the long term. Neither, necessarily, is the plea to care for the environment. Researchers have shown that concern for environmental values is widespread in the United States but that it is shallow and superficial.[34] There is, however, another more positive approach that focuses on the fact that much of the behavior outlined above is both environmentally unsustainable and also socially and personally harmful. It is by focusing on the goal of promoting well-being for the citizens of the world that we can best motivate ourselves towards change.

Well-Being

We have noted that most Westerners today are on average wealthier than at any time in the past. We have observed that we spend more than any previous generation and, accordingly, own more stuff. We have remarked that we travel further than any previous age.

Several other observations might be placed alongside these. We live longer than ever before—life expectancy is almost ten years greater now than in 1970. We are considerably less likely to die from history's major killers, such as tuberculosis. We are less likely to experience the tragedy of infant mortality, which has fallen from 26 deaths per 1,000 births to under 7 since the 1960s.[35] Most of us have never had it so good.

Except that we don't think so. Life satisfaction, or well-being as it is more popularly known, is notoriously difficult to measure, but by most accounts and in spite of the unprecedented economic growth and material advances of the post-Second World War period, we are no more and may indeed be less satisfied with life today than we were 50 or even 30 years ago.

The ways in which we recognize, report, and record depression, crime, and other such indicators have changed over the years, necessitating caution when drawing conclusions about long-term well-being trends. Nevertheless, we can discover some symptoms of our society's unease from such data. Dr. Marc Miringoff of Fordham University and his colleagues believed that the Gross Domestic Product does not give a complete picture of the nation's social health. Combining statistics from sixteen social indicators affecting various stages of a person's life, they devised a single number "Index of Social Health." In 2005, this Index fell for the fifth year in a row. Ten of the indicators had worsened since the 1970s. These included: child poverty, child abuse, teenage suicide, unemployment, wages, income inequality, and access to affordable healthcare and housing.[36] These statistics demonstrate a certain level of frustration, anxiety, hardship within an otherwise prosperous society.

When Dr. Miringoff compared nine of the indicators to the Gross Domestic Product from 1959 onward, he found a close correlation until 1975 when social health began to decline while GDP continued to rise. In 2000, he commented: "It used to be that a rising tide lifted all boats, but at a certain point in the 70s, social health and per-capita income split apart."[37]

By 2001, Americans worked more hours, with fewer and shorter vacations, than any other nation in the industrialized world.[38] Decade by decade we seem to be adding hours to our work schedule, a full week per year just between 1990 and 2000. Total work hours by all members of the family increased by 11 percent between 1975 and 2002. This trend is counter to what is happening in other industrialized countries.

A report by the United Nation's International Labor Organization (ILO) in 2001 showed that per person American workers are more productive but not necessarily as efficient (hour by hour) as those in other countries. Americans work about twelve and a half weeks more per year than the Germans, five weeks more than the British or Brazilians, two and half weeks more than the Japanese or Canadians. According to the ILO Director-General Juan Samovia:

"The number of hours worked is one important indicator of a country's overall quality of life. . . . While the benefits of hard work are clear, working more is not the same as working better."

Working more also may not be the same as improved quality of life. Many of the reasons for the increased commitment to work are valid. Families have chosen to move further from work to ensure a safe environment and good schools for their children, often resulting in a longer commute. Dual income families are much more common today than in the 1970s, a response to the rising cost of living, housing costs, and the lure of consumption. Jobs are not as secure as a result of the recession in the 1980s, company downsizing, and globalization. For some, "defensive overwork" has become a way to demonstrate productivity and protect their jobs.

But as a result, work has been eating away at our personal lives. According to Joe Robinson, the founder of the Work to Live campaign, "We really turned the concept of the work ethic into an overwork ethic. The fact is that many of us don't have another identity other than our job title. . . . We are defining ourselves through our labor, and it's only gotten more extreme." Lawrence Jeff Johnson, the leader of the study for the United Nations International Labor Organization, and an American, said that "We have blurred the line now between what is work and what is play. But we don't want to give up that edge. We American workers don't want to take time away from work." Nor, perhaps feel that we can.

Perhaps surprisingly, this not only has consequences for our families and our own health but it also has implications for climate change. A recent study by the Center for Economic and Policy Research found that if Americans were able to continue their high levels of productivity while following the European example in work hours and vacation time, the nation would use 20 percent less energy. In fact, if this practice had been in effect in 2002, the United States would have produced 3 percent less carbon dioxide than it had in 1990, only 4 percent above the suggested level of emissions under the Kyoto Protocol.

Such objective measures of well-being are well supported by the more subjective ones found in social studies that record what people say about their own lives.[39] Self-reported happiness in the United States has remained the same for the past 30 years. In 2006, as in 1972, 50 percent of Americans reported themselves as "pretty happy" and just over 30 percent as "very happy."[40] This trend can be seen in other high-income nations. Despite a sixfold increase in income per head since 1950, the Japanese have recorded no increase in happiness. In Belgium, the percentage of people who were very satisfied with their life fell from 44 percent in 1973 to 18 percent in 2001.[41]

This decoupling of wealth and well-being, unprecedented and unpredicted in the West, has forced upon us, with renewed urgency, the age-old question: "What does make us happy?" In as far as social science has an answer, it claims that a number of factors, such as age, gender, looks, IQ, and education have negligible impact, and others, like genetic inheritance or health, have some impact (although not as much as one might intuitively think).[42] There are, however, half a dozen or so factors, including one's work, family and community life, personal values, and relationship with the divine, whose impact is significant and important, and several of these factors are related to two of the three areas discussed above: travel and consumption.

This link is important and worth exploring for two reasons. First, it suggests that there may be something to gain from responding to the challenge of climate change: it needn't all be hard work with no obvious return. And second, it places center stage the observation that you cannot hope to understand environmental issues in isolation from social ones, an observation that resonates strongly with the biblical social vision, as we shall see in Part 2.

Travel and Well-Being

The way in which we travel can have a considerable impact on our well-being, specifically in the way it impacts our relationships. This is best understood by looking at three concentric circles: first, the innermost and most intimate, our family relationships; second, local, community relationships; and third, more generally the social atmosphere that our excessive or "hyper"-mobility breeds.

Transport and Family

No other factor is more strongly or positively correlated to personal well-being than a good relationship with friends, colleagues, community, God, and family. Put simply, close, helpful, trustworthy, and intimate relationships make life worth living.[43] Marriage is consistently shown to be the most important single contributor to a happy life. Married people tend to be happier than those who never married or those who have divorced, separated, or been widowed, a fact that holds across cultures and when income and age are taken into account.

There are, of course, innumerable reasons for family discord and break-up but one that is rarely noticed is transport, or, more specifically, the way in which our hypermobile lives stretch relationships too thinly.

People in the United States today travel further to school, work, shop, and for leisure than ever before. The average commute is over 12 miles (it used to be to just over 9 miles thirty years ago), the average shopping trip 7 miles (compared to 5), the average family and personal business trip 7.5 miles (up from 6.7), and the average leisure trip 12 miles (compared to just over 10). These may not seem to be major changes, but combined with the number of trips made each year the average American family traveled 4,000 miles more per year in 2001, for everyday tasks, than they did in 1990.

Commuting has also changed. By 2005, the average travel time to work had increased to 25 minutes each way. Three million workers face an hour and a half or longer daily commute. Rush hour congestion has spurred many more workers to leave home earlier in the morning and to stay later at night. In 2006, one in every eight workers left for work by 6 am. In 1990 it had been one in nine.[44]

Such hypermobility can put a severe strain on family life. Parents live divided lives, with their time stretched between home and work. Children's lives are similarly stretched between home and school. Broadly speaking, more time spent traveling to and from these various places means less time spent together as a family.

At a different level, a culture of necessary job mobility, which demands time-consuming business travel or wholesale relocation, can compound this lack of family interaction time, removing parents from the home for prolonged periods or tearing entire families from whatever social network they have developed around them.

This is not to suggest that the more you travel the worse your family life will be. Our lives and families are far too complex to draw such easy, simple conclusions. Nor is it to imply that we should return to a pre-mobile culture in which people rarely traveled more than two miles from their front door. That is the straw man that opponents like to demolish in this debate.

It is, however, to state that a stable family life contributes enormously to our well-being but demands time, and that our regular or long-distance travel devours that time and can weaken the family ties and our well-being accordingly.

Transport and Community

Not only do Americans travel further today but the *number of trips* they take has also increased dramatically. In 2001, the average household undertook 262 more vehicle trips than they did in 1990. While trips for commuting rose only by 6 percent, shopping trips grew by a third, family and personal business by almost as much, and social or recreational trips by 26 percent.[45]

What this really means is that we are using our cars, vans, and SUVs more and more as our primary means of transport. The result of these trends is that we spend far more of our time sealed inside our cars. Not only is this true, but more of these trips seemed to be spent alone. In 2007, approximately 85 percent of workers drove by themselves to work.[46] Considering all trip purposes, in 2000, the average number of occupants per vehicle was 1.6 down from 1.9 in 1977.[47]

Not only has this decreased the time available for relationships with family and friends, but it has led to a severe decrease in "local interaction time," that time spent in our local community during which we form relationships with others who share our immediate physical space. In his book *Bowling Alone,* Robert Putnam estimates that for every 10 minutes of additional commuting time there is a corresponding 10 percent decline in all forms of social interaction.[48] Because there are only ever 24 hours in a day, the more time we travel by car the more thinly we spread ourselves.

This is more serious than simply being a case of people missing a nice, warm, neighborly feeling and a few garden-fence conversations. A little way beneath good family relationships as a correlate to personal well-being comes good community ties. Not surprisingly, living among people you know, like, trust, and can depend upon tends to make life more secure and enjoyable.

Again, as with family life, no one suggests that our hypermobility is the sole cause for fractured or non-existent community relations. Television, affluence, and time-famine (due to other reasons) all play their part. But, as with family life, the more time we spend sealed off from our immediate physical space in our cars—and, correspondingly, as we shall note below, the less time we spend in our immediate retail space—the less time and opportunity we have to form those relationships that, no matter how casual, contribute to our sense of feeling at home where we live.

Transport and Society

The third way in which our hypermobility affects our well-being is more nebulous. Studies have shown that the weight of traffic in a neighborhood is, broadly speaking, inversely correlated to the number of local friends and acquaintances people have. More traffic equals fewer friends.

Not only does this erode the relationships that make life worthwhile but it also helps foster the perception of a more hostile, dehumanizing environment. "Mobility fosters anonymity and anonymity fosters crime."[49] A local "community" which is largely anonymous and fluid makes it comparatively easy to commit crime, especially home burglary and car crime. Householders are less likely to be at home, neighbors less likely to observe the culprits, and bystanders less likely to challenge their behavior. Moreover, "people are far more willing to steal from strangers and institutions than from personal acquaintances."[50]

Crime itself fosters a surveillance society. This means a rising number of neighborhood watch schemes, one of the most effective and economical means of preventing crime. But on the negative side, it means ever more resources devoted to domestic security measures and video surveillance, an increase in gated communities and private roads, and, more generally, a pervasive siege mentality in which public space feels hostile and potentially dangerous.

This sense of hostility is particularly serious for children. A study in 1980 concluded that residential and arterial traffic "was the one universal factor above all others that restricted the development of children's spatial range, thereby limiting children's knowledge of the community environment—including its natural characteristics and components."[51] Since that time a new factor has been added, the fear of "Stranger Danger." The boundaries of a child's world have shrunk to a ninth of what they were in 1970.[52]

As a substitute for time to explore the woods, fields, and surroundings in a neighborhood, many more children now interact primarily with television or video games or participate in organized sports. Today the US Youth Soccer Association has nearly 3 million members, up from 100,000 in 1974. To a parent, organized sports would certainly seem a better alternative than watching television or playing video games. But the proportion of children's time that is highly structured has also increased. By 1997, children spent 27 percent more of their time in organized sports than in 1981. Recent studies have shown that, for children, *unsupervised* time in natural surroundings helps build creativity, lessens stress, and encourages confidence, knowledge, and appreciation of the natural world. Modern children suffer from "nature-deficient syndrome." Not only are there implications for a child's physical and mental health, but also social development.

The ultimate—if slightly extreme—consequence of all this is a society in which, unless supervised, children cannot play outside (because it is too dangerous), cannot visit the shops (because there aren't any within walking distance), and cannot go unescorted to schools (because of fear of pedophiles).

The now familiar caveat demands repetition here. No one suggests that hypermobility is the sole or even most significant contributor to crime rates or the erosion of childhood; merely that the anonymous, fluid society that it generates helps facilitate these unwelcome trends. Once again, the point made is that reducing our levels of mobility need not be pure "stick," a troublesome but necessary limitation of hard-won freedoms in order to save the climate. It could also be "carrot," an opportunity to re-examine who we are, what we value, and to reshape our lives around it. This, as we shall explore in Part 2, is certainly the attitude that the biblical social vision would encourage in us.

Consumption and Well-Being

As with trends in personal mobility, our changing levels and patterns of consumption have a significant impact beyond the obviously environmental sphere.

Consumption Levels and Well-Being

Money doesn't buy you happiness. Nor does stuff. The message is not new. Centuries ago the teacher of Ecclesiastes wrote about the "grievous evil" of "wealth hoarded to the harm of its owner" (Eccl 5:13), and the Apostle Paul about the "ruin and destruction" that trap "people who want to get rich" (1 Tim 6:7). Superficial readings of such verses have led some to claim that Christianity hates wealth and demands penury of all. Although the truth is subtler, the unavoidable fact is that biblical writers recognized the dangers of wealth—specifically its misleading claim to guarantee salvation—and were therefore nervous about, and often hostile towards it.[53]

What is (relatively) novel is the way in which the social sciences are beginning to gather evidence in support of this view. Studies consistently show that personal well-being is more closely linked to relative than to absolute levels of wealth. Beyond a certain basic level, how happy we are is influenced more by how much other people have than it is by how much we have. It is important to understand this precisely. There is no positive correlation between happiness and poverty, still less between happiness and unemployment. Money and the consumption it enables does improve well-being—but only up to a point. The problem comes when we, and wider society, fail to recognize or respond to that point.

We may hear that possessions don't make us any happier, but if our whole culture is still oriented around the idea that buying, owning or doing more makes us happier, we end up trapped on a "hedonistic treadmill," exhausting ourselves in the chase for more, when more does not mean happier.

It is worth repeating that money itself is not the problem. Nor, strange as it may seem, is wealth. The problem is when wealth owns us, rather than we it, and begins to blind us to the consequences of our actions. Without realizing it, we find ourselves consuming stuff that we don't need and hardly want; stuff that fails to makes us any happier but does make the planet marginally unhealthier. In the colorful words of Jonathan Porritt, "if people aren't getting any happier as they go on getting richer, why do we continue to trash the planet and turn people into consumptive zombies in pursuit of economic growth?"[54]

Consumption Patterns and Well-Being

The way we consume also affects our well-being.[55]

Over the last decade, we have moved decisively away from local, small-scale retail outlets, towards larger, out-of-town chain stores. They are cheaper and tend to be more convenient, at least for the car-driving majority of the population. But the transition has come at a cost, not only for our own towns but around the world.

The quest for the lowest price on goods has given great power to the consumer. The big-box retailers, such as Wal-Mart, are able to keep their customers happy by "driving any excess costs out of the supply train." This means pushing for lower costs from their suppliers—translated into lower wages for their employees, often not only wages for the store, but also for the seamstress in far away Bangladesh. Studies have shown that when these large scale retailers move into a town, wages in other retail stores often drop in order for the smaller stores to remain competitive. A small independent retailer's wholesale cost for an item is higher than the retail selling price by a large big-box retail store due to the latter's greater purchasing power. The reward to the consumer is more stuff, more cheaply. And perhaps lower personal wages.

In the process, town and village centers, small shops, and shopping districts are disappearing. Quality, uniqueness, and civility are lost in the process. Small retailers who attempt to find a niche through good customer service and unique, high quality merchandise are often criticized for higher prices. Town developers have tried to recapture the small town feel by creating shopping centers that resemble old "Main Streets." Yet the shops that are able to survive are often ones connected to national chains. So there is an increasing homogenization of the shopping world. Malls may be larger, contain more or different restaurants or ways to entertain shoppers, but the stores are likely to be similar no matter where you shop. As the author Tom Wolfe wrote in his novel, *A Man in Full:* "the only way you could tell you were leaving one community and entering another was when the franchises started repeating and you spotted another 7 Eleven, another Wendy's, another Costco."[56]

One additional reason why this matters is that local shops, post offices, bank branches (and, of course, transport services), are all important in helping people to develop and maintain relationships with the people with whom we share our immediate physical space. They provide an intimate and locally-rooted forum in which people can meet, share news and information, give advice, ask and offer favors, as well as shop. Shopping malls try to replicate this, but they are commonly too large, impersonal, and distant from home to do it well. Local interaction, which is facilitated by lively town and village centers, is, accordingly, linked directly to high levels of trust (and inversely to levels of crime and anti-social behavior) and indirectly to well-being.

It is only fair to recognize that local communities can also be suffocating, myopic, and constricting. There is no shortage of literature testifying to the need of individuals to "spread their wings" and escape. We are mistaken if we envisage paradise in a 1950s market town. Nevertheless, insufficient local interaction is more likely to be a threat to our well-being today than too much.

Advertising, directly linked as it is to our consumption patterns, also has a discernible impact on our well-being. The average America views approximately 20,000 TV broadcast advertisements each year. Thirty percent of network news programming is devoted to commercials.[57] By 2005, over 107 million phone numbers had been added to the National Do Not Call registry—an indication of the frustration Americans felt with advertising invading their homes through telemarketers. In 2005, US companies sent more than 300 pieces of bulk mail for every man, woman, and child in the United States.[58] The production and disposal of all this junk mail consumes more energy than 3 million cars.

And what of advertising to children: Companies are now spending 2.5 times more money (about $15 billion) on advertising directed at children than they did in 1992. The average child is exposed to 40,000 advertisements a year on television. Even the in-school TV channel, Channel One, includes advertisements for food, movies, and games.

Even churches are not exempt from the infiltration of consumerism. This may show up in simple ways such as a food court or coffee shop—ways to encourage fellowship or outreach. But to some large companies, the megachurches have become a prime distribution and marketing channel. In a 2007 study on the rise of megachurches, Barry Harvey, a professor at Baylor University in Waco, Texas, said: "The church is essentially becoming indistinguishable from its biggest competitor, the mall. To allow the commercial enterprise to come into the church is to allow the desire for accumulating things, buying things, to dominate even the relationship with God." Of course, not all churches follow this course but it does show the great pressure on people, from all sides, to consume.

One final effect of our consumerism is more subtle. According to Richard Harwood who has conducted surveys across the United States over the past decades, the messages of consumerism are so pervasive that people have "built a protective barrier of skepticism around themselves, which often prevents even genuine messages from penetrating their awareness. The barriers do not simply keep external forces out; ultimately they confine the individual to a personal space that keeps people inward, in the process making them indifferent, or even resistant, to their full involvement in the public realm."[59] In other words, we have withdrawn more and more from engagement in the large issues of life and from participation in political or civic affairs. However, Hartman also found a sense of hope, and an expectation that change in national well-being will begin with individuals, will be based on people's character, requires an engagement with the real issues that affect their lives, plus a move to take personal responsibility and a commitment to something larger than themselves.

Summary: Sustainability and Well-Being

This chapter has explored the human face of climate change: sustainability. Superficially, a single, vast, and impenetrable problem, climate change is really billions of small, seemingly insignificant, wholly solvable ones. The way we use energy at home, the way we travel, and the manner in which we consume lie at the heart of climate change. Unless they change, it won't.

There is, however, another side to the coin: well-being. Responding to the challenge of climate change and our unsustainable energy use need not be a "hair shirt" option. Issues of environmental and social sustainability are inextricably linked, and if we use the opportunity afforded by the first to examine the second, and respond accordingly, we may find that not only do we not suffer but we may actually benefit in the long run.

This is certainly, as we shall see in Part 2, the approach that the biblical social vision would promote in us. What of a biblical environmental vision—the other half of the climate change equation? What place does involvement with environmental issues have in a Christian's life? It is to this we now turn.

Part 2

THE BIBLICAL PERSPECTIVE

3

THE BIBLICAL VISION OF CARE
FOR THE ENVIRONMENT

SUBSEQUENT CHAPTERS WILL OUTLINE what a distinctively Christian response to climate change might look like. This chapter examines a more fundamental issue: what is the foundation of a Christian's care for the environment? It argues that God cares about the material world, since he created and sustains it. He values it independently of human existence, and Christians are called to imitate the concern of God for maintaining and taking care of creation. Human flourishing is deeply bound up with our attitude towards creation, and part of becoming fully human is to take responsibility for the physical world in which we live and to which we belong. Care for the natural world is inseparable from the command to love our neighbor, and recognizing human nature as being fundamentally physical and embodied means that to love other people means not only to communicate the good news of the gospel verbally but also to care for their material needs and the effects of our actions on their welfare. Moreover, Christians care for creation because it has an eternal destiny in Christ: it will be redeemed and transformed along with our own bodies in the new creation, and the work we do now to shape and to care for the world is of eternal significance.

Why Care? Historical Perspective

There is a long history of positive Christian engagement with the environment, and, although we cannot make a full review here, a few examples will give a flavor of that engagement.[1] The attitude to the natural world of the early Greek Fathers such as Basil the Great and John Chrysostom was exemplified by the way they fostered positive attitudes to animals. Benedict, the sixth-century founder of Western monasticism, propounded a similarly gentle attitude to nature and to animals within his Rule. Indeed the wide-spread development and influence of monasteries led to the domestication both of the land and of animals (notably of sheep, which transformed the pastoral landscape of Europe).[2] Throughout the medieval period there was an understanding of the need to steward the Earth, particularly for successful long-term agricultural productivity.

John Calvin in 1563 was one of the first people explicitly to expound the commands in Genesis as a requirement for sustainable use of the Earth's resources. He wrote:

> Let him who possesses a field, so partake of its yearly fruits, that he may not suffer the ground to be injured by his negligence; but let him endeavour to hand it down to posterity as he received it, or even better cultivated . . . Moreover, that this economy, and this diligence, with respect to those good things which God has given us to enjoy, may flourish among us; let every one regard himself as the steward of God in all things which he possesses.[3]

A century later, Sir Matthew Hale, sometime Lord Chief Justice of England, published similar views, writing that man was created as God's viceroy, steward, and bailiff and was given dominion to curb the fiercer animals, protect the tame and useful ones, to preserve and improve plant species, to check unprofitable vegetable growth, and "to preserve the face of the Earth in beauty, usefulness and fruitfulness."[4] Many of the early Fellows of the Royal Society, founded around the same time, were committed to understanding the world around them as part of their Christian duty. They saw the pursuit of science as a way of discovering God's handiwork and using their understanding of nature for the good of humankind. In the nineteenth century the founders of the London Missionary Society were similarly committed to using science to improve the lot of humanity.[5]

Despite this long history of Christian engagement with the environment, cases of negligence and exploitation have also sometimes been reported as being sanctioned by the command in Gen 1:28 that mankind should have dominion over the world. As we discuss below, that is a grossly incorrect reading of the Genesis text, as well as being historically inaccurate.[6] Contemporary Christian environmental concern is often relegated to a back seat in favor of more individualistic, "spiritual" concerns. Many have considered environmental issues to be secondary to more important matters of salvation or of care for the poor, the underprivileged and the vulnerable. There has sometimes been a little articulated but powerful underlying assumption that the Earth will some day, maybe quite soon, be burnt to a frazzle, so it is not important or even appropriate to put resources into long-term environmental policies. Some Christians have felt a need to distance themselves from a Green agenda, because they suspected overtones of pagan nature-worship or New Age spirituality. As a result, throughout the latter half of the twentieth century the environmental flag was flown mainly by the largely secular Green movement.

Yet from a scriptural perspective, Christians of all people should have been active in the environmental agenda.[7] The very existence of this universe is the result of God's creative activity, bringing into being a world that he pronounced "very good" and that he then lent to humankind to subdue and tend (Gen 1:28–31; 2:15). For Christians, there should be no sense that the "material" is in any way inferior to the "spiritual." God shows his commitment to the material world not only by upholding it moment by moment through Jesus (Heb 1:3), but by becoming incarnate in it, by taking a human body in the person of Jesus with all its limitations and finitude.[8] This world is one that still displays the creator's glory and purposes, though marred by the effects of sin; a world with the certain hope of a renewed future; a world in which we are called to work to God's praise and glory.

Why Care? Because God Does

First, we care about the environment because God cares about it. This is quite clear in the Genesis creation story. God existed before the universe and is separate from it. He chose to create it of his own free will and for his own purposes. He was not beholden to anyone or anything, and the entire natural order is, and remains, his possession. The very first verse of the Old Testament makes this clear: "In the beginning God created the heavens and the earth." The first verses of John's Gospel echo the same truth: "Through him [Jesus] all things were made"—and just in case we didn't get the message John continues by making the same point again: "without him nothing was made that has been made" (John 1:3). Our care for creation is predicated on the fact that God owns it and that he is sovereign over it: "The earth is the Lord's and everything in it; the world and all who live in it" (Ps 24:1).

The picture of God in the early chapters of Genesis is of a hardworking and conscientious laborer: of honest day's work, of rest at the end of the week and of satisfaction at a job well done, with the frequent affirmation that "God saw that it was good." This is a God who gloried in his creation and whose creation, in turn, reflected something of his character. "The heavens declare the glory of God," says Ps 19:1. Paul comments in his letter to the Romans: "since the creation of the world God's invisible qualities—his eternal power and divine nature—have been clearly seen, being understood from what has been made" (Rom 1:20).

God created a world that is good and beautiful, independent of our presence in it. According to Ps 148, the Sun, Moon, stars, waters, mountains, hills, weather, vegetation, animals, birds, and sea creatures all praise the Lord. The goodness of the Earth does not derive solely from the presence of people in it. The Bible is also clear that this material world is one which God sustains, through Jesus, all the time, day by day, moment by moment: "The Son [Jesus] is the radiance of God's glory and the exact representation of his being, *sustaining all things by his powerful word*" (Heb 1:3). Without him it would fall apart into chaos: "For by him [Jesus] all things were created . . . He is before all things, and *in him all things hold together*" (Col 1:16–17).

God cares for his creation. In the book of Job, the Lord asks rhetorically, "Who cuts a channel for the torrents of rain, and a path for the thunderstorm, to water a land *where no man lives,* a desert with no one in it, to satisfy a desolate wasteland and make it sprout with grass" (Job 38:25–27). In chapters 38–39, he gives a long list of all the ways in which he cares for and exercises his sovereign rule over his creation: his dominion ranges from the stars to the Earth's very foundations; through the inanimate creation, including the sea, light, snow, hail, thunderstorm, and lightning; to care for animals like the lioness, the raven, wild donkeys, oxen, and horses; to watching over the birds such as the ostrich and hawks.

Even eagles, those most independent and powerful of birds "soar at his command."

Psalm 65:9–13 describes God as intimately involved in caring for creation, "You care for the land and water it; you enrich it abundantly . . . You drench its furrows and level its ridges; you soften it with showers and bless its crops. You crown the year with your bounty, and your carts overflow with abundance." The language of blessing the Earth, of richness and abundance portray God not as merely maintaining the created world, but as lavishing his goodness upon it, caring for it. This superabundant goodness of God towards the Earth is met with a response of joyful praise: "The grasslands of the desert overflow; the hills are clothed with gladness. The meadows are covered with flocks and the valleys are mantled with grain; they shout for joy and sing."

The language here of God's loving care for the Earth, and the Earth's joyful response, suggests that God's sustenance of creation is more than a mechanical exercise to provide a habitat for humanity. Rather it implies that God delights in the world he has created and loves to pour out his goodness upon it. Throughout the Old and New Testaments, God is named and praised as the creator and sustainer of all things.[9] His involvement with creation is an expression of his character. God's care for his creation is *independent* of human agency or presence.

When God himself came to Earth in the person of Jesus, he showed this same concern. Jesus explicitly reminded his hearers of the value that God places even on the lowliest of creatures: "Are not two sparrows sold for a penny? Yet not one of them will fall to the ground apart from the will of your Father" (Matt 10:29). Jesus also showed his authority over the so-called forces of nature. While out with the disciples in a squall on the Sea of Galilee the disciples became terrified that the boat would be swamped and would sink, but Jesus calmed the sea with a word. "Who is this?" asked the disciples in awe, "even the wind and the waves obey him!" (Mark 4:41).

From the environmental perspective, by caring for the non-human created order we are also worshipping God by allowing it to give glory to God as he intended it to. We shall return to this theme later in this chapter. And of course, the converse is true: if we neglect, abuse, and despoil it we are not only damaging something that is precious to God but also preventing the created order from reflecting God's glory fully.

If we don't care for the world in which we live, we are acting rather like the teenagers who with a wild party have wrecked a family home that has been lovingly created for them by their parents, or have simply treated it as a hotel with a fridge to be raided for food and a place to dump dirty clothes. Or, to use a different analogy, imagine Michelangelo completing the Sistine Chapel ceiling, sharing all his learning, experience, and skill with his apprentices, and then offering them the use of his paints for their own artistic expression—only to find that they have used them to scrawl ugly graffiti across his masterpiece.[10] God's relationship with creation is a long way from the all-too common idea that it is simply the stage on which the drama of human salvation is worked out. Rather, the created world is God's masterpiece: he crafted it as a place of fruitfulness and abundance that reflects his character, and he continually sustains it. To understand and appreciate this is to realize the importance of taking care of it: God's attitude to creation indicates that it is precious and wonderful, irrespective of any utility it possesses for us. To love Jesus and to grow to be like him is to care for the things that he cares for, to take care of the things he has created and has blessed us with. This alone ought to be sufficient to motivate us to take responsibility for the world around us.

Many national and international groupings of Christians are active in promoting care for the environment from a specifically Christian perspective. The John Ray Initiative in the UK brings together scientific and Christian understanding of the environment to promote the twin themes of sustainable living and environmental stewardship.[11] In the USA, the Evangelical Declaration on the Care of Creation in 1994 set out clearly a broad agenda of environmental concern;[12] while the Evangelical Climate Initiative in 2006 focused on the issue of global climate change.[13] The National Religious Partnership for the Environment draws together efforts in evangelical, Catholic, Jewish, and mainline Protestant congregations on a variety of environmental issues, including climate change.[14] Chapters of the Interfaith Power and Light Campaign help congregations across the United States assess their energy use in light of climate change, provide alternatives and education programs.[15] A Rocha focuses on practical, local, conservation issues, including climate change, and has branches in the United States and Canada (as well as 16 other countries).[16] The involvement of Christians has had major impacts on social issues in the past, including the abolition of slavery,[17] the establishment of American civil rights, the overthrow of repressive communism in eastern Europe, and the fall of apartheid in South Africa: it may well be that Christians could have a similar impact on action to address global climate change.

Why Care? Because It Is Part of What It Means To Be Human

Before we move on to consider humankind's place and responsibilities within God's created order, we need to remind ourselves that the universe God created is not a timeless, unchanging place. We are not called to preserve the world as it was in some presumed golden age 50, 500, or 5,000 years ago. God's creation is a fruitful, developing place, with a sense of direction to it, and it is right that we should use scientific understanding and technological skill to govern our interaction with it.

The biblical story paints the same picture, of a definite direction, a development in God's interaction with his people. This is apparent both in God's dealings with Israel recounted in the Old Testament[18] and also in the lives of individual believers. In the daily walk with God the Christian believer becomes more like Jesus, the example of what it means to be fully human, being "transformed into his likeness" (2 Cor 3:18). This idea of development is important to a proper Christian engagement with the environment, not least when the secular language is so often only that of "preservation" and "conservation."

Our Well-Being Is Tied Up with That of the Environment

God's relationship to creation is not the only reason why Christians ought to care about the environment. Another significant motivation can be found in what the Bible teaches about our own relationship to the rest of the world. The opening chapters of Genesis highlight the commonalities between humanity and the rest of the animate creation.[19] Genesis 2 uses the same word to describe how animals, birds, and humans were "formed" from the ground. Humans were formed specifically from the *dust* of the ground—that hardly constitutes an accolade of superiority (Gen 2:7; 1 Cor 15:47). Humanity shares the same food as other animals (Gen 1:29–30), and the same breath of life is given to animals and humans alike.[20] Psalm 104:10–30 describes how humans have the same needs as other animals, all of which the creator God provides in abundance. To care for creation is therefore to care for a system of which we are a part and upon which we are utterly dependent.

Human flourishing and the well-being of the rest of creation are inextricably linked in the biblical narrative. When humans rebelled against their creator God, the consequences of their sinfulness were detrimental both to the physical environment and to their own well-being: living in the land became immediately much more dangerous, both from wild animals and from other people (Gen 3:15; 4:14); the joy of procreation was scarred by an increase of pain in childbirth (Gen 3:16); even the production of food from the earth became painful toil (Gen 3:17–19). In these curses that came as a result of human sin, we see the alienation of humanity from the land. According to Genesis, humanity's continuing sin perpetuates the corruption of the ground (Gen 4:11–13), and throughout the Old Testament there is a connection between human obedience and the fertility of the land (Gen 26:12; Lev 26:3–6; Deut 11:13–15); and conversely between human disobedience and its infertility (Deut 11:16–17; Isa 24:1–13; Hos 4:1–3; Hag 7:1–11). As part of creation, we suffer when creation suffers, and it is our sin that causes creation to suffer.

The Blessing of Rule Over Creation

Humans are part of the created order, yet the Bible asserts that there is something special about us. We are more than animals, even though we share with them our material and genetic make-up. Genesis says that humans, uniquely among creation, are made "in God's image" (Gen 1:27) and are given a command by God to rule over and to take care of both the living and the nonliving creation (Gen 1:28; 2:15). Both of these have implications for the way we should relate to nature.

The term "image of god" is found in ancient Mesopotamian and Egyptian culture contemporary with the writing of Genesis. The king was sometimes described as being in the image of god, meaning that he was god's representative on earth. This has the sense of carrying responsibility with it, making humankind vice-regents, ruling on behalf of God. In Babylon, for example, the king handed back his insignia to the high priest every year and to get them back had to give a detailed statement that he had been a faithful ruler. The Genesis reference to humans as being "in the image of God" almost certainly carries overtones of this sense of ruling on God's behalf and also of being accountable to him for the way in which we rule, and suggests that this is an essential component of what it means to be human. However, uniquely among the cultures of the Ancient Near East, the Genesis account designated not one king, but the whole of humanity as being "in the image of God," using the plural form of the verb in Gen 1:26 to describe their role in ruling over creation.

Along with giving humankind the privilege of ruling and having dominion over the Earth, God *blesses* humanity in Gen 1:28. Genesis 2:15 also states that, "The Lord God took the man and put him in the garden of Eden to work it and take care for it." The word translated "work" is *abad,* which carries the sense of "to serve," and the word translated "take care of" is *shamar,* which means "to keep, guard, protect." The dominion that humanity is given over nature is not to be one of exploitative and selfish rule, but rather one of careful and just service. And within that service, which should be part of the worship of God, there is blessing.

Although some have claimed that much of the wanton exploitation that has caused current environmental degradation is a result of ideology developed from the command in Gen 1:28 that humankind should have dominion over the Earth,[21] there is little historical basis for this. In any case, this is a gross misreading of Gen 1,[22] which, set in its context, implies instead that we are given the privilege of carrying out the mandate of delegated dominion in a way that reflects the character and values of God's loving and compassionate kingship.[23]

Within a Christian framework, there are limits set to our oversight of creation: "the highest heavens belong to the Lord, but the earth he has given to man" proclaims Ps 115:16. God is still ultimately sovereign, and the responsibility to care for creation is one for which we are answerable to him. The modern concept of "stewardship" captures some elements of this responsibility to care for creation, but it is limited in that it has the sense of management of an inanimate thing rather than the caring relationship that the kingship model of Genesis suggests. A more helpful image of the way in which we are to have dominion over the Earth is that of the shepherd or servant king,[24] the role given to the kings of Israel (Ps 72) and explicitly adopted by Jesus when he came to Earth. This rule is directed entirely to the benefit of God's kingdom and glory and not at all to the gain of the king himself.

In the Old Testament laws intended to govern Israel's dominion over the land, we see a graphic model of the right way to relate to God's creation, although in reality Israel rarely if ever lived up to this ideal. Israel is depicted as a tenant in God's vineyard, given the land only insofar as they keep the covenant, and they are held to account by their heavenly king. Respect for animals and land is enjoined in the Old Testament regulations, and tithing and the giving of first fruits acknowledge that the land is God's.

Biblical literature depicts right rule over the land as an essential part of what it means to be human, but there is also the suggestion that failure to rule justly diminishes our humanity. Apocalyptic literature depicts exploitative empires as beasts. When King Nebuchadnezzar openly disobeyed God, his authority was removed from him and he became, literally, like a beast: "He was driven away from people and ate grass like cattle. His body was drenched with the dew of heaven until his hair grew like the feathers of an eagle and his nails like the claws of a bird" (Dan 4:33). The implication seems to be that it is not simply dominion which sets humanity apart from the rest of creation, but specifically just and caring rule over the land and the people, and that by failing to rule as they were originally intended to, humans deface the image of God which makes them uniquely human.

To be fully human, then, is to rule over the Earth in a way that reflects our role as God's vice-regents. We are to exercise dominion through servanthood. Of course, we will inevitably fall short of this ideal. As humans, our sin has profoundly damaged both ourselves and the world in which we live, and living in a fallen world means that as well as the blessing or joy it was originally intended to be, caring for the Earth is often difficult and costly. However, in Jesus we find both the model of perfected humanity and the means by which we may begin to live in a way that is pleasing to him.

To see what it means to be fully human, we need to look to Jesus, who "is the image of the invisible God" (Col 1:15). Jesus is the hallmark, the living standard of what it means to be truly human. The rest of us, marred by our rebellion against God, yet created by him and offered salvation by him, are "human becomings," on the way to full humanity.[25] Christians, committed to following Jesus and partaking of his perfected humanity, are therefore called to work towards the exercise of servant rulership over the whole created order. The created earth is not a resource to be exploited but a domain entrusted to our care and protection. We are called to this servant rule as one of the means by which we may become fully human and flourish as we were originally intended to.

Why Care? To Obey the Command to Love Our "Neighbors"

A third reason why Christians care for the physical world is that this is an important element of loving other people. According to Jesus, the two greatest commands are "Love the Lord your God with all your heart and with all your soul and with all your mind and with all your strength" and "Love your neighbor as yourself" (Mark 12:30–31). We are commanded in the same breath to love God and to love our neighbor. That "love" is something that involves the whole person, heart, soul, mind, and strength.

When considering what it means to "love our neighbor," we need to beware of stressing people's spiritual needs at the expense of their material needs. To do so would be to fall into an unbiblical dualism, to fail adequately to acknowledge the reality that humans are embodied. It is not possible to be a human without a body, either in this world or the next. Jesus himself drew attention to the reality of his post-resurrection body when with his disciples, who were amazed and frightened because they thought that he was a ghost. He told them "Look at my hands and my feet. It is I myself! Touch me and see; a ghost does not have flesh and bones, as you see I have" (Luke 24:39).

A significant element of Jesus' earthly ministry was tending to people's physical needs at the same time as he addressed their pressing spiritual needs. So when a paralytic was carried on a mat to Jesus by his friends, Jesus saw the faith of the friends and told the paralyzed man: "Take heart, son; your sins are forgiven." Although he was making the point that the man's greatest need was to have his sins forgiven, Jesus went on to cure the man physically as well (Matt 9:2–7). Sometimes people seeking physical healing came to Jesus, and he responded first by healing them but then went on specifically to seek them out and show them the importance of faith in their lives. For example, when the woman who had been bleeding for twelve years touched his cloak in a crowd, Jesus immediately healed her. He then explicitly asked the woman to reveal herself to him in front of the crowd, which she did, allowing Jesus to reinforce her faith, saying, "Daughter, your faith has healed you. Go in peace and be freed from your suffering" (Mark 5:25–34).

On other occasions Jesus took the initiative in healing those who were suffering. John 5:1–14 reports him coming across a man by a pool in Jerusalem who had been an invalid for 38 years, and asking him, "Do you want to get well?" Not surprisingly, the invalid did, and Jesus healed him. But apparently the man did not know who Jesus was. Later, Jesus sought him out at the temple, where he made the obvious point "See, you are well again," and went on to add the spiritual point by telling the man to "stop sinning." Jesus time and again made it clear, as he did in this case, that people need to be made whole both spiritually and physically. We too need to keep that balance in our love for others.

It is notable that when Jesus tells the parable of the Good Samaritan to illustrate who is the neighbor of the second great commandment (Luke 10:25–37), he specifically chooses a person with whom many Jews would prefer not to associate. Our neighbors include all those of different beliefs and different cultures. And in that same parable, the love of neighbor quite obviously includes caring for their physical needs and their safety.

The gospel is "good news" for the whole person, and so it is important that Christians should seek to tell unbelievers the good news of Christ crucified and risen again, while living out the good news of the gospel by caring both for the material needs of other people and for the creation of which they are a part.

The "Neighbor" We Cannot See

One of the key messages of Jesus' parable of the Good Samaritan is that our neighbors are not restricted to those with whom we share ethnic, cultural, or geographic links. All fellow humans are neighbors, and thus demand our love and care, irrespective of how far away they live. Space is no bar to neighborly love.

Nor is time. Just as those living on the other side of the planet are our neighbors, so are the unborn, the men and women of future generations whom we cannot see but who will inherit from us the consequences of our actions, and flourish or suffer accordingly. As Margaret Thatcher said: "No generation has a freehold on this earth. All we have is a life tenancy—with a full repairing lease . . . we are its guardians and trustees for generations to come."[26]

The Bible places a strong emphasis on exercising responsibility for the good of future generations, with the Old Testament repeatedly stating the call to preserve God's name and his blessings "through all generations." In the New Testament the concern to do so is maintained but is transformed into the command to honor and spread "the name of Jesus" throughout all peoples.

Global climate change is a particularly striking example of the truth that my activities here and now that produce greenhouse gases will have inevitable consequences for people living elsewhere: from the other side of the planet to the other end of the century. As we saw in chapter 1, these consequences of increased weather extremes, warmer average temperatures, and rising sea levels are real and are potentially life- or livelihood-threatening to people living in already marginal circumstances in some low-income areas of the world. Moreover, the consequences of our greenhouse gas emissions today are liable to be felt in climate change and rising sea levels for decades and centuries to come.

This is not to say that we should never drive to visit relatives, or that we should sit shivering in unheated houses, but it does highlight the fact that everything we do in this life is likely to have consequences for other people, so we should be conscious of that as we make decisions about our activities.

Christianity is a deeply counter-cultural religion. We are called continually to consider how our actions affect other people, and where necessary to give up some of our rights for the sake of others. Thus Paul wrote that although there was no bar to him eating meat that had been offered to idols, "if what I eat causes my brother to fall into sin, I will never eat meat again, so that I will not cause him to fall" (1 Cor 8:13). When writing to the Philippians he broadened this application by telling them, "Each of you should look not only to your own interests, but also to the interests of others" (Phil 2:4). The reason, he goes on to say, is that "Your attitude should be the same as that of Christ Jesus . . . [who] made himself nothing, taking the very nature of a servant" (Phil 2:5–7).

Why Care? Because of Our Hope for the Future

A final strand of this chapter's argument that Christians care for the environment is the theme of eschatology, that is, our theology of the "last things." We care about creation because of its eternal destiny, because God's plan "to reconcile to himself all things" (Col 1:20) really does include all things. We ought to work for the restoration and flourishing of creation as part of our work for the kingdom of God, to see God's will "done on earth as it is in heaven," and to work in this world in the confidence that what we build that is trustworthy and true will not be rendered futile by the future coming of Christ and judgment, but will be taken up into Christ and fulfilled in the new heaven and new Earth.

There can be few stronger statements of God's commitment to the material world and to humankind in particular than that he chose to become incarnate in the world as a human. That Jesus assumed a physical human body, then, means that our bodies can be redeemed through Christ, and this can be seen in the emphasis found throughout the New Testament on the resurrection of the body. Paul sees the promise of the resurrection of the body as central to the Christian gospel: "If there is no resurrection of the dead, then not even Christ has been raised. And if Christ has not been raised, our preaching is useless as is your faith" (1 Cor 15:13–14). This hope of physical resurrection indicates God's commitment to the whole of human nature, physical and spiritual.

Creation Yearning in Hope

Of the physical world, though, it is not just our bodies that are in need of and receive the promise of redemption in Christ.

The biblical picture is that human sinfulness has put the whole of creation out of joint. This is partly because of the intimate connectedness between humanity and the rest of creation, but also, more significantly, because of the role given to humanity in Gen 1 and 2 to be the servant rulers of the created order. As Paul teaches in his letter to the Romans, humans, made in God's image to rule creation and to enable it to glorify God to the full extent of its created potential, have turned their backs on God and ignore him in their daily lives. This means that the created order in which they live is itself prevented from playing its part, in concert with humans, in giving glory to God. By our own sinful neglect of God, by the absurdity of a life lived with no ultimate reference point to either God or eternity,[27] humanity has also prevented all of our surroundings from reflecting God's glory fully. Paul asserts that this human frustration of God's original designs has affected the whole of creation.

Paul's discussion in Rom 8:19–23 is worth quoting in full:

> The creation waits in eager expectation for the sons of God to be revealed. For the creation was subjected to frustration, not by its own choice, but by the will of the one who subjected it, in hope that the creation itself will be liberated from its bondage to decay and brought into the glorious freedom of the children of God. We know that the whole creation has been groaning as in the pains of childbirth right up to the present time. Not only so, but we ourselves, who have the firstfruits of the Spirit, groan inwardly as we wait eagerly for our adoption as sons, the redemption of our bodies.

Why is creation frustrated and groaning? Partly it is because humans have not fulfilled their God-given mandate to care for it as servant kings. Just as subjects in a nation ruled by a despotic king long for the day when he will be replaced by a just and caring ruler who allows them to live properly fulfilled and free lives so that they can develop their full potential, so creation itself longs for a similar release. While humans refuse to play their part in ordering and ruling creation on behalf of God the creator, creation itself is prevented from reaching its full God-given potential and so it cannot reflect God's glory fully in the way he intended it to do.

In striking contrast to the popular caricature of the Christian hope as one which sees humans escaping a world destined to be burnt up, Paul draws a parallel here between the groaning of creation and our own sufferings as we await the age to come, and contrasts it with the glory that both God's children and creation itself will experience in the new creation. The "glory" is the full splendor of God, eternal, incorruptible, and immortal, which will one day "be revealed." When this new creation comes, the Earth will no longer be subject to the decay, to the cycles of life and death that are an inevitable part of life in the present world. Creation itself will be liberated, along with God's children, to share in the eternal glory of Christ. Paul uses the picture of childbirth to describe the transition from the old to the new creation. Labor pains are a heavy burden to bear, and are often accompanied by more vocal outbursts than just groaning, such is the pain. Yet they are the herald of a new life, of a new beginning. Paul says that, as with childbirth, the pain experienced now by humanity and the whole of the physical creation longing for the promised freedom is bearable because of the hope of new life shortly to come to reality. Creation is groaning not in its death-throes because it is destined to be destroyed, but in its birth pangs as it waits for renewed life.

The redemption and restoration of this world is spoken of by several New Testament writers. Jesus talked about the future new birth of all things (Matt 19:28); Paul of the reconciliation of all things (Eph 1:10), and other writers of the new heaven and Earth where all sorrow, pain and death will be absent (2 Pet 3:13; Rev 21; 22). Jesus is the creator and sustainer of the universe, but also the means by which it is redeemed and reconciled to God: "For God was pleased to have all his fullness dwell in him [Jesus], and through him to reconcile to himself all things, whether things on earth or things in heaven, by making peace through his blood, shed on the cross" (Col 1:19–20). It is not just the spiritual world that will be redeemed, but the whole of the created order. Since *all things* were created by God acting through Jesus, so all things can be re-deemed and restored by him. Nothing is beyond his reach, nothing is beyond his reconciling work.

New Earth: Different but Similar

There is both continuity and discontinuity in the biblical pic-ture of the re-creation of all things.[28] Paul likens the resurrection body to the growth of a new organism from a seed (1 Cor 15:35–40).

An acorn does not look at all like an oak tree, yet it bears in itself all that is needed to grow into the giant oak. It is as if the new creation in the future will be the full reality of which the present creation is but a faint shadow.[29] Although the biblical authors struggle to describe the new creation in our earth-bound, limited terms, yet still they paint a picture of a place where we will feel completely at home, where we will have recognizable physical bodies, where the environment will be one in which we fit precisely, where we will know one another, and where we will love and be loved. In our present life we may experience many of the blessings and "rightness" or contentment of heaven in a transient sense: in the new creation this will always be the steady, settled reality. When Christians look forward eagerly to the return of Jesus, then, it is not to their escape from the Earth, but to their reconciliation with it and with all things, and the transformation not only of themselves but of the whole creation.

The discontinuity of life now compared to that in the new heavens and Earth is emphasized by Peter when he writes that "the day of the Lord will come like a thief. The heavens will disappear with a roar; the elements will be destroyed by fire, and the earth and everything in it will be laid bare" (2 Pet 3:10). Peter's reason for writing is made clear in the next sentence: "what kind of people ought you to be?" in the light of the new creation that will one day come into being. And his answer is forthright: "You ought to live holy and godly lives as you look forward to the day of God" (2 Pet 3:11). Unlike our present times, awash with unrighteousness and sin, Christians "are looking forward to a new heaven and a new earth, the home of righteousness" (2 Pet 3:13). And the return of Jesus will come suddenly and unexpectedly in the same way as does a thief. So, writes Peter, Christians ought to "make every effort to be found spotless, blameless and at peace with him [Jesus] . . . grow in the grace and knowledge of our Lord and Savior Jesus Christ" (2 Pet 3:14, 18), as we wait for the return of Jesus.

Peter's comment that "everything will be destroyed" before the new creation needs to be read alongside the parallel that he draws in this same passage between the cleansing that will be brought by the new creation and the destruction that accompanied Noah's flood. In speaking of Noah's flood Peter writes that by those waters "the world of that time was deluged and destroyed" (2 Pet 3:6). We know that the same physical Earth emerged after the flood, but that it was purged and cleansed: in the same way, Peter suggests, the new creation will be one cleansed of the sinfulness that pervades it now, re-created and transformed to how God always intended it to be. This radical transformation, this renewal of the entire cosmos captures both the sense of continuity and of discontinuity suggested by the biblical authors. God is not going to "make all new things": but he *is* going to "make all things new" (Rev 21:5).[30]

Although the citizenship of Christians is in heaven (Phil 3:20), they are currently living in that in-between state between the first coming and the final return of Jesus at the end of time. The kingdom of heaven is near, said Jesus (Matt 10:7), but the full consummation of God's redeeming act will not occur until the creation of the new heaven and new Earth. This will bring the fullness of life that God always intended and purposed for his creation: a place where people will again be truly at home in their environment, and redeemed humanity will worship and glorify God along with the rest of creation. As in the Garden of Eden where God walked with Adam in the cool of the day, it will be a place restored to order where God himself will dwell with his people in the new creation, but more fully than Adam and Eve could imagine (Rev 21:1–4).

The Coming of God's Kingdom

We have established that God cares about the Earth, that along with redeemed humanity it will be redeemed, and that Christians are to live in the certain hope of the future transformation of all things. But the question remains: how does this affect our attitude to the physical creation as we await the consummation of the kingdom of God?

Christians are called to live in a way that announces the future kingdom of God, and to model the reality that, at least in part, the kingdom of God is here already, while realizing that it will only be brought about completely by the decisive intervention of Christ's return. In the period between the first and second comings of Christ, in which we now live, Christians are not simply to wait expectantly, but are to work actively in God's world. As Jesus told his disciples, when Christians pray they should say, "Your kingdom come. Your will be done on earth as it is in heaven" (Matt 6:10).

We live in the "now and not yet" period of history. Christ has done his redeeming work on the cross, but the full manifestation of his kingdom rule is awaiting his return when the new heaven and new Earth will be born. It is promised and it is certain, but in the meantime we are a work in progress. We can choose either to align ourselves to God's transforming work or we can ignore it. The gospel is the good news of the kingdom of God, and the role of the church is to announce the kingdom by declaring and living out its values. If, as discussed above, the transformation of creation is a part of the message with which we are entrusted, then our role is to declare that God cares about the world and will redeem it.

The picture of the future we find in the New Testament means that we should live out the reality of trusting God who has promised to redeem all of his creation. It liberates us from the belief that we can bring about utopia through our own efforts, a hope that is shipwrecked time and again by the reality of human sinfulness. It is seen in the way that God's perfect future reaches down into the present, first and foremost by the incarnation of Jesus, and subsequently through the indwelling of God the Holy Spirit in every believer. Christians are not striving to create the future through their own exertions, but seen in this light are participants in the transformation and restoration of the world that is willed and purposed by the sovereign God. And which will give all the glory to him. It liberates Christians to be obedient to God in their daily lives, one aspect of which includes their care for creation.

The Heavenly Value of Earthly Work

Our work on the Earth, however, is not merely a sign of the end, and a demonstration of hope.[31] To bring the kingdom to Earth is not just to create a poor approximation of the kingdom which will be done away with when the kingdom really comes with the return of Christ, any more than to preach salvation to the people around us is to promise them a reality which they will only experience in the distant future. Rather, the decisions we make in this world, the things we do and say, our personalities, will all in some sense carry forward to the world to come. What we build on this Earth will be purified ("as if by fire" writes Paul in 1 Cor 3:12–15), and transformed: if what we built has good foundations, it will last into eternity.

The Earth is still innately fruitful, even though it labors under the dissonance of human sinfulness. The orderliness of the created order and our God-given ability to understand it and to make use of it through science and technology ought to allow us to work for the good of all. There is sufficient food in the world to feed everyone, yet we allow mountains of food to grow in one part of the world while people starve to death in another. People in one country die for lack of common medicines while medical resources are poured into needless cosmetic surgery in another. This disconnection between the possibilities for good in our use of the environment and the consequences of its misuse either by intent or by neglect is because abuse of the environment is not only unwise or unfair but is actually a sin against God, its creator and sustainer.

The new heaven and Earth are represented in the New Testament not only by a restored "natural order," but also by a city. A city is a human construct, a place of community, of the possibility of intense interpersonal relationships, of creativity and technology and the "glory and honor of the nations will be brought into it" (Rev 21:26). This implies that at least some of the things that humans have done on this Earth will be transformed and carried into the glorious fulfillment of the new creation.

In Luke 24:36–43 Jesus appears to the disciples and shows them the marks of crucifixion that he still bears in his body. In Revelation, at the center of the worship of heaven is "a Lamb standing as if it had been slaughtered" (Rev 5:6). The crucifixion was the work of human hands, the consequence of human sin. Yet even in the heavenly realms the work of humans, though transformed and glorified, leaves its mark on the body of Jesus. If some of the consequences of human sin can carry over in this way into eternity, how much more significant will be the work of humans obedient to God, building on the "foundation" that is Jesus Christ (1 Cor 3:10)? First Corinthians 15:27 talks of "the end" when God will "put all things in subjection under his feet," and, as argued above, this must refer not only to humanity but also to the whole of creation, implying that our work, which shapes and affects creation, will in Christ be brought under God's feet in the new creation, though purified and perfected.

The biblical authors write that although this world is flawed by human sinfulness, we need to work at using it for good. The certain hope of a renewed future creation is not a license to abandon care for this one. Rather, the opposite is the case: because there is some continuity between this world and the next, because it will be the fulfillment of God the creator's plans for this universe, there is every incentive to foster and to use the innate underlying goodness and fruitfulness of this material world to do what is pleasing to God in our time and place. As Luther is supposed to have remarked: "if I knew Jesus would return tomorrow, I would plant a tree today."

Summary

Should Christians care about the environment? Emphatically, yes. Historically, Christian attitudes to the created world have varied wildly, with both inspiring stories of pioneering creation care and depressing stories of negligence and exploitation. But whatever our history, as this chapter has argued, there is a strong mandate for the church now to engage with these issues and to begin to challenge, both within our own community and in the wider world, the attitudes and behaviors which have led to such widespread environmental degradation in the world which God has entrusted to us. Those of us who live in the high-income industrialized nations with standards of living purchased on the back of profligate use of natural resources have a particular responsibility in our use of resources, an imperative to care for those elsewhere in the world marginalized by global climate change.

"From everyone who has been given much, much will be demanded; and from the one who has been entrusted with much, much more will be asked" (Luke 12:48).

4

THE BIBLICAL VISION OF SUSTAINABLE LIVING

Introduction: The Need for a Vision

If Christians have a duty to care for creation we need to ask "how?" What should we actually *do* if we are to care properly for God's Earth? More specifically, what should we do, both individually and corporately, if we are to answer the challenges posed by climate change and our unsustainable use of energy in a way that demonstrates a love of God and neighbor?

There is much biblical material on which to draw in answering this question, but it would be a mistake to proceed directly to it without first standing back and asking a broader question. What is our guiding and unifying vision? What ideas or images can we draw on that will help us to frame and order our responses to the challenges before us?

There are (at least) two reasons for asking this question. First, visions help to "join up" responses. Without a clear idea of what the "ends" look like, the means of getting there are liable to be inefficient at best or contradictory at worst. Without a unifying vision, we purchase energy efficient bulbs for our homes before flying to Rome for the weekend, or we buy food from a farmer's market but take a job which involves a 600-mile weekly commute and cuts 10 hours a week from our family time.

Second, visions inspire. One of the biggest obstacles to a serious, concerted response to the challenge of climate change is that observed in chapter 2: for most people, it seems like too much effort for too little reward. Although the discussion of well-being in that chapter suggests that this need not be the case, the fact is that beginning our response with a list of dos and don'ts is likely to reinforce this "hair shirt" perception.

Articulating a vision can help circumvent these problems. At its best, it can clarify, unify, and inspire: exposing the possible, outlining its contours, and motivating those who might otherwise succumb to resignation or despondency. "Where there is no vision, the people perish" (Prov 29:18).

What, then, is our guiding and unifying vision? What picture do we have of life that is truly "sustainable," of creation as it should be? What image best captures the ends to which we aspire? There are various passages and motifs running through the biblical story to which we might refer, but the most substantial and significant stands in the detailed and multifaceted vision presented within Isa 40–66.

Isaiah 40–66: A Vision to Inspire

Jesus began his public ministry in Nazareth, according to St. Luke, by appropriating the prophet Isaiah (ch. 61). "The Spirit of the Lord is on me" he told the attentive synagogue, "because he has anointed me to preach good news to the poor. He has sent me to proclaim freedom for the prisoners, and recovery of sight for the blind, to release the oppressed, [and] to proclaim the year of the Lord's favor." "Today," he concluded, "this scripture is fulfilled in your hearing" (Luke 4:18–20).

Chapters 40–66 of Isaiah are truly visionary. They are poems of hope, joy, and celebration. They imagine the deliverance and restoration of God's people, the vindication of God's rule, and the inauguration of a renewed order that reflects God's plans for creation. They present a vision of life as it is meant to be, a vision of the renewed order that is not only joyful but also "sustainable."

Accordingly, they are also of foundational importance for the New Testament, in particular for the way that New Testament writers conceived and understood Jesus' mission and achievement. The book of Isaiah is quoted or referred to in the New Testament more often than any other, Psalms excepted. The manner in which Jesus used Isa 61 in his "Nazareth Manifesto" alerts us to its significance in his ministry. Matthew draws on Isa 42 for the same effect (Matt 12:15–21). These glimpses from Isaiah capture the essence, and are central to our understanding of the kingdom of God.

All the gospel writers quote Isa 40 when writing about John the Baptist and his ministry of preparation.[1] All understand the seminal chapter, Isa 53, as prefiguring and explaining Jesus. Jesus uses Isa 56:7 to justify his attack on the temple reported in the Synoptic Gospels.[2] His parable of the weeds in Matt 13 is a restatement of Isa 65:1–8. His advice, in Matt 6, "not [to] store up for yourselves treasures on earth, where moth and rust destroy," indirectly references (among other sources), the words of Isa 50:9 and 51:8. Indeed, the whole, deliberately counterintuitive pattern of the Beatitudes (Matt 5:3–12) seems to echo the passage in Isaiah from which the Nazareth Manifesto is taken:

> The Spirit of the Sovereign Lord is on me . . .
> to comfort all who mourn,
>   and provide for those who grieve in Zion
> to bestow on them a crown of beauty
>   instead of ashes,
> the oil of gladness
>   instead of mourning,
> and a garment of praise
>   instead of a spirit of despair . . .
> Instead of their shame
>   my people will receive a double portion,
> and instead of disgrace
>   they will rejoice in their inheritance. (Isa 61:1–7)

Similarly, just as this passage from Isa 61 goes on to say that "all who see them will acknowledge that they are a people the Lord has blessed" (Isa 61:9), Jesus proceeds to tell his disciples to "let your light shine before men, that they may see your good deeds and praise your Father in heaven" (Matt 5:14).

Revelation derives much of its inspiration from Isa 40–66. Jesus' talk of "the first and the last" in Revelation is rooted in Isaiah.[3] The winepress of God's judgment in Rev 14 is derived from that of Isa 63 (itself related indirectly to the song of the vineyard in Isa 5). In particular, Rev 21, the New Testament's most complete and inspiring vision of the fulfilling of all things is especially indebted to Isaiah. The picture that "the old order of things has passed away" in Rev 21:4 is based on Isa 42:9 ("See, the former things have taken place, and new things I declare"). The idea that "the foundations of the city walls were decorated with every kind of precious stone" (verse 19), comes from Isa 54.[4] The vision of "a new heaven and a new earth" is derived from Isa 65, and the idea that God, rather than the sun or moon, would be the people's light in the redeemed creation has its roots in Isa 60. All told, the way in which the New Testament in general, and Jesus and the book of Revelation in particular, draw on Isa 40–66 to describe and explain the intent and action of God for all creation confirm that passage as an important and inspiring vision.

But is it a vision of sustainable living? At first glance, the answer appears to be "no." The author obviously had no knowledge of our modern, "secular" concept of sustainability. However, sustainability, as we noted in chapter 2, has a range of subtly different definitions, which revolve around the idea that life should be lived without drawing on tomorrow's capital. As we noted in the previous chapter, this idea finds a biblical parallel in Israel's concern to preserve God's name and blessings "through [or for] all generations."[5]

The biblical sources assert that the way we live today needs to accord with *the right order of things,* with God's plan for all creation, not least of which is the call to love not only our living neighbors but also our unborn ones. For all its particular context and circumstantial detail, Isa 40–66 contains some of the most inspiring images we have within Scripture of "the right order of things." The terminology of modern secular views and biblical authors may be different but there remains a common idea. Ultimately, both speak, albeit from different perspectives, about how life should be lived. We turn to Isa 40–66 not for an exegetical account of sustainability but for a vision of what "the right order of things" looks like.

Social and Environmental Sustainability Are Closely Linked

Isaiah 40:26 entreats the reader to "lift your eyes and look to the heavens [and ask] who *created* all these?" In doing so, it uses the verb *bara,* which occurs in the first Genesis creation narrative and is only ever used with God as a subject.[6] The God of Isaiah is explicitly the creator God.

God is the one "who has measured the waters in the hollow of his hand . . . marked off the heaven . . . held the dust of the earth in a basket . . . weighed the mountains on the scales and the hills in a balance" (Isa 40:12). He "sits enthroned above the circle of the earth . . . stretches out the heavens like a canopy, and spreads them out like a tent to live in" (Isa 40:22). Time and again, we hear that this creator God is creator of the whole natural order. Parentheses in the text remind us of this:

> For this is what the Lord says—
> he who created the heavens,
>> he is God;
> he who fashioned and made the earth,
>> he founded it;
> he did not create it to be empty,
>> but formed it to be inhabited—
> he says:
> "I am the Lord,
>> and there is no other." (Isa 45:18)

Given this emphasis, it should not surprise us to read how the redemption of this "natural order" is central to the overall vision of renewal. God the creator is also God the re-creator. Isaiah 41:18–19 records God declaring:

> I will make rivers flow on barren heights,
>> and springs within the valleys.
> I will turn the desert into pools of water,
>> and the parched ground into springs.
> I will put in the desert
>> the cedar and the acacia, the myrtle and the olive.
> I will set pines in the wasteland,
>> the fir and the cypress together.

This interest in "environmental" regeneration will surprise only those who have uncritically accepted the popular idea that biblical Christianity is interested only in soul-saving and is actively antagonistic to the material—in particular the non-human material—world.

Having said that, the vision of Isaiah makes it clear that this redemption of the natural order is not simply a matter of rebuilding nature for its own sake. Rather, as observed in the previous chapter, humanity and "environment" are intimately and inextricably linked. Both are part of the total created order.

Thus the redemption quoted above is uttered in response to a particular human need voiced in the previous verse: "The poor and needy search for water,/ but there is none;/ their tongues are parched with thirst./ But I the Lord will answer them;/ I, the God of Israel, will not forsake them" (Isa 41:17).

The detail and interest in environmental redemption expressed here and elsewhere in Isaiah (and the Old Testament) reminds us that nature does not exist simply to be humanity's larder. Instead, the message is that environmental regeneration is not to be understood in isolation from social redemption, just as neither can be understood separately from the spiritual dimension of humanity's relationship with God. The rejuvenation of the desert, beautifully described as it is, is not solely for its own benefit, but rather, as we hear in the same chapter, "so that people may see and know,/ may consider and understand,/ that the hand of the Lord has done this,/ that the Holy One of Israel has created it" (Isa 41:20).

The restoration of the *entire* created order is part and parcel of God's overall plans for restoring his people and revealing himself. The redemption of the non-human creation is intrinsic to the redemption of all creation and not to be judged separately. Thus, two chapters later God says:

> I am doing a new thing! . . .
> I am making a way in the desert
>   and streams in the wasteland.
> The wild animals honor me,
>   the jackals and the owls,
> because I provide water in the desert
>   and streams in the wasteland,
> to give drink to my people, my chosen,
>   the people I formed for myself
>   that they may proclaim my praise. (Isa 43:19–21)

God's plans envisage symbiosis: the non-human creation honors God for his saving action towards his people. It is through his people that he receives praise (verse 21) and, as Paul declares in Rom 8:21, through them that the rest of creation is "liberated from its bondage to decay."

This idea may seem obvious but it presents a serious challenge to two important, contemporary ideas. The first is the view, found in some Christian and humanist circles, that the natural world is not particularly important, that it is at best a sideshow, at worst an irrelevance. Either the material is an inconsequential distraction from the spiritual or it is putty in human hands, to be molded as we see fit. Social rather than environmental problems demand our attention.

The second is the other extreme, a view rooted in "deep ecology," that it is humans who are an irrelevant distraction or, worse, the problem itself. Were it not for us, nature would be able to take care of itself. It is environmental rather than social problems that demand our attention.

The vision we find in Isa 40–66 (and, indeed, throughout the whole Bible)[7] is that both are important. Addressing one in isolation from the other ends up doing violence to both. Social and environmental are, in effect, two sides of the same coin. Both demand our attention.

Sustainable Living Is a Moral Issue

Humans may be part of creation but, as explored in the previous chapter, they are not *just* a part of it. Rather, we play a uniquely moral role within it, and sustainable living demands that we fulfill that role.

Isaiah 56 begins with a call to "maintain justice and do what is right," for God's salvation "is close at hand" and his righteousness "will soon be revealed." Subsequent verses and chapters spell out what this involves. The people are to "keep the Sabbath without desecrating it" (Isa 56:2) and to "hold fast to my covenant" (Isa 56:4). Those who have historically been excluded or discriminated against, such as eunuchs and the foreigner "who has bound himself to the Lord," are to be incorporated into the community, "given an everlasting name . . . within my temple and its walls" (Isa 56:3–7). The nation is to turn from idolatry, renouncing pagan practices, in particular the abhorrent practice of child sacrifice (Isa 57:5–9). It is also to engage in "true fasting," a practice that demands rather more than a bowed head and prostration "on sackcloth and ashes" (Isa 58:4–5). "Is not this the kind of fasting I have chosen?" God asks in chapter 58:

To loose the chains of injustice
   and untie the cords of the yoke,
to set the oppressed free
   and break every yoke?
. . . to share your food with the hungry
   and to provide the poor wanderer with shelter—
when you see the naked, to clothe him,
   and not to turn away from your own flesh and blood?
                                              (Isa 58:6–7)

"If you do away with the yoke of oppression," God promises several verses later, "with the pointing finger and malicious talk, and if you spend yourselves on behalf of the hungry and satisfy the needs of the oppressed," then "your light will rise in the darkness, and your night will become like the noonday" (Isa 58:9–10). You will, in other words, be fulfilling the role that you were originally charged with: that of proclaiming, by word and deed, the right relationships that characterize the kingdom of God.

Should God's people follow these commands and fulfill their role, they will flourish, as Isaiah describes by means of a natural metaphor: "The Lord will guide you always;/ he will satisfy your needs in a sun-scorched land/ and will strengthen your frame./ You will be like a well-watered garden,/ like a spring whose waters never fail" (Isa 58:10–11).

In the language of chapter 65, the redeemed people

will build houses and dwell in them;
   they will plant vineyards and eat their fruit.
No longer will they build houses and others live in them,
   or plant and others eat.
For as the days of a tree,
   so will be the days of my people;
my chosen ones will long enjoy
   the works of their hands. (Isa 65:21–22)

This chapter goes on to describe how God will "extend peace to her like a river, and the wealth of nations like a flooding stream," a peace that is reflected in the natural world, as the well-known verse declares: "The wolf and the lamb will feed together,/ and the lion will eat straw like the ox,/ but dust will be the serpent's food./ They will neither harm nor destroy/ on all my holy mountain,/ says the Lord" (Isa 65:25).

These chapters 56–66 still see humanity as part of the created order: human prosperity, justice, and security are part of the same tapestry as ecological fruitfulness and environmental sustainability. However, the role they assign to human righteousness and justice in the redemption of creation reminds us that the overall vision of Isa 40–66 is inescapably moral.

In itself, this observation merely complements much of the material explored in the previous chapter. Our role as servant kings is inherently moral. What is interesting about Isaiah's moral message is its comprehensiveness (an idea to which we will return in the following chapter). The focus is as much on economic and social justice as it is on idolatry and religious observation. Moreover, nowhere is there the suggestion that it is environmental ethics specifically that govern environmental issues. Although one must always be careful not to press arguments from silence too far, the ethical vision of Isaiah seems to suggest that the *entirety* of our moral life is relevant to the issue of sustainable living, of living life as it should be.

Once again, this may not, in itself, seem particularly revelatory. Isn't it obvious that well-rounded moral living is the key to sustainable living? The answer is no. There is today a deep-rooted conviction that technology is able to fix anything. New energy sources, cleaner fuels, more efficient machines will be able to rescue us from even the worst of our excesses and allow us to go on living pretty much however we want to. Even when we recognize the moral element in our attitude to environmental sustainability, we are liable to focus on the obvious categories of environmental ethics, such as waste management or energy use, rather than thinking about the way we spend time at the weekend, our attitude to the poor, or, ultimately, our relationship with God. The vision of Isa 40–66 (which, again, is not limited to these chapters)[8] suggests that, whether we like it or not, there is an irreducible and far-reaching moral element to the issue of sustainable living. The created order is inherently moral and, if we wish to sustain it, we cannot ignore our moral obligations.

We Need Both a Broad and a Narrow Perspective

One of the truly remarkable things about Isa 40–66 is the breadth of its vision. Israel had always lived as a small, vulnerable people, squeezed between superpowers. Its eventual conquest in the early sixth century BC should, by any logic, have been its end. The fact that it wasn't is noteworthy. The fact that it resulted in the universal vision of these chapters is remarkable.

In reality, the good of other peoples had always been a strand in Israel's national history. Abram is told in Gen 12 that "all peoples on earth will be blessed through you" (Gen 12:3). His descendants are told to observe the decrees and laws carefully, "for this will show your wisdom and understanding to the nations, who will hear about all these decrees and say, 'Surely this great nation is a wise and understanding people'" (Deut 4:6–8). The people were continually reminded of their duty to welcome and protect the alien and the stranger (e.g., Lev 19:33–34). To this extent, an "international" outlook had always been in Israel's blood.

Even so, the insistent emphasis on the redemption of *all* in Isaiah is striking, not least given Israel's virtual nonexistence at the time. The opening chapter talks of how "all mankind together will see" the glory of the Lord (Isa 40:5). The justice that was to mark out the people of God as distinct would now extend to all peoples: "Listen to me, my people;/ hear me, my nation:/ The law will go out from me;/ my justice will become a light to the nations" (Isa 51. 4). Salvation was now for all: "Turn to me and be saved,/ all you ends of the earth;/ for I am God, and there is no other" (Isa 45:22).

Time and again, the narrative draws attention to the fate of "all the nations," "the peoples," "the Gentiles," "the ends of the earth," "the islands," and "foreigners." "My justice will become a light to the nations," God says in 51:4. "I will lift up my banner to the peoples," in 49:22. "All the ends of the earth will see the salvation of our God," he says in 52:10. "[To] foreigners who bind themselves to [me] I will . . . give joy in my house of prayer," he declares in chapter 56:7. The call to bless all the nations that had been part of Israel's identity for so long emerges as crucially important.

What is of particular interest in this is *how* this universal blessing was to be achieved. There is no sense whatsoever in Isa 40–66 that the focus on the particular, on Israel's unique call and role has been lost. "'Do not be afraid, O worm Jacob, O little Israel,'" we touchingly hear in 41:14, "'for I myself will help you,' declares the Lord." "You are my servant, Israel, in whom I will display my splendor" (Isa 49:3). And then, in 51:1–3, in verses that reconfirm Israel's original blessing and highlight the link between the redemption of the people and the rest of creation:

> Listen to me, you who pursue righteousness
> and who seek the Lord:
> Look to the rock from which you were cut
> and to the quarry from which you were hewn;
> look to Abraham, your father,
> and to Sarah, who gave you birth.
> When I called him he was but one,
> and I blessed him and made him many.
> The Lord will surely comfort Zion
> and will look with compassion on all her ruins;
> he will make her deserts like Eden,
> her wastelands like the garden of the Lord.
> Joy and gladness will be found in her,
> thanksgiving and the sound of singing.

"Little Israel" was still God's special servant people. "I have . . . not rejected you," God reassures them in chapter 41. "Fear not, for I have redeemed you; I have summoned you by name; you are mine" (Isa 43:1). It is simply that their *particular* role and task was to herald *universal* blessing. God's servant was to be "a light for the Gentiles, that you may bring my salvation to the ends of the earth" (Isa 49:6).

It is in this way that the dual emphasis on the universal and the particular—an emphasis that the modern mind finds hard to understand or accept—was reconciled. Isaiah reminds us that it is not either/or: *either* you focus on the good of a particular group and forget the rest *or* on the good of all and ignore, minimize, or eliminate particular allegiances. Instead, the good of all is realized only through the good of some.

This is instructive for debates over climate change, where the question of *how* we should respond often gets stuck in the issue of *who* should respond and, in particular, in the somewhat sterile national versus international debate. Individual nations won't do anything unless the international community does, but the international community can't do anything unless individual nations do.

Isaiah reminds us that for a thing to happen *every*where, it needs first to happen *some*where. If we are serious about responding to the challenge of climate change, we need to maintain both a broad and a narrow perspective, seeking the good of all by being the good for some. This idea should have particular purchase on Christians who not only have a moral duty to care for God's creation and care for their neighbors, as discussed in the previous chapter, but inherit the call to be a light and a blessing to the peoples. The way Isaiah maintains a dual focus on the redemption of the people of God *and* of all peoples and creation, tells us that the church should be that somewhere where the redemption of everywhere begins.

God Is a Faithful Creator and There Is Reason for Hope

The last three sections have done more to outline the unifying aspects of the vision than the inspiring ones. They have suggested that the biblical vision for sustainable living shows social and environmental concerns to be inextricably linked; that there is an irreducible and pervasive moral element to our living well; and that our focus needs to be both particular and broad. Such points help outline that vision but are less likely to inspire.

Two other points from Isa 40–66 may supply that inspiration. The first relates to God's role in redemption and the hope it breeds (the second will be examined in the following subsection). Important as is Israel's moral response, there is no indication that redemption is dependent on, or achievable by it. From the first words of Isa 40, it is clear that the role of God as creator is key. Thus, not only does the writer tell us about God "creating" in the manner of the Genesis creation story, but he also draws on imagery from a creation myth that was widespread in the ancient Near East to describe God's character and role. The writer blends this with the story of Israel's own creation through the Red Sea to emphasize the "new thing" that God is doing:

> Was it not you who cut Rahab to pieces,
>   who pierced that monster through?
> Was it not you who dried up the sea,
>   the waters of the great deep,
> who made a road in the depths of the sea
>   so that the redeemed might cross over? (Isa 51:9–10)

The expectation of redemption and a new creation that is expressed in these verses is founded not on the "natural" order of things, still less on human merit, but on God's sovereignty and creative genius. That alone underpins the promise to redeem the people of God and, through them, all creation.

This understanding of God's creative power, and with it the idea that in spite of everything that had happened he remained faithful to his promise and plans for creation, is the basis for the hopefulness that pervades Isaiah. That hopefulness is based on who God is. It is not so much a hope *for* as a hope *in,* specifically a hope *in* God or *in* his law. Thus, the verses at the end of Isa 40 place hope in God above human strength: "Even youths grow tired and weary,/ and young men stumble and fall; but those who hope in the Lord/ will renew their strength" (Isa 40:30–31).

Two chapters later the poet describes how "in his [the servant of the Lord's] law the islands will put their hope" because "he will bring justice to the nations" (Isa 42:4, 1). As part of the description of the restoration of Israel in Isa 49, God affirms to his people, "then you will know that I am the Lord; those who hope in me will not be disappointed" (Isa 49:23).

The sense of hopefulness in these chapters is not, of course, limited to those instances when hope is specifically mentioned. As we shall note below, the entire passage echoes with a sense of joy and celebration, central to which is a sense of hope and expectation.

Yet the particular construction of this hope—hope *in* God who has not lost faith in his creation—is important. The challenge set before us by climate change is immense. Some, such as James Lovelock, have already said it is too late. Others, less iconoclastic, speak of a window of opportunity that is closing rapidly. The attitude urged on us by the vision of Isaiah is emphatically not one of complacency—that God will intervene and sort everything out so we don't need to worry—but of faith that, in spite of the task ahead of us (just as for Israel it was in spite of the trauma of exile) the creator God is trustworthy. It *is* worth making the effort.

Sustainable Living Is Joyful

If there is one thing that clearly differentiates Isaiah's vision of a redeemed created order from the modern idea of sustainable living, it is its emphasis on joy.

The sheer energy and exuberance of the vision as it is outlined in these chapters is irrepressible. Everlasting joy, singing for joy, shouting out loud, bursting into song, clapping hands, giving thanks, rejoicing, feeling glad: all are recurring motifs. "I have swept away your offences like a cloud, your sins like the morning mist," says God in 44:22, proceeding to say something that captures not only the moral dimension to the re-creation ("return to me . . .") but also the tight bond between human and non-human creation:

"Return to me,
        for I have redeemed you."
Sing for joy, O heavens, for the Lord has done this;
        shout aloud, O earth beneath.
Burst into song, you mountains,
        you forests and all your trees,
for the Lord has redeemed Jacob,
        he displays his glory in Israel. (Isa 44:22–23)[9]

As this quotation suggests, the joy of the vision is rooted primarily in Israel's change of prospects: the return from exile, the forgiveness of sins, the end of affliction, and ultimately the coming of the kingdom. Thus the poet sings: "Your watchmen lift up their voices;/ together they shout for joy./ When the Lord returns to Zion,/ they will see it with their own eyes" (Isa 52:8).

Yet it would be a mistake to see the rejoicing as simply a transitional emotion. It is more than simply being overwhelmed by a change of fortune. Joy is a characteristic of the new creation as Isa 51:11 indicates "Everlasting joy will crown their heads./ Gladness and joy will overtake them,/ and sorrow and sighing will flee away."

Isaiah 58:13–14 goes on to link this joy with the moral dimension of the vision:

If you keep your feet from breaking the Sabbath
    and from doing as you please on my holy day,
if you call the Sabbath a delight
    and the Lord's holy day honorable,
and if you honor it by not going your own way
    and not doing as you please or speaking idle words,
then you will find your joy in the Lord,
    and I will cause you to ride on the heights of the land
    and to feast on the inheritance of your father Jacob.

"I will make you the everlasting pride and the joy of all generations,"
God says later in chapter 60, and again, in the climax of the poem:

Behold, I will create
    new heavens and a new earth.
The former things will not be remembered,
    nor will they come to mind.
But be glad and rejoice forever
    in what I will create,
for I will create Jerusalem to be a delight
    and its people a joy.
I will rejoice over Jerusalem
    and take delight in my people;
the sound of weeping and of crying
    will be heard in it no more. (Isa 65:17–19)

This emphasis on joy is instructive. It reminds us that in spite of the size of the problem and the moral demands it places upon us, the conclusion is a cause for celebration. Echoing the discussion of well-being in chapter 2, it suggests that we should understand the challenge of sustainable living not so much as a burdensome limitation of our freedom as an opportunity morally and socially to reorient ourselves, and to rediscover the idea that living within the constraints of the created order is a matter for celebration rather than complaint.

Isaiah 40–66 offers not a substitute for the modern concept of sustainability, but an inspiring vision of what sustainable living could look like. It is almost breathless with anticipation and draws on vivid and emotive language and imagery to convey that vision. And it serves as a reminder that all our efforts to address the problems of climate change and inculcate the principles of sustainable living will come to naught if there is no vision to guide and inspire us.

Redemption Demands Sacrifice

The vision laid out in Isa 40–66 is a hopeful and joyful one. It insists that living sustainably, according to God's ordering of creation, under his kingship, is a matter for celebration. It is articulated with energy, exuberance, and a palpable anticipation, partly because it heralds a transition from darkness to light, but also because that light is, in and of itself, a good thing. Although its irreducible moral component presents us with a real challenge, it is still a vision to inspire.

That said, the *means* by which that vision is achieved is particular and counter-intuitive, and bears examination. It is best understood by looking at the biblical idea of *shalom*, a word that is untranslatable but can be roughly approximated in English to "well-being" or "wholeness." We shall return to the concept of *shalom* shortly as a potential, more authentically biblical alternative to "sustainable living." For the meantime, however, we should note that *shalom* is often used to describe life lived according to and blessed by God's ordering of creation, and that it is used in such a way at a pivotal moment in Isaiah.

"He was pierced for our transgressions . . . crushed for our iniquities," we are told in the seminal chapter, Isa 53. "The punishment that brought us peace was upon him, and by his wounds we are healed." The word here translated peace (other translations use "whole" or "well-being") is *shalom*. Chapter 53 tells us that the wholeness of all creation is achieved by an act of unmatched self-sacrifice, by the way of the cross.

This is liable still to appear counter-intuitive to us, just as it did to Jesus' contemporaries who expected him to inaugurate the kingdom by means of violent revolution. If *shalom* is a vision of joy, surely the road towards it is joyful, paved with anticipated "wholeness"? Yes it is, but only in part, Isaiah seems to say. Yes, the new thing God is doing is a reason for celebration, but because the present state of things is so sorry, the way in which it is achieved is costly.

In Isaiah that cost is borne by the servant of the Lord, and, accordingly, Isa 53 became a paradigmatic text for the first Christians. While they had no sense that they *needed* to suffer in the way their Lord had done, or that their suffering effected redemption in the way that his did, there was a clear sense that they were "in Christ," and as such would share the cost of his sacrifice as they did in the glory of his blessings.

It is in this way that Isa 53 becomes a model for the attainment of the sustainable life today. If complete *shalom* is achieved only by God's matchless self-sacrifice, and we are called to belong to that sacrifice, to share in the "attitude . . . of [him] who . . . made himself nothing" (Phil 2:5–6), then our response to the challenge of sustainable living will also demand sacrifice.

On further reflection, therefore, this may appear less counter-intuitive. The new life of *shalom* should indeed be one of joy and celebration. However, adopting that new life in the context of an old and broken one, in which our hearts are not fully attuned to its attractions and our situation fails to recognize its validity or, worse, is actively hostile towards it, is rather harder. To take a concrete example from the following chapter, the rest and respect that characterize the Sabbath should, in themselves, be reasons for celebration. However, not only do we fail to understand this fully but, even if we do, ring-fencing Sabbath time when the world in which we live races on at breakneck speed can be very challenging.

All this points to the Christian concept of repentance. As with so many religious ideas, this one has often been individualized and over spiritualized and is often taken to mean apologizing to God for one's personal sins. While personal contrition is undoubtedly at its heart, we are liable today to lose both the corporate element that is often implicit in the term, and the active and demanding element of "turning away" that is there. Repentance involves doing things differently, as a community just as much as an individual. It involves being transformed by the direction in which a renewed mind leads you. That direction is homeward, towards the light and the kingdom, and is based on our faith in God's promises, but the road there can be narrow and testing. The goal of repentance is rewarding but the process may be costly, the ends joyful but the means taxing.

It is worth emphasizing that repentance and moral reorientation are not the whole story. The "way of the Lord" is not simply onerous and the tone of Isa 40–66 is hardly troubled. Doing things God's way means taking up the cross and following him. But it also means taking up an easy yoke and a light burden. If there is a tension in this, it appears to be a basic fact of the Christian life, one that is a recurrent theme in the epistles, which talk frequently about joy and affliction in the same breath.[10]

Instead, the whole story, in so far as it can be summarized, is that (a) redemption demands sacrifice; (b) that although we cannot satisfy that demand, we can participate in it; (c) that our participation may be costly; but (d) the joy of the destination should lighten that burden and inspire us to do that which we would not otherwise be inclined to do.

Summary

If we have dwelt on the poetry of Isa 40–66 at some length it is because it offers the fullest vision the Bible has to offer of a joyful, renewed, and lasting creation.

The vision does not speak the language of the Brundtland Report, and it would be unfair and misleading directly to compare one with the other. Nevertheless, the difference in language, tone, and context should not blind us to the fact that both address the same topic: life on Earth as it should be lived. Modern reports discuss the policies and practices intended to achieve this objective. The biblical social vision, to which we shall turn in the following chapter, outlines its own principles and paradigms. But both are founded on a conception or vision of life lived within its correct limits. Biblical teaching understands and expresses this vision in a particular way: it is life lived under the just and loving rule of God, a vision that is described in Isaiah, albeit in prospect, with an exhilaration and detail unmatched elsewhere in the biblical narrative.

That vision is one of hope, focused, and dependent on God, and in particular on his authority and creativity. It insists that there is an indissoluble link between human activity, in particular the nature and structure of human relationships within society, and the prosperity (or otherwise) of the rest of the created order, both animate and inanimate. It has both a broad and a particular focus. It is positive rather than negative, suggesting that we should live now in the light of the coming kingdom of God, rather than simply scale down our lifestyles until we are in a position to maintain them at that level for the foreseeable future. Instead of being about the restriction of our enjoyment of material things, it is about finding the space to become whole people living in right relationship with God, each other and all of creation.[11] Altogether, it offers a vision of the full flourishing of a redeemed creation, a vision of what the kingdom of heaven is like, a vision that is joyful and is closer to Martin Luther King's "I have a dream" than to some modern environmental "jeremiads."

5

THE BIBLICAL PRACTICE OF SUSTAINABLE LIVING

ISAIAH 40–66 SETS BEFORE us a vision of life as it should be lived. Its language, tone, and imagery are those of inspiration rather than explanation. Its intention is not to describe in detail what a redeemed life according to God's plan for creation would be like, but rather to present a picture and a promise of what it should and, one day, *will* look like. For our purposes, we may use it as a vision of hope and joy to inspire our commitment to living sustainably and as an outline to shape and guide that commitment.

We are left, however, with the task of filling in that outline. How was this vision of "sustainable living" to be put into practice? An initial response to this question must be that it wasn't—at least not fully. The disciples may have been told to "be perfect . . . as your heavenly Father is perfect" (Matt 5:48), but nowhere in the biblical story is there an expectation that perfection, the kingdom of God, will be realized by human effort alone. When Jesus told his disciples at Bethany that they will always have the poor with them (Matt 26:11), he wasn't contradicting the advice of Deut 15:4 ("there should be no poor among you") but rather highlighting the premise on which the law was given. As the psalmist and after him Paul wrote, "there is no one righteous, not even one" (Ps 14:3; Rom 3:10). In the words of Immanuel Kant centuries later, "Out of the crooked timber of humanity, no straight thing was ever made."[1]

Such an observation is liable to depress and deter action if divorced from the idea, which pervades Isaiah and is, of course, central to the New Testament, that God has acted and will act, and that humans are required not to work alone but rather to participate in God's action. It is an observation that should remind us of the limitations and provisionality of political power, of our inherent fallibility, and of our ultimate dependence on God. Its intention (in as far as it has one) is to avert new Babels rather than to deter new building projects; to prepare us for the weeds we will find, rather than to discourage us from cultivating the garden in the first place.

It is in this context—of assessing how we can cultivate rather than guarantee sustainable life—that we shall explore the practical manifestations of the vision outlined above. That practical manifestation can be seen, in different forms, at every juncture of the biblical story—in the life of the early church, in Jesus' teaching and ministry, in the prophet's critique of the people—but it is rooted in the life and practice of early Israel as articulated in the Torah.[2]

The life and practice articulated there and traced throughout the rest of the Bible is an integrated whole. Every part is linked, somehow or other, to every other part, and to extract and study certain particular areas is inevitably artificial and limiting. That noted, the key themes outlined in Part 1—our engagement with the environment, our consumption habits, our attitude to mobility, etc.—point us towards six areas—some specific, others more diffuse—that speak *directly* to the vision of sustainable living. We begin with one on which we have already touched.

Jubilee

In Luke 4 Jesus reads aloud in the synagogue a description of a Jubilee or "the year of the Lord's favor" from the book of Isaiah. This is sometimes refered to as the "Nazarene Manifesto." A few scholars have suggested that he was intending to summon the nation to a literal year of Jubilee, in which debts were cancelled and families returned to their ancestral lands. But if that were his intention, he is more likely to have headed straight for Lev 25, in which the idea originates and the legislation is laid out in some detail. Instead he is quoting from Isaiah's broader and more nebulous promise.

That said, it is clear that the Jubilee did inform his proclamation. Not only did he promise "the year of the Lord's favor" but he used a phrase, "to release the oppressed," the Hebrew verb for which, *deror,* is used in Lev 25:10. To an audience that included many who may have been mired in debt (the first thing that rebels did at the start of the Jewish war three decades later was to burn the Treasury in which debt records were kept), the implications would have been clear.

N. T. Wright suggests that "although Jesus did not envisage that he would persuade Israel as a whole to keep the Jubilee year, *he expected his followers to live by the Jubilee principle among themselves.*

He expected, and taught, that they should forgive one another not only 'sins' but also debts."[3] If this is true it reinforces the idea, originating in the Torah, that the Jubilee and the principles behind it were an important part of God's plan for human flourishing.

In exploring the Jubilee we should be careful not to see it simply as a debt-focused or even economic decree. Economics, environment, and society were fused together at the time, and to understand the Jubilee we need to see it in its full context. In pre-industrial societies land was of inestimable importance. As the source of food, income, security, and, to a large degree, identity, land provided the means by which one could grow and mature as a human being. Although our situation in the modern West is not quite as different as we sometimes think—it was only two generations ago that the British were frantically cultivating every scrap of land to avoid wartime starvation—we are less alert to the importance of land and the implications of landlessness than were our ancestors. For Israel, the land was never simply a neutral stage on which history was enacted. Instead, it was a sign of the covenant that declared various things about who God was and what he wanted his people to be.[4]

First and foremost, the land was God's. In the same way as Ps 24:1 proclaims, "the earth is the Lord's, and everything in it" (with the Hebrew word *eretz*, here translated "earth," also meaning "land"), Lev 25:23 has God declare, "the land is mine and you are but aliens and my tenants." This (rather deflating) pronouncement, analogizing the Israelites to the vulnerable aliens who lived among them, reminded them that it was God rather than they who were the land's ultimate freeholders. They lived simply by the grace of their landlord.

Second, the land was a good gift and thus, again, a microcosm of all creation. The elegant description in Deut 8:7–9 testifies to a deep aesthetic and practical appreciation of that land's goodness:

> [It is] a land with streams and pools of water, with springs flowing in the valleys and hills; a land with wheat and barley, vines and fig trees, pomegranates, olive oil and honey; a land where bread will not be scarce and you will lack nothing; a land where the rocks are iron and you can dig copper out of the hills.

At the same time, the abrasive words in the following chapter inform the Israelites that it is also a gift, a reminder of God's sovereignty and their dependence: "It is not because of your righteousness that the Lord your God is giving you this good land to possess, for you are a stiff-necked people" (Deut 9:6).

Third, land was to be distributed equitably. Chapters 26 and 34 of the book of Numbers and chapters 13–19 of Joshua record in considerable detail the division of the land between the Israelites "according to their clans," the rule of thumb being that each should receive land according to its size and need. This was central to Israel's social order, its identity as a people of justice and righteousness, and as a light to the nations, ensuring rootedness and family cohesion over time. When the principle of the Sabbath year, in which debts were cancelled, is outlined in Deut 15, Israel is told: "There should be no poor among you, for in the land the Lord your God is giving you to possess as your inheritance, he will richly bless you, if only you fully obey the Lord your God and are careful to follow all these commands I am giving you today" (Deut 15:4–5).

This reflects the idea that God has provided richly for his people, both in terms of natural resources and human ingenuity.[5] It also, however, highlights the fact that the inheritance will only remain rich if God's commands are obeyed. No such gift can survive unrestrained profligacy. In this instance, "obeying the Lord" involved following commands that helped to ensure economic equity and justice, and family cohesion across society, and this was to be achieved, in part, by guaranteeing equitable access to natural capital in the form of the land.

It is here that environment, economics, and society come together. In most other cultures of the time, land was owned outright by a king under whom the rest of the population subsisted as tax-paying tenant farmers. Not so with Israel. For them, God was sole owner, all people were tenants, and the land was distributed equally so that everyone would have access to natural (and thereby financial) capital, in such a way as to create a socially cohesive society. This was the logic behind Micah's vision of the last days in which, "every man will sit under his own vine and under his own fig tree" (Mic 4:4).

Fourth, land was distributed inalienably. This is where the Jubilee legislation came into play. "Count off . . . forty-nine years," the Israelites are instructed in Lev 25, "then have the trumpet sounded . . . [and] proclaim liberty throughout the land." "Each one" of the Israelites was "to return to his family property and each to his own clan." Debts were cancelled and land that had been sold since the last Jubilee was to be restored to its original owners. This meant, as verses 15–16 indicate, that what was in fact being sold was usufruct, meaning "the legal right to use and derive profit from property that belongs to another person, as long as the property is not damaged" (lit. "using the fruit") rather than property rights:

> You are to buy from your countryman on the basis of the number of years since the Jubilee. And he is to sell to you on the basis of the number of years left for harvesting crops. When the years are many, you are to increase the price, and when the years are few, you are to decrease the price, because what he is really selling you is the number of crops. (Lev 25:15–16)

In the year of Jubilee, the land itself was to enjoy a period of rest: "Do not sow and do not reap what grows of itself or harvest the untended vine" (Lev 25:11).

There is some debate not only about the precise mechanism by which the Jubilee was to be implemented but also about whether it ever actually happened.[6] Whether or not it did, its promise of freedom and restoration for people and land epitomizes the spirit of the law. Families who had been compelled to sell their land out of economic need, or who had mortgaged it to a creditor, or who had been split up through debt servitude could once again be united in what was, by the grace of God, theirs. In this way the Jubilee re-enacted the exodus.

The Jubilee legislation was intended to be at the hub of Israel's social, environmental, and economic life, a central idea on which many other laws rested. Not only were the people to enjoy "rights" to the land on an equal basis but those rights were to be inalienable. This would not, as we shall explore below, prohibit market interactions, but it should prevent the economic polarization that marked other societies of the time and remains a mark of most today.

Thus, at a single stroke the Jubilee law would have achieved two of the central ambitions of modern policy making: equality of opportunity and a stakeholder economy. In guaranteeing equal access to natural capital according to clan, it gave all parties a stake in society, helped maintain the cohesion and relevance of local life, or "civil society" as we now call it; and it sought to avert the economic and social polarization that characterizes so many societies.

That the nation failed to live up to these objectives, as the prophets constantly reminded it, may be because the Jubilee was too challenging and morally demanding ever to be instituted successfully. It is no accident that the legislation is punctuated by more general exhortations: "do not take advantage of each other, but fear your God. I am the Lord your God," as detailed in Lev 25:17.

Irrespective of how demanding it was or whether it was ever actually implemented, however, we see in the Jubilee legislation an important way in which the biblical vision of sustainable living was intended to be realized: equitable, protected and assured access to land and thereby economic opportunity, and with it guaranteed "rest" for the land.

Wealth

If the Nazareth Manifesto marked the start of Jesus' public ministry, the "cleansing" of the temple in Jerusalem marked its effective end. Jesus said and did many things in the final week of his life, but after his behavior in the temple courts he was a marked man.

Precisely what Jesus did that day and why did he did it are still matters of debate. It seems likely that his actions enacted and symbolized the imminent destruction of the temple system for having failed to obey God's commands, for alienating Gentiles, for exploiting Jews, and for providing a haven for violent revolutionaries.[7] What can be said with certainty is that the popular idea that he was making some sort of primitive anti-capitalist protest is wrong. The fact that "he [drove] out those who were buying and selling there . . . [and] overturned the tables of the money changers" (Mark 11:15–17) does not mean that he was implacably opposed to commerce. The problem was not trade in itself, nor even its presence in the temple courts, as if Jesus were trashing a cathedral gift shop, but the way in which money was corrupting Israel, a long-standing problem as the prophecies of Amos 5 and Isa 5 indicate.

If this evaluation seems at odds with Jesus' other, undeniably harsh judgments on the dangers of money, it is because we are too used to hearing them quoted out of context. "The eye of a needle," "treasures in heaven," and "the root of all evil" are still occasionally cited in public discourse, usually to "prove" how Christianity demands penury of its followers. The truth is subtler.

Such popular monetary aphorisms tend to be plucked from contexts that have more to do with the way in which money corrupts the human heart than with its allegedly intrinsic evil. Thus, when Jesus told his disciples that "it is easier for a camel to go through the eye of a needle than for a rich man to enter the kingdom of heaven," it was after he had seen an eager, faithful young man, faced with a straight choice between God and wealth, choose wealth (Luke 18:18–30). When he told his audience on the Mount not to "store up for yourselves treasures on earth," his initial explanation that no earthly banking system is truly secure soon gave way to a deeper reason: "where your treasure is, there your heart will be also" (Matt 6:19–21). When he talks about the poor widow in the temple treasury, he tells his disciples that whereas the rich donors "gave out of their wealth . . . she, out of her poverty, put in . . . all she had to live on" (Mark 12:41–43). Her heart, in other words, was where her treasure was: in her relationship with God.

Paul wrote in the same vein in his first letter to Timothy, speaking not about "people who own money" nor even "the rich" but about "people who want to get rich." It is acquisitiveness that leads to "many foolish and harmful desires." The context is not money but the obsessive pursuit of it, and, of course, it is not money but the love of it that "is the root of all kinds of evil," leading "some people . . . from the faith [to] pierce themselves with many griefs" (1 Tim 6:6–10).

In all this, Jesus and Paul were continuing a theme that can be traced from the Old Testament. As we have seen, the equitable and inalienable division of land across Israel was intended to check avarice, protect the poor, and prevent economic polarization. As we shall see below, this was one measure among many intended to discipline rather than disallow market exchange. Greed rather than trade was the problem.

A number of proverbs echo these sentiments. We tend to treat wealth as if it were a "fortified city" (Prov 10:15) or "unscaleable wall" (Prov 18:11). Ultimately, "wealth is worthless in the day of wrath, [whereas] righteousness delivers from death" (Prov 11:4). Whereas "a kindhearted woman gains respect . . . ruthless men gain *only* wealth" (Prov 11:16).

Several psalms endorse these opinions. Psalm 52 talks disap-
provingly of the man "who did not make God his stronghold but
trusted in his great wealth" (Ps 52:7). Psalm 39 speaks of wealth in
the same disparaging breath as it does man's "fleeting life":

You have made my days a mere handbreadth;
    the span of my years is as nothing before you.
Each man's life is but a breath.
    Man is a mere phantom as he goes to and fro:
He bustles about, but only in vain;
    he heaps up wealth, not knowing who will get it. (Ps 39:5–6)

It is the teacher of Ecclesiastes, however, who is supremely eloquent
on the subject:

Whoever loves money never has money enough;
    whoever loves wealth is never satisfied with his income.

[. . .]

As goods increase,
    so do those who consume them.
And what benefit are they to the owner
    except to feast his eyes on them?

I have seen a grievous evil under the sun:
    wealth hoarded to the harm of its owner. (Eccl 5:10–11, 13)

None of this indicates an outright hostility to money or even wealth.
Proverbs 10:22 remarks that "the blessing of the Lord brings wealth."
The teacher of Ecclesiastes goes on to say, "when God gives any man
wealth and possessions, and enables him to enjoy them, to accept
his lot and be happy in his work—this is a gift of God" (Eccl 5:19).
And one of the themes of Isaiah is the promise of wealth for Zion:

the wealth on the seas will be brought to you,
    to you the riches of the nations will come . . .

Your gates will always stand open,
    they will never be shut, day or night,
so that men may bring you the wealth of the nations—
    their kings led in triumphal procession. (Isa 60:5, 11)

Money in itself is not the issue. Rather, it is the way that money is pursued "to the harm of its owner" and the detriment of others; the way it is used for purposes other than God's is the real problem.

The precise nature of those purposes is most clearly articulated by Jesus in his parable of the shrewd manager. This story, sandwiched in Luke's Gospel between that of the prodigal son brought to his senses through his experience of poverty and that of the rich man brought to his doom by his meanness to Lazarus, records how the manager, called to account, "acted shrewdly" not so much in his swift debt recovery but in the way he used his position to ensure that he would be welcomed into other people's houses should he need help. In spite of the fact that the manager is dishonest and had been wasteful, he is the example Jesus lifts before his disciples. "The people of this world are more shrewd in dealing with their own kind than are the people of the light," he tells them, before going on to advise them to "use worldly wealth to gain friends for yourselves, so that when it is gone, you will be welcomed into eternal dwellings" (Luke 16:8–9).

Money, in other words, is a function of relationships, a tool by means of which we can shape creation so as to achieve God's plans and reflect God's being. It is a means rather than an end. To miss this is to do violence to oneself, to others, and to God.

The Jubilee legislation instituted (in theory) a stakeholder society and equality of opportunity within Israel through its equitable and inalienable access to natural capital. The biblical attitude to money underpinned that legislation, in as far as it insisted that the secure, stable, and equitable relationships that such legislation was intended to ensure were more important than the trading and moneymaking that it permitted. In modern parlance, a nation's "social capital" or "civil society" is a better measure of its health than GDP per capita.[8]

This has relevance to the challenges posed by climate change and sustainable living in a number of ways. It is, in part, as observed in chapter 2, our omni-consumerism that is causing climate change, while eroding the very things that make our own lives worth living. Our unthinking equation of per-capita income with development or progress cements this harmful confusion. At a general level, there is a crying need to use our worldly wealth to make friends, bringing the human and relational cost into our economic equations.

Trade

Shortly after Jesus told his disciples the story of the shrewd manager, he told a larger crowd another tale with a similar outline (Luke 19:11–27).[9] The rich man is replaced with a newly crowned king, his manager by ten servants, and his "possessions" by ten "minas," each of which would have been worth about three months wages. The tale proceeds to describe how the servants had managed or failed to make the money with which they were entrusted work for its owner. Despite the fact that the parable is primarily about the judgment that God's return will visit on (some of) his people,[10] some have taken the narrative device of "putting the money to work" as an indication that Jesus was overturning the Old Testament prohibition on interest.

It is, to put it mildly, highly improbable that this was his intention. The matter of interest is an incidental detail rather than the focus of the parable. If anything, the implication is that charging interest is the sign of a hard man who reaps where he has not sown.[11] Nowhere in his recorded teachings does Jesus encourage the charging of interest,[12] and, in any case, the ban on interest was deeply rooted in the law that Jesus explicitly affirmed (Matt 5:17–19). This prohibition may seem obsolete (or even naive) to us today but it points us in the direction of a nexus of laws and attitudes that constitute a third strand in biblical teaching on sustainable living.

Early Israel had a relatively free market system in which work was lauded, trade permitted, and growth expected.[13] In spite of the way that some of Jesus' and Paul's teachings have been plucked from their context and used to justify a largely alien line of thought, commerce was the social norm. Indeed, the Bible's near-obsessive focus on the poor hardly makes sense in any other light.

Thus, in the words of Paul Mills,

> apart from the ceremonial food laws and the observance of the Sabbath [see below], the only constraints on trade in biblical law are the exhortations to merchants to maintain fair weights and eschew adulteration.[14] There is no notion that trading for profit is inherently "wrong" (although profit from an artificial monopoly is condemned in Prov 11:26). There is also ample evidence that trade was relatively commonplace and Israel participated in the international trading networks of the time (Deut 28:12; 1 Kgs 10:14; Neh 13:16; Ezek 27:17).[15]

"We can thus infer," Mills continues, "both the acceptance of competitive markets and the presumption that the 'just price' for a good is that which results from fair competition."

In addition to this, there was a capped and proportional rate of income tax through the tithing system (although the number of tithes in any single year remains unclear), a limited and constrained role for the state (see below), a stable monetary system and price level, and a strict legal code that established property rights. All this might seem to point towards a traditional, right wing, neo-liberal economic system, like that which is commonly associated with the USA. Such a reading would, however, be based on a partial reading of the text. Balancing this apparent laissez-faire economic system were laws that took the economy in a very different direction.

The first is the equitable and inalienable land distribution that we have observed in the Jubilee legislation and other laws governing land transfers in Lev 25. The runaway effect of laissez-faire economies was kept in strict check by restrictions on land transfer.

The second is the ban on interest. The Torah repeats this ban three times. Twice (Exod 22:25 and Lev 25:36–37) the ban is made in the context of lending to the poor and once, in Deut 23:19–20, universally within Israel:

> Do not charge your brother interest, whether on money or food or anything else that may earn interest. You may charge a foreigner interest, but not a brother Israelite, so that the Lord your God may bless you in everything you put your hand to in the land you are entering to possess.

This repetition reflects its importance, as does the way Ezekiel links interest with theft and idolatry (Ezek 18:13). The book of Proverbs juxtaposes the man who charges interest against the one who is kind to the poor (Prov 28:8), and Nehemiah reimposes the ban on interest after the exile (Neh 5:1–13).

As with the biblical attitude to wealth, the ban on interest sought to make money subservient to relationships.[16] Loans are a part of life and accepted as such within the Bible. They allow an individual to achieve, through the grace and generosity of another, what they could not achieve on their own. However, as soon as interest is charged, whether modest or extortionate, the loan and its "relationship-reinforcing potential" is transformed into a different animal, one in which self-interest rather than love of the other is the motivating force. Paul Mills explains this with the example of the proverbial "cup of sugar" that one neighbor might borrow from another:

> Repayment terms are not specified and the loan will be made good either in kind or in the form of reciprocal favors. However, if the lender specifies when the sugar is due to be returned and how much more sugar the borrower is to return for the privilege, then the loan is transformed into something that "neighbors" do not engage in.[17]

The fact that this ban was limited to fellow Israelites, at least until the Christian era in which Jerome first proposed its universalization on the grounds of universal brotherhood, simply underlines this logic. The ban on interest was not motivated by some early anti-capitalist leanings, or even on the recognition that interest bred debt, but by the logic that the people of God should "use worldly wealth to gain friends," in other words to build relationships.

The third nexus of laws were those restricting the labor market. Employers were required to pay wages punctually (Deut 24:15) and to be responsible for their workers' safety (Exod 21:28–29). The Sabbath restrictions (see below) provided further protection against worker exploitation. Slaves were to be offered the opportunity of freedom after six years, and their owners were placed under legal restraint with regard to their treatment (Exod 21:20–21, 26–27).[18] In this way, the allowances for and the expectation of economic growth were not to be at the expense of the safety, security and basic humanity of workers.

The combination of these laws suggests, in modern terms, that the biblical vision favored a market-based system (over and against a centralized or planned one), which was free for goods but restricted for resources. Crucially, however, it was a market system that was oriented around people rather than profits, structured to safeguard and strengthen relationships, avoid long-term indebtedness, protect the poor, and, as we shall see below, safeguard the natural environment.

Roots

"Foxes have holes and birds of the air have nests, but the Son of Man has nowhere to lay his head" (Matt 8:20). Jesus spent his ministry as a peripatetic teacher, living on the support and hospitality of others. His disciples were expected to follow him or were sent out ahead of him (Luke 10:1). His tale of the Good Samaritan cut right across ethnic and cultural boundaries, the true neighbor being the hated foreigner rather than the religious leader or lay associate with whom the victim would have shared his land (Luke 10:25–37). He told the woman at the well in Samaria, "a time is coming when you will worship the Father neither on this mountain nor in Jerusalem . . . when the true worshippers will worship the Father in spirit and truth" (John 4:21–22). His parting words in Matthew's Gospel are "go out and make disciples of all nations" (Matt 28:19). A sense of place seems largely irrelevant in the Gospels, Jesus' call overriding all local loyalties.

Paul appears to endorse this. Believers are first and foremost "in Christ." The cross has dissolved the boundaries between communities: "You are no longer foreigners and aliens but fellow-citizens with God's people" (Eph 2:19). Paul himself led an itinerant life. He reasoned to the Christians in Rome:

> How can they call on the one they have not believed in? And how can they believe in the one they have not heard? And how can they hear without someone preaching to them? And how can they are preach unless they are sent? As it is written, "How beautiful are the feet of those who bring good news!" (Rom 10:14–15)

The gospel spread (in part) because believers like Paul were prepared (or forced) to leave their homes and embrace a life of travel. All in all, the New Testament appears to mark the end of the importance of place, an importance that had been painfully evident in the Old. Chris Wright has remarked that "the physical territory of Jewish Palestine is nowhere referred to with any theological significance in the New Testament."[19] The manner in which possession of the land had been "a huge, symbolic, tangible proof to every Israelite householder that he, his family, and his people had a special covenantal relationship with the Lord,"[20] was now subverted by and into Jesus himself. "For the holiness of place, Christianity . . . fundamentally . . . substituted the holiness of Person: it . . . Christified holy space."[21]

This is not the whole truth, however. For every rich young man told to sell his possessions and follow Jesus, there is a healed demoniac told to "return home and tell how much God has done for you" (Luke 8:39). The unique glimpses of Jesus' ministry offered by John's Gospel, not least his relationship with his friends at Bethany, remind us that being a disciple did not always necessitate leaving "all we had to follow you" (Luke 18:28). Quite apart from anything else, if sharing proximate space with other people, that is, being their neighbor, was now genuinely irrelevant, it would make no sense to use the metaphor of *neighborliness* in the way that Jesus does in the story of the Good Samaritan. In actual fact, Jesus does not abandon the concept of neighborliness so much as use it to exemplify the standard of behavior God demands from all.

In a similar way, Paul was rather different from the communities between which he spent much of life traveling. As Graham Tomlin has written:

> To the embarrassment of many an evangelist over the years, the epistles of the New Testament hardly ever contain appeals to Christians to go out and tell their friends about Jesus . . . The focus of these letters instead lies on getting these small communities to order their lives under the rule of God, ensuring they are marked not with petty jealousies, arguments and competition, but instead by love, compassion and holiness.[22]

The task set out in the New Testament for most of the church community is to live *rooted but open* lives: lives that are dedicated to the location in which they are lived, which forge the stable and secure communities and public space that human life needs in order to flourish, while at the same time maintaining a "mobile" or fluid mindset, one that is open to the fact that the call of God may override that of place and circumstance.

This subtly balanced attitude to rootedness and mobility ties in with one of the foundational ideas within this chapter: the importance of relationships. Ultimately, relationships require physical space in order to flourish fully. Notwithstanding the modern trend away from local communities and towards "virtual" communities of interest, the fact remains that humans are bodily creatures, in Chris Wright's phrase, "animals among animals . . . earth-creatures—*Adam*, from the soil, *ădāmâ*."[23] "To be human is to be placed," writes Timothy Gorringe.[24] Although a sense of belonging and permanence can be dangerous—humans have an inclination to move from rootedness into xenophobia—securing and maintaining a sense of place is necessary if one is to safeguard families, sustain welfare networks for the disadvantaged, foster civic life, secure economic equity, and preserve environmental stability. This opens up challenges for us today on two separate fronts. First, we do not own the territory beneath our feet. Everything we have, whether that is our possessions or our local or national identity, is on loan to us from God. As David prayed at the consecration of the temple:

> Everything comes from you, and we have given you only what comes from your hand. We are aliens and strangers in your sight, as were all our forefathers. Our days on earth are like a shadow, without hope. O Lord our God, as for all this abundance that we have provided for building you a temple . . . it comes from your hand, and all of it belongs to you. (1 Chron 29:14–16)

We must not fall into the error of thinking that just because we have been given leasehold of the ground beneath our feet we own it. We, like the Israelites, are tenants not landowners.

Second, we may not own the ground beneath our feet, but we have responsibility for it, a responsibility that requires from us some sense of the value of place in developing and nurturing sustainable life. This is not to imply we should abandon the car and return to a world in which "a stranger from a village five miles away . . . [might be] looked upon as 'a furriner.'"[25] It is, however, to suggest that if we are genuinely interested in living sustainably, we need to recognize the importance of place.

Nature and Sabbath

It may seem strange that we have not until now explored the most obvious element of sustainable living, namely how we treat our natural resources. The reason for this is to emphasize a point that has recurred throughout Part 2 of this book: that one cannot engage with the biblical vision for the environment in isolation from its vision for human society.

This point was noted in Isa 40–66 and is repeated time and again in the biblical story. Deuteronomy 29 talks about how the people's insincere, hypocritical response to the law would turn "the whole land [into] a burning waste of salt and sulphur—nothing planted, nothing sprouting, no vegetation growing on it," and this warning is repeated from different angles by the prophets. Hosea explicitly links the sin of the people to environmental devastation:

> Hear the word of the Lord, you Israelites,
>   because the Lord has a charge to bring
>   against you who live in the land:
> "There is no faithfulness, no love,
>   no acknowledgment of God in the land.
> There is only cursing, lying and murder,
>   stealing and adultery;
> they break all bounds,
>   and bloodshed follows bloodshed.
> Because of this the land mourns,
>   and all who live in it waste away;
> the beasts of the field and the birds of the air
>   and the fish of the sea are dying." (Hos 4:1–3)

Two centuries later, Jeremiah brings out this connection with particular clarity. He writes how the people "do not say to themselves, 'Let us fear the Lord our God, who gives autumn and spring rains in season, who assures us of the regular weeks of harvest'" (Jer 5:24). Instead they "have become rich and powerful . . . fat and sleek," and "do not plead the case of the fatherless . . . [or] defend the rights of the poor" (Jer 5:27–28). The result is judgment, although it is made clear that the judgment is self-inflicted. "Your own conduct and actions have brought this upon you" (Jer 4:18). The punishment sounds strangely familiar:

> The nobles send their servants for water;
>   they go to the cisterns
>   but find no water.
> They return with their jars unfilled;
>   dismayed and despairing,
>   they cover their heads.
> The ground is cracked
>   because there is no rain in the land;
> the farmers are dismayed
>   and cover their heads.
> Even the doe in the field

deserts her newborn fawn
because there is no grass. (Jer 14:3–5)

"I will weep and wail for the mountains," Jeremiah laments in chapter 9:

> [I will] take up a lament concerning the desert pastures.
> They are desolate and untravelled,
>   and the lowing of cattle is not heard.
> The birds of the air have fled
>   and the animals are gone. (Jer 9:10)

"What man is wise enough to understand this?" he asks a few verses later. "Why has the land been ruined and laid waste like a desert that no one can cross?" God replies, "It is because they have forsaken my law, which I set before them; they have not obeyed me or followed my law" (Jer 9:12–13).

"How long will the land lie parched and the grass in every field be withered?" Jeremiah responds several chapters later, before repeating the fundamental charge: "Because those who live in it are wicked, the animals and birds have perished" (Jer 12:4). God's response is typically elliptical, offering hope and a moral challenge, but not a timetable:

> After I uproot them, I will again have compassion and will bring each of them back to his own inheritance and his own country. And if they learn well the ways of my people and swear by my name, saying, "As surely as the Lord lives" . . . then they will be established among my people. (Jer 12:15–16)

Two points are established in these (and other) passages concerning environmental collapse. The first is that environmental degradation is a direct consequence of disobedience: violating God's law not only offends God and harms others but damages the shared environment on which we depend. The second, reflecting a point made in the previous chapter, is that there is no distinctive feature of those laws that relate to environmental consequences. They are not all economic, or all cultic, or even all environmental.

This last point is noteworthy. There is a number of what we might call specifically environmental commands in the Torah: "Do not slaughter a cow or a sheep and its young on the same day" (Lev 22:28); "Do not muzzle an ox while it is treading out the grain"(Deut 25:4); "When you lay siege to a city for a long time, fighting against it to capture it, do not destroy its trees by putting an axe to them" (Deut 20:19); "If you come across a bird's nest beside the road . . . do not take the mother with the young"(Deut 22:6). The fact is, however, that none of these is ever cited as the specific reason for the environmental degradation about which the prophets warn. Although one needs to be careful not to push this argument too far—the prophets were not concerned to make a full inventory of Israel's sins and, as noted in the previous chapter, arguments from silence must necessarily be tentative—it seems to point to the fact that it wasn't (and isn't) simply environmental commands that had environmental consequences. Rather, it is the entirety of humanity's relationship with God and with each other that affects the environment.

This point is underlined by the fact that when the prophets do list Israel's sins in the context of environmental degradation, they seem to us, at first sight, rather detached from the issues of environmental awareness and sustainable living. Hosea (as we have noted) cites Israel's "cursing, lying and murder, stealing and adultery" (Hos 4:2). Jeremiah cites Israel's lies, deception, disobedience, idolatry, and, among other things, the way the people have prioritized money and power over "plead[ing] the case of the fatherless . . . [and] defend[ing] the rights of the poor" (Jer 5:27–28). When the prophet Joel talks, in lavish detail, of the environmental disaster that will overcome Israel (Joel 1:7–12), he does not point the finger at particular "environmental" sins but instead calls the people to "return to [God] with all your heart, with fasting and weeping and mourning" (Joel 2:12–13).

All this should encourage us away from searching for a neat "natural resources" category that will explain the environmental "bit" of sustainable living. In a very real way, the Jubilee legislation, the attitudes to wealth, to trade, and to roots each have environmental implications, despite being more obviously about social, cultural, or economic issues.

Having recognized this, it is worth highlighting the way in which one piece of legislation in particular, the Sabbath, while having a primarily social and economic impact also has a significant environmental scope. The Sabbath is outlined twice in detail, in Exod 20:8–11 and Deut 5:12–15, and twice more in summary in

Exod 23:12 and 34:21. In each of the longer commands the Israelites are told to keep the day holy, working for the remainder of the
week but resting on that day. The Sabbath is not simply a day of rest
for householders, however, but also for "your son . . . daughter . . .
manservant or maidservant . . . ox . . . donkey . . . [all] your animals
[and] the alien within your gates."

The reasons given for the Sabbath legislation are varied. In Exodus, the rationale is the creation order, reminding Israel that God
is the source of life: "For in six days the Lord made the heavens
and the earth, the sea, and all that is in them, but he rested on the
seventh day" (Exod 20:11). In Deuteronomy, the Sabbath is a way
of protecting the vulnerable by remembering "that you were slaves
in Egypt and that the Lord your God brought you out of there"
(Deut 5:15).

In addition to the reasons explicitly stated, the Sabbath legislation would have had a wide-ranging effect on many areas of life in
Israel. It would have functioned as an economic measure, placing a
check on what might otherwise become unrestricted trading, and
also as a social one, guaranteeing leisure time for those who would
otherwise not enjoy it, "ring-fencing" relationship time for families
and communities. While all these were, in their own way, religious
measures, the Sabbath was also, of course, a more narrowly religious edict, reorienting the whole community back towards the
God who created, rescued, delivered, and protected them.

On top of all these things, it was also an environmental command, as the explicit inclusion of livestock in the commands
indicated. Its environmental credentials are clarified by the corresponding legislation concerning the Sabbatical Year in Exod 23
(and Lev 25):

> For six years you are to sow your fields and harvest the crops, but dur-
> ing the seventh year let the land lie unploughed and unused. Then the
> poor among your people may get food from it, and the wild animals
> may eat what they leave. Do the same with your vineyard and your
> olive grove. (Exod 23:10–11)

As these verses make clear, there were environmental *and* social
concerns behind the Sabbatical Year. The land was not to be exhausted by overuse. The poor were to be given access that would not
otherwise have been theirs. The law even allowed for wild animals

to consume what the people left, thereby suggesting that agriculture (and other human activities) should not be permitted to destroy nonhuman life, ascribing value to nonhuman ecology, and implying that awe and respect for God's creation should not "give way to an exploitative and managerial approach to nature."[26]

The consequences of ignoring the Sabbath principle are spelt out clearly, both in the law and the prophets. Leviticus 26:34 warns the Israelites that if they do not allow the land its Sabbath, God will: "Then the land will enjoy its sabbath years all the time that it lies desolate and you are in the country of your enemies; then the land will rest and enjoy its sabbaths."

This warning is picked up by the narrator at the end of 2 Chronicles when he says that, during the time of the exile, "the land enjoyed its Sabbath rests; all the time of its desolation it rested" (2 Chron 36:21). The prophets are equally clear that Sabbath desecration was one of the sins for which Israel came under God's judgment, with Ezekiel paying it particular attention. "I gave them my Sabbaths as a sign between us, so they would know that I the Lord made them holy. Yet the people of Israel rebelled against me," God says in 20:12–13.

The Gospel writers record Jesus having six encounters on and about the Sabbath, five relating to him healing people and the sixth to eating.[27] Each was controversial, with his opponents accusing him of desecrating the holy day. In reality, however, his apparent subversion of the Sabbath was more of a rescue mission than an abandonment of the principle. Rather than being a time of rest, reorientation and a symbol of redemption, the Sabbath had been turned into a burden, a day in which those who were hungry or sick were held captive by their misfortune. Jesus' multiple healings and his corn-eating debate were rescuing the original intent of the law, while pointing forwards, in himself, to that "great Sabbath day when all [Israel's] enemies would be put to shame, and she herself would rejoice at God's release."[28]

The Sabbath, like the Jubilee, was a multilayered law, encompassing cultural, religious, social, economic, and environmental concerns. As such, it represents well the practices that sprang from the biblical vision of sustainable living, gesturing simultaneously in the direction of the environmental principles that marked the people's (intended) engagement with the rest of creation *and* in the direction of the social and economic laws and attitudes that were intended to shape the nation and make it a light to the Gentiles.

Vulnerability

Jesus began his "Nazareth Manifesto," in which he proclaimed "the year of the Lord's favor," with the claim that he had been anointed by "the Spirit of the Lord . . . to preach good news to the poor." Even allowing for the fact that he was quoting Isaiah this is significant. The Beatitudes begin with a blessing for the poor, "in spirit" being added in Matthew's Gospel (Matt 5:3; Luke 6:20). When John's disciples ask Jesus who he is, Jesus instructs them to tell their master what they hear and see: "The blind receive sight, the lame walk, those who have leprosy are cured, the deaf hear, the dead are raised, and the good news is preached to the poor" (Matt 11:5; Luke 7:22). When dining with a "prominent Pharisee" Jesus tells him "when you give a banquet, invite the poor, the crippled, the lame, the blind, and you will be blessed," adding, "although they cannot repay you, you will be repaid at the resurrection of the righteous" (Luke 14:12, 14). Although he tells his disciples that they will always have the poor with them (echoing the sentiments of Deut 15:11), it seems equally clear that he always has the poor on his mind and in his heart.

In this, he is doing no more than living out the values of the Law and the Prophets. The Sabbath year was intended, at least in part, as we have seen, to allow the poor to obtain food from un-plowed land (Exod 23:11), and the law on gleanings had a similar intent (Lev 19:10; 23:22). The poor were to be treated equally in all legal matters (Exod 23:3; 23:6; Lev 19:15) but given special dispensation in matters of ceremony (Lev 5:7, 11; 14:21) and personal redemption (Lev 27:8). Israelites were repeatedly instructed to bail out fellow countrymen who had fallen on hard times (Lev 25:25, 35, 39, 47; Deut 15:7), and not to exploit those with whom they had commercial contact (Deut 24:10–15).

Prophetic pronouncements on the poor are too many even to scratch their surface. Isaiah pronounces woe on those who "deprive the poor of their rights . . . withhold justice from the oppressed of my people, making widows their prey and robbing the fatherless"

(Isa 10:2). Among the many charges Jeremiah lays at Israel's door is that "wicked men" among them have failed to "plead the case of the fatherless to win it [or] defend the rights of the poor" (Jer 5:28). Ezekiel reports how "the people of the land practice extortion and commit robbery; they oppress the poor and needy and mistreat the alien, denying them justice" (Ezek 22:29). Amos proclaims God's condemnation of Israel for "sell[ing] . . . the needy for a pair of sandals . . . trampl[ing] on the heads of the poor . . . and deny[ing] justice to the oppressed" (Amos 2:6–7), and Zechariah records God's command to his people as they returned from exile, "Do not oppress the widow or the fatherless, the alien or the poor" (Zech 7:10).

Concern for the poor is a recurrent, perhaps even *the* recurrent social concern of the Law, the Prophets, and the Messiah. But—and this is an important but—we fall into a dangerous and characteristically modern error if we see poverty in *purely* material or financial terms. Just as we are alert to the fact that being financially rich does not make one rich in biblical terms (and can, indeed, be the very opposite), we need to be alert to the fact that being financially poor does not make one absolutely poor. To recognize this is emphatically not to romanticize poverty or to prioritize "spiritual" encouragement over material assistance. Instead, it is to broaden our understanding of poverty and, in doing so, to frame that understanding in more biblical terms.

Care for the poor is a recurring motif in biblical social ethics, but that motif is usually evident in a more inclusive format. Those termed "poor" are characteristically found alongside aliens, widows, orphans, and others. The verses from the prophets quoted above, for example, mention widows (twice), the fatherless (three times), the needy (twice), the alien (twice), and the oppressed (once), as well as the poor (five times).

Jesus follows this practice. His Nazareth Manifesto places the blind, the prisoners, and the oppressed alongside the poor. The Beatitudes begin with the poor in spirit (in Matthew), and go on to mention (among others) the meek, the mourners, and the persecuted. As we have already noted, Jesus' message to John's disciples cited "the blind . . . the lame . . . the leprous . . . [and] the deaf," and the redrawn guest list he offers the unnamed Pharisee in Luke 14 includes "the crippled, the lame, [and] the blind," alongside the poor.

The poor, in other words, take their place alongside those other people who, for whatever reason, are socially vulnerable. They may be physically impaired, or socially ostracized, or without an immediate social network on which to rely in hard times. Whatever the reason, it is these people whose lives are to be lifted and transformed with the coming of the kingdom. It is weakness rather than strength that commands attention in God's order.

In saying this, it is important to note that Israel was part of a wider ancient Near Eastern culture that recognized and addressed the realities of poverty and vulnerability. Care for the weak did not begin with the exodus. That said, the manner in which the exodus became Israel's founding, paradigmatic event, "an act of liberation and removal of the poor from the system that oppressed them," determining the nation's identity and self-understanding and thereby shaping its culture *was* distinctive.[29] To be Israel was to know what vulnerability was like. It was to know "how it feels to be aliens" (Exod 23:9).

This self-identification with the vulnerable was a recurrent theme in the early church. Peter wrote his first letter to "God's elect, strangers in the world, scattered throughout Pontus, Galatia . . ." at a time when Christians, particularly in Rome, were believed to be a malign and untrustworthy foreign body whose very existence jeopardized the foundations of the empire—a fear remarkably similar to that of the Israelites in Exod 1. The identity of the stranger suffering under an oppressive empire must have seemed all too appropriate to Peter. A few decades later, Clement of Rome began his (so-called) *First Letter to the Corinthians* (perhaps the earliest surviving Christian document outside the New Testament) "From the Church of God which is transiently sojourning in Rome," and in doing so used a technical term that denoted temporary rather than permanent residence.[30] Similarly, the anonymous writer of the slightly later *Letter to Diognetus* declared: "Though [Christians] are residents at home in their own countries, their behavior there is more like that of transients; they take their full part as citizens, but they also submit to anything and everything as if they were aliens."[31]

The first Christians knew they were God's "holy people" but identified with aliens and strangers of the world because they understood that the two were the same. God's values demonstrated and demanded a particular concern for the vulnerable.

Unlike the points made in the previous section on trade, this concern for the vulnerable offers no specific practices that might act as templates. The Jubilee land legislation and the ban on interest were specific measures intended, among other things, to prevent social and economic polarization, limit debt, and secure family and neighborhood networks. The concern for the vulnerable outlines no comparably precise policies but, instead, insists that unless the plight of the vulnerable is our lodestar as we respond to challenges of sustainable living and climate change, we will be heading in the wrong direction. Given the fact that the main beneficiaries of fossil fuel consumption over the past century have been high-income countries and the brunt of its consequences has been and is likely to be borne by the low-income ones, this concern for the vulnerable is particularly important for our response to climate change.[32]

Ultimately, the concern for the vulnerable should act like the ground beneath the feet of other practices. It is, to change metaphors, like Amos's plumb line, a measure to be placed beside policies to determine how "true" they are. Or it is, to paraphrase an altogether different source, UK Conservative party leader David Cameron, a reminder that the acid test for biblically derived policies (in any area and not just sustainable living) will not be how they affect the better off, but how they protect, help, and transform the lives of the vulnerable.

Summary

The concepts outlined in this chapter—jubilee, wealth, trade, roots, nature and sabbath, and vulnerability—were not expected to establish the kingdom of God, and they didn't. As contemporary readers we come to these concepts in the light of the vision outlined in Isa 40–66 and its inauguration in the New Testament, seeing them as responses to what God is already doing to create that new life, rather than as a blueprint for sustainable living.

These teachings were rooted in the particular circumstances of the period, and that advises us that if we are to draw on them to develop the response to our current challenges, we need to treat them with care, deriving principles that are both biblically valid and applicable to our current situation. It is to those principles that we now turn.

Part 3

THE CHRISTIAN RESPONSE

6

A Vision of Sustainable Living Today

What, then, should we do? If (as we discussed in Part 1) climate change is real, caused by humans, potentially catastrophic, and driven ultimately by our unsustainable levels and patterns of consumption, travel, and domestic energy use; if (Part 2) the command to love God and neighbor presents Christians with the duty to care for all creation as part of our worship of and obedience to him, as he makes "all things new," then what (Part 3) should we *do* about it? How can we translate the biblical vision and principles of sustainable living into our modern setting?

This question can be separated into two parts. First: what are we aiming for? What would a sustainable society actually look like today? What, in modern terms, is the vision of sustainable living to which we aspire? And second: how might we achieve it? What policies and practices should we adopt in our pursuit of this vision? What—on personal, communal, national, and international levels—should we be doing or campaigning for?

We shall explore the first of these questions below and the second in the next chapter.

Eight Principles for Sustainable Living

In drawing principles from biblical teaching that are intended to shape our social vision, we need to be alert to the potential for legitimate debate. Christians can and do disagree on which material to use and how to apply it.

In drawing on the breadth of material that we have presented in Part 2, we have sought to obviate the first problem, going beyond the small number of familiar passages and attempting to grasp the total biblical vision for sustainable living. But that still leaves two related questions: what principles should we derive from that teaching, and how specific or abstract should they be?

The Jubilee legislation offers an example of this problem. The Jubilee can be understood as intended to secure long-term, family cohesion or to maintain social capital; to prevent permanent indebtedness or to prevent a culture debt; to maintain economic equity or to avert economic polarization; to secure equitable and inalienable access to natural capital or to do the same for financial capital—or any combination of the above. None of these "principles" would be incorrect, as such, and none is mutually exclusive. Issues of family, wealth, indebtedness, and access to capital are, after all, closely linked. But which combination of which principles to what level of specificity is open to debate.

That debate is, at least in part, derived from the question of what the big idea should be. What ultimately matters? Does the center of gravity lie in the biblical social vision? In economic equality? Freedom? Family life?

Drawing on the work of the Jubilee Centre,[1] we have taken *the quality of relationships* with God and between human beings to be the controlling idea. Far from being in tension with principles like those just mentioned, the quality of relationships includes and often necessitates the principles listed above. It is hard to see how a relationship marked by severe inequality, oppression, or emotional brokenness can be deemed genuinely good. That said, in judging the quality of relationships as of primary importance, we implicitly relegate other principles to a secondary rank: important, but as tools rather than goals. Ultimately, it is relational well-being that should inform a Christian vision of society. The right ordering of our relationships, personally and institutionally, creates the context in which environmentally sustainable living becomes both a possibility and a joy.

This concept is explored in greater detail in the book *Jubilee Manifesto.*[2] For our purposes it is important simply to be open about the presupposition that underlies the principles that we believe should inform and shape our attempt to live sustainably.

1. **We should value and protect creation, seeing that as a joy rather than a burden.** The themes that structured chapter 3 point to the significance of creation, both human and nonhuman.

Creation matters to God but is entrusted, in an act of considerable "self-emptying," to humans, so that they may order, subdue, work, and care for it. That care should, however, be a joy rather than a burden, a way of fulfilling our proper relationship with God. To ignore the detrimental consequences of our actions on creation is, in part, to distort our relationship with the creator. This principle suggests that we should not offload the costs of our lifestyle onto the environment, but rather be prepared to "internalize" them, to pay the full cost of them. Less tangibly, we should speak positively of sustainable living, insisting that it is a goal to which we should aspire willingly and hopefully, rather than a "hair shirt" that we must don in order to survive.

2. **We should reflect the close bond between society and environment in our decisions.** Many of the themes within Part 2 emphasize the intricate link between human and environmental concerns. Humanity is part of creation, with a special responsibility for it. To care for creation is to love God and to love neighbor. Accordingly, to claim to love our neighbor while harming the environment we share is deeply misguided and is ultimately impossible. Renewal of society demands care for creation, and vice versa. Supposedly "social" or "economic" policies have a significant impact on "environmental" issues. This close link should act as a lens through which we can evaluate policies, highlighting those that have a double effect. It might, for example, lend weight to policies that seek to reduce carbon emissions by encouraging people into cleaner cars but lend more weight to those that sought to encourage people to drive less in the first place and to invest more time building relationships in their locality.

3. **We should pursue justice for the vulnerable and marginalized.** Concern for the vulnerable runs like a spine through the biblical narrative. It aims to foster a culture in which the interests of the weak are defended by the strong and might is not right. The Bible does this at least as much through concrete social and economic commands as through general moral exhortation. Given the disproportionate consequences of climate change on the global poor, this is particularly relevant. As with the previous principle, this can act as a lens through which policies may be judged. How does a particular policy affect the vulnerable? If it

communal (i.e., public transport) forms of transport, encouraging us, all the while, to invest more time and energy in our locality. It may also act as another lens through which to judge policy options: does a policy invest power and responsibility in a locality, or does it attempt to solve its problems for it?

7. **We should aim to offer just and equitable access to natural resources.** As observed earlier, the Jubilee legislation can be understood in many ways: as a way of ensuring family connectedness, of managing wealth equality, of reducing indebtedness. One key principle that may be drawn from it relates to shared access to "common goods": society should be structured in order to secure equitable and inalienable access to natural and, thereby, financial capital. This, as noted in chapter 5, corresponds closely to the modern notions of a stakeholder economy and equality of opportunity: everyone has a share and everyone has an equal opportunity to optimize their share. These two ideas are something akin to the Holy Grail for modern policy makers.

8. **We should respond seriously and with hope.** Underpinning all these principles is the idea that the commands to love God and neighbor demand a response. Espousing social and environmental concerns without doing anything about them is hypocritical. The prophets have disturbing things to say of people who merely "honor [God] with their lips" (Isa 29:13). If we are serious about loving God and loving our neighbor, however distant or unseen, we need to be serious about responding to God's commands. That noted, a serious response should also be a hopeful one. God has not abandoned creation to our corrupt and ineffective devices but rather laid the foundation stone for its renewal in person and promised fulfillment in the fullness of time. A serious response to his commands should also be a hopeful response to his promises.

These principles between them provide the foundations for a sustainable modern society. They help frame our response to the challenges of climate change and sustainable living in a way that is consistent with the vision of the good life the Bible presents to us.

Principles tend not, however, to fire the imagination, so it is worth thinking, a little creatively, about what they might actually *look* like in practice.

A Vision of Sustainable Living

There is no obvious and incontrovertible vision of sustainable living to which we should aspire. There will be as many impressions of the genuinely sustainable society as there are people to advocate them. Imagining a sustainable society does not demand a kind of ecofascism that seeks to impose its vision of the future on all, threatening violence to recalcitrants and skeptics.

What follows, therefore, is a vision, not a template, of what sustainable living might look like at some point in the not-too-distant future.

People are far more conscious of energy issues. They are acutely aware that they do not live in autonomous bubbles, but that every decision they make has an impact on someone somewhere. They recognize the connection between their energy use and the impact on forests, rivers, mountains, wildlife, and people, whether locally or further away, which results from burning fossil fuels or the generation of electricity. Fellow Americans living in Appalachia or Alaska, subsistence farmers and the families in sub-Saharan Africa or surrounding the Bay of Bengal are not simply struggling or starving figures on the 10 O'Clock News but are real people who are taken into account in everyday energy, transport, and consumption decisions.

Accordingly, use of renewable energy suppliers has increased, both for households and businesses. There is more localized and micro energy generation, as well as a growing market in "domestic combined heat and power" boilers, producing both electricity and heat from a single fuel source.

The great majority of households and businesses have implemented energy saving measures, such as wall and roof insulation and energy efficient appliances, which significantly reduce energy wastage. Substantial government grants are available for those living in or near "fuel poverty" to help them improve their homes. This has resulted in millions across the country, not least the poorest, saving money on fuel bills. In particular, the grotesque situation whereby the poorer you are the more you pay in real terms for your domestic energy is now a thing of the past. This, in turn, has helped (slightly) to narrow the gap between rich and poor.

New housing developments are built to far stricter energy standards, with many utilizing the LEED (Leadership in Energy and Environmental Design) rating systems for new homes. Green building designs have become more popular and affordable. Existing communities, as well as new developments, are taking steps to become carbon neutral.

Along with a recognition of the contribution made by the extended family structure to social cohesion, there is a growing awareness of the way denser living populations have less of a negative affect on the environment. There has been a steady rise in the marriage level and a slow decline in divorce, as well as more cohabitation and colocation of relatives, and a greater emphasis on local employment and shorter commuting times. More people are able to work closer to home, giving them more time to spend with family and local friends.

More generally, there is also greater recognition of the unpriced yet invaluable contribution to social order, cohesion, and well-being made by those men and women who have chosen to stay at home and look after children or elderly and frail relatives, rather than earn a wage—a recognition that has significantly lifted the status of the housewife/husband and helped encourage many extended families to restructure their lives accordingly.

Car use is lower than used to be the case and is still falling. There is greater use of and investment in public transport, with public space and infrastructure being planned around pedestrians, cyclists, and public transport rather than cars. People talk about a return to the age of the train. New housing developments are built into an established and spreading integrated transport network, which makes buses, subways, and trains a cheaper, easier, and more attractive option than cars. Infrastructure investment has done much to address past criticisms about the infrequency, lateness, and unreliability of public transport. Car sharing and teleworking is also more popular. Those car journeys still made depend more on electric vehicles or cleaner and more efficient (but more expensive) fossil fuels. As a result, cities are cleaner with fresher, healthier air, green spaces, and clean water.

Aircraft use has begun to fall, and airport expansion has been checked. Taxes on airline tickets are significantly higher than at present. Genuine progress has been made in persuading the International Civil Aviation Organization to renegotiate the 1944 Chicago Convention, which allows an exemption from taxes on air fuel.

At the same time, there has been a marked rise in domestic vacationing (and with it a significant boost to the North American tourist industry), as well as a notable trend towards vacations by train, bus, and boat. In the business world, an expansion of (vastly improved) video-conferencing facilities has helped reduce business air miles. People still fly to visit relatives living at a distance but do so less frequently and for longer periods. A high proportion of people who still fly voluntarily contribute to carbon-offset schemes. More generally, there is a much more cautious attitude to the whole business of moving long distances from loved ones.

All but the smallest businesses now participate in a compulsory carbon-trading scheme. This has focused their minds on energy efficiency, with two effects. First, businesses now see it as strategically and financially sensible to make serious efficiency measures in their premises and the vehicles they use. Second, those that have been unable to make such measures are spending a large and growing sum on financing carbon-offset schemes in poorer countries. Some still complain about this, but the steady investment in low-income countries is making a difference to their economies and is popular with the public at home. Moreover, there is every sign that the carbon-trading scheme will become more rather than less demanding.

Agriculture, the food chain, and grocery retailing is more localized. Shoppers make greater use of local grocery retailers who, in turn, are more inclined to source from local suppliers. Supermarkets also make greater use of local suppliers and have modified their supply network so as to minimize the food mileage accrued. There is a significant rise in online grocery shopping, with supermarkets boasting about the reliability of their in-store "pickers & packers" (hence overcoming a long-standing consumer fear). Delivery is by electric vans, a modern, grocery version of the milk truck.

The localized grocery infrastructure has helped revitalize North American agriculture and agricultural communities, as has considerable investment in renewable energy sources, both wind power and biofuel and biomass production. Regions have been able to focus on developing their best assets. The prairie states have not only harnessed the ever present wind, creating a new source of income for farmers, but have also helped to restore the prairie grasslands and reintroduced species such as free range bison, an additional source of high quality food and income. Best management practices have been instituted for biofuel and biomass production insuring low impacts on both wildlife and natural ecosystems. Local agriculture and renewable energy production has helped dwindling rural communities to re-establish their economic viability. Small shops, post offices, local banks, and grocery stores are now reopening, and farmers' markets are no longer limited to the rich suburbs. Commentators now talk about a "rural renaissance."

While the localized grocery infrastructure has significantly reduced the grocery trading links that rely on long distance truck haulage and airfreight, international trade remains strong in other ways. Freight transport by sea remains steady, and those economies that had relied on air-freighting raw food products to the West, now rely far more on shipping processed food products. In doing so, they earn a larger share in a more profitable sector of the grocery market, which has significant positive effects in their own economies. Like all other fuel, that used for air travel, freight, and for shipping produces less pollution and is more efficient than ever before.

There is greater recognition of the principle of rest. A grassroots movement to "give us a break" and protect workers' family time has grown significantly and puts real pressure on government and large retailers. Accordingly, Sunday trading became increasingly cost-ineffective, and supermarkets, which are now involved in the carbon trading scheme outlined above, now recognize a day of rest as one of the most cost-effective ways to meet their emissions targets. There is mounting pressure to tighten regulation on Sunday trading, with only shops under 3,000 sq. ft. being permitted to trade, for social and environmental reasons.

Public pressure has also helped establish a clear, well monitored, labeling system for products sold in the United States and Canada, guaranteeing fair wages, treatment, and investment to overseas workers, and sustainable agricultural practices. Advertising stickers on new vehicles include estimates of greenhouse gas emissions along with fuel efficiency ratings.

Corporate Social Responsibility is now taken seriously. The old joke—"Get real, John! We're talking about business ethics, not ethics!"—no longer reflects reality. There is now widespread recognition that companies that pay serious attention to stakeholder concerns rather than just shareholder concerns actually perform better, securing better quarterly results, more robust brand reputation, and attract some of the most able young recruits to work for them. Environmental and social accounts are based on reliable and respected metrics, and are submitted and audited with the seriousness of financial accounts. There is genuine public interest in these results, and companies stand to damage brand image and lose significant consumer support for falsifying accounts or failing to live up to stated corporate objectives. Those "green" companies that moved early into the supply or use of renewable energy have become market leaders as the price of fossil fuels has rocketed and other companies have been left with obsolete infrastructure. Their share prices have risen steeply.

There is broad acceptance that Gross Domestic Product is only part of the picture. Several other measures of national health, such as Relational Well-Being (RWB), have been informally adopted and are used to shape policy. These go beyond simple market growth to incorporate a range of other factors, such as health, education, reported well-being, national income distribution, levels of relationship breakdown, the value of domestic labor, the impact of environmental pollution, and crime.

Both nationally and internationally, there is growing recognition that human beings should "farm" rather than "mine" environmental resources, and that each human being has the same farming rights. In other words, global inequalities are unacceptable and it is recognized that everyone, no matter where they live, has the right to an equal share of the planet's resources. Accordingly, a far greater proportion of the budget of high-income countries is spent on overseas development and, at an individual level; a greater proportion of personal income is donated to domestic charities and international development organizations.

There is also recognition that carbon rationing (Contraction and Convergence on an international level and cap and trade programs on a national one—see chapter 7 for both) is the only just and fair means of apportioning pollution "rights." Even those high-income nations who might appear to stand to lose, at least at first, from such arrangements, now recognize that the domestic impact of climate change, and the need to liberate themselves from vulnerable, overseas energy supplies, now support the idea of "fair shares," and are helping to develop the international mechanisms by means of which they might be implemented.

North America is a world leader in this whole sphere and is widely regarded as the model from which other nations adopt and adapt policies. The introduction of carbon "rationing" and taxes; the growth of energy saving measures and of the renewables industry; the precipitous decline in greenhouse gas emissions that has occurred without damaging the economy; the increase in reported well-being—all these factors have cemented North America's position as the model for how modern societies can live sustainably. Environment ministers from other countries study the region's transition. Both the United States and Canada's position as world leaders in this field gives them unprecedented weight on the world stage, and these nations are using this to push through an ambitious framework for international targets, as well as developing mitigation funds and carbon-trading schemes that are further reducing carbon emissions worldwide.

It is equally widely regarded that the changed national consciousness and raft of new policies has been effected, in large part, by the role of the churches. By insistently pushing this agenda, thinking innovatively about policy options and mobilizing a grass-roots campaign, the churches caught the public imagination and created the space for government policies that would, only a few years ago, have been deemed impossibly idealistic.

This vision will not please everyone. Some will object to the details. Aviation fuel taxed!? Car use reduced!? Pollution rights rationed!? Others will dismiss it as pie-in-the-sky. Will we ever transfer our allegiance from private to public transport? What are the odds of getting the USA, or any country, to renegotiate the 1944 Chicago Convention exempting aviation fuel from taxation, let alone signing up to international carbon rationing?

All such objections may be valid but, for the time being, immaterial. This vision of sustainable living is not offered for its appeal (although hopefully much of it *will* appeal), or for its feasibility (although, again, much of it should be feasible). Rather, it is offered as one picture of how the principles of this book could be implemented in a modern Western economy like that of the United States or Canada.

That noted, and assuming that there is a level of agreement, if not consensus, concerning this vision, we are still left with the bigger question(s) of how we get from here to there. It is to these that we now turn.

7

THE PRACTICE OF SUSTAINABLE LIVING TODAY

THE GREAT MAJORITY OF households and businesses have implemented energy saving measures, such as wall and roof insulation and energy efficient appliances. . . . North America has become a world leader in the whole sphere (climate action) and is widely regarded as a model from which other nations adopt and adapt policies. . . . It is equally widely regarded that the changed national consciousness and raft of new policies has been effected, in large part, by the role of the churches."

How is this going to happen? How can this become more than just a wonderful vision? Is it even possible? Perhaps a first step is to understand that we are already in the midst of social changes needed to bring this vision about. In order to deal with climate change, we are seeking to change a relationship—that with our use of energy. We are being asked to change how much energy we use, how we use it, what type we might choose, and how we obtain this energy. For some 2007 was a "tipping point," perhaps an environmental tipping point, but certainly a social one. Increasingly the issue for the public, business groups, and even governments has ceased to be whether climate change is real, but rather what should we do about it.

Historically, we have made these types of changes before. Consider our relationship with birds. Birds were once considered either pests to farmers or sources of feathers and adornment to the fashionable. Yet now birds and their habitats are protected and they are valued as examples of the beauty of nature. In 1910, the millinery industry and "feather" trade were worth millions of dollars and employed thousands of people. Whole or pieces of birds adorned women's clothing. Anyone could use a neighborhood bird for target practice. Changing our relationship with birds presented practical and moral challenges similar to those we face with climate change. However, volunteers and professionals who wanted to protect birds used their talents to overcome barriers in law, economics, science, religion, psychology, and culture. One scientist analyzed 37,825 bird stomachs to prove to farmers that birds ate insects, not necessarily their crops. Other people wrote and distributed books on natural history, awakening children to the beauty and personalities of birds. Activism on the part of nonprofits was very important, with one using their own funds to hire wardens to protect bird colonies during breeding season. The resistance to this change in the treatment of birds was so strong that one of these wardens was murdered. Change has never been easy. Eventually, county, state, and national laws were passed, and also the International Migratory Bird Treaty, insuring the protection of migratory birds across North America.[1] It took decades, but in the process a cultural shift occurred. We still have a social and economic relationship with birds, but a *different* one than in 1910. By 2007, "bird watching" had become a $25 *billion* per year activity in Canada, the United States, and Mexico. One fifth of all Americans feed or "watch" wild birds—over 50 million people.[2]

There are other examples of huge changes in public perception and consequent actions. Smoking was a ubiquitous symbol of sophistication, and now it is banned from restaurants, taverns, public places, and work places across North America. Change is possible, though it may be difficult, impact the economy, take time, and require adaptability. Achieving sustainability will also be fraught with moral and practical complexity, but it can be done.

This chapter is divided into five sections for five areas of response—personal, communal, governmental, technological, and international. This reflects the fact that addressing climate change and moving towards sustainability demands engagement on all available fronts. Each section, although focused on the immediate issue of reducing carbon emissions and energy use, is also marked by the close link between environmental and social concerns that has run through this book.

Personal Response

According to Richard Harwood, people have become wary of politicians and the media because "many issues are framed in terms of supercharged emotions and false battle lines, where the nature of the problem is exaggerated, where choices do not reflect people's real concerns, where real costs are underestimated, and where potential results are oversold." People have withdrawn into circles of friends and local communities where life is manageable and they find people they can trust.[3] It is in this type of setting that personal energy choices can influence more than just our own "carbon footprint."

Many of the personal responses to reducing energy use are also ways of saving money or promoting a more sustainable life-style—ideas that have appeal even for those not convinced of climate change. Some aspects of sustainability can be "caught" from a friend.

Do personal choices make a difference? In early 2008, the state of Maryland sought advice on how to meet the state's growing demand for electricity and help consumers reduce their soaring energy bills. Should the state build new power plants (coal fired with some nuclear)? Or transmission lines from out of state? The American Council for an Energy-Efficient Economy reported that the best strategy for the state was to reduce the demand for electricity. "Energy efficient policies can more than offset projected load growth in the state over the next 18 years, deferring costly new electric power generation and transmission projects and reducing the risk of blackouts over the next 3–4 years. . . . Reducing demand for electricity with efficiency will also reduce air pollutant emissions from the combustion of fossil fuels at power plants, giving the state a cleaner energy future at an affordable cost."[4] The report also linked reduced demand to the state's efforts to combat the impact of global warming and support a vibrant economy. One recommendation was a law requiring a 15 percent per capita energy reduction by 2015 related to 2007 per capita consumption. A state government may be reluctant to legislate energy efficiency, but this demonstrates the cumulative impact our small steps to energy savings can have. It is worth remembering that the residential sector is the largest consumer of electricity in the United States, followed by our office buildings, retail stores, and other efforts that make up the commercial sector.

There are several personal responses that can be seen as "easy wins" (see Box 7.1). Most demand little more than a moment's thought and effort, and, in return, they reduce carbon emissions *and* save money. There is little excuse for ignoring them.

Box 7.1 "Easy Wins"

- Turn off unnecessary lights. Make greater use of daylight whenever possible.

- Unplug appliances or use a power strip to turn off home electronics such as TVs, DVD players, CD players, computers, and monitors. Don't leave them on standby!

- Turn your heating system down by 1ºF and air conditioner up by 1ºF. Change filters on forced air systems monthly.

- When it gets cooler, reach for a sweater before turning up the thermostat.

- Close curtains during day in summer to keep rooms cooler, but at night in winter to keep them warmer.

- Set your water heater thermostat at 120ºF.

- Ensure that the washing machine, dryer, or dishwasher is full when used.

- Defrost the freezer regularly. Use a thermometer to keep the freezer temperature at 3º F and the refrigerator as close to 37º F as possible. Keep the refrigerator coils clean.

- Hang your washing outside or in a warm room instead of using a dryer whenever possible.

- Consider collecting condensation water from air conditioning units, or using rain barrels, to water plants and lawns.

There are also many personal responses that cost money (at least in the immediate term). Typically they involve ways of altering a home so that it is more energy efficient; some of these ideas are listed in Box 7.2. For a Christian who takes their responsibility towards God and neighbor seriously many of these are also easy wins, the possible exception being among those for whom the more expensive adaptations would entail a sacrifice in other more important areas (such as rent or food). In the United States, the Department of Energy's Weatherization Assistance Program helps low income families reduce their energy bills (and energy use) by installing energy efficient changes in their homes. Each state administers its own program. Box 7.2 contains contact information for this program and links to other forms of assistance such as tax credits for implementing energy saving choices in the home.

Box 7.2 Will Save Money in the Long Run But May Cost Money in the Short Run

– Replace incandescent light bulbs with energy efficient compact fluorescent bulbs.

– Seal air leaks. Use caulk, spray foam, or weather stripping around windows, doors, outlets, pipes, wires, and baseboards.

– Insulate walls and attic spaces. Seal air leaks in attics, basements and crawl spaces.

– Give your electric hot water heater an insulating jacket. Insulate the first 6 inches of the supply and return pipes with foam pipe wrap.

– Install a high efficiency hot water heater, or an on-demand water heater if appropriate. Use water efficient faucets, shower heads, and toilets.

– Consider replacing your heating and cooling system if more than 15 years old and your refrigerator if more than 10 years old.

– Install a programmable thermostat.

– Look for the Energy Star label when replacing old appliances or purchasing new ones.

– Replace old windows with energy efficient double glazed windows.

– Install solar panels if you can.

For more information see: Power Scorecard: www.powerscorecard .org; Energy Star Web site: www.energystar.gov; Energy Efficiency and Renewable Energy Network: www.eere.energy.gov/consumer/ tips for a wide variety of ideas on saving energy at home.

For "green building construction" ideas see Environmental Building News: www.buildinggreen.com; Sustainable Building Sources: www.greenbuilder.com; and US Green Building Council: www.usgbc.org.

For tax credits and grants for energy related home improvements
see: www.energystar.gov in US; ecoENERGY Retrofit in Canada:
www.nrcan-rncan.gc.ca. Other helpful sources are: Tax Incentives
Assistance Project: www.energytaxincentives.org; and Database
for State Incentives for Renewable Energy: www.dsireusa.org. For
the Weatherization Program see: http://apps1.eere.energy.gov/
weatherization/state_contacts.cfm.

A third response is to switch to renewable or "green" electricity,
otherwise known as green power. There are three ways to do this,
and a lot depends on where you live in the United States or Canada.
In some states and provinces, electricity markets are open to competition and customers can purchase their power directly from renewable energy suppliers. In other areas, the local utility company
provides a service called "green pricing." Customers can choose to
pay a premium on their electric bill which then allows the utility
to purchase renewable energy, or invest in renewable technologies
as part of the regional energy grid. The wind or solar power may
not come directly through the transmission lines to the particular
consumer's home, but their choice creates a greater percentage of
renewable energy to fossil fuel generated electricity in their region.
It is a way of demonstrating consumer demand for renewable energy or working to lower the impacts of coal fired power plants in
a local area. Currently there are over 750 utility companies across
the United States that offer green pricing.

A third way to influence the amount of renewable energy is purchasing a "renewable energy certificate" otherwise knows as a "green
tag." In effect, the consumer purchases the environmental benefits
of a certain amount of renewable energy. The cost of the certificate
pays for renewable energy that may be generated in a totally different part of the country. This is one method people use to offset
their own carbon emissions. Green power is an emerging industry.
Currently there are no common and enforced industry standards.
Box 7.3 provides some resources for the wise consumer in locating
and evaluating green power suppliers and certification programs.

The next step up from using renewable electricity is to generate
your own. So-called "micro-generation" technology is becoming
increasingly available to the general public. Solar PV (photovoltaic)
systems use cells to convert solar radiation into electricity. Solar

---

Box 7.3 Resources on Green Electricity Suppliers

- Green Power Network: www.eere.energy.gov/greenpower US Department of Energy site lists, by state, companies and available plans for purchasing "green power," "green pricing," and "green tag certificates."

- Environment Canada's Green Power site: www.ec.gc.ca provides links to their Environmental Choice Program.

- Power Scorecard: www.powerscorecard.org site rates green power suppliers.

- Environmental Resources Trust's EcoPower: www.winrock.org/feature_ert_200802.asp and Green E Certification Program: www.green-e.org certify green energy certificates.

- Pembina Institute: http://climate.pembina.org provides information on renewable energy in Canada.

---

water heating systems use the Sun's heat to supplement conventional water heaters. Ground source heat pumps transfer heat from the ground into a building to provide space heating and cooling, and in some cases, to pre-heat domestic hot water. Small-scale building-integrated wind turbines suitable for urban locations are currently being developed, as are micro-hydro plants, and there are several ways of using biomass or biofuels to supplement domestic energy. Some of these options are explored in greater detail in the section on technological responses below. More information on each is available from the Energy Efficiency and Renewable Energy Network (www.eere.energy.gov).

A less direct approach, but one that underlies the far-reaching implications of climate change and sustainable living, is one's choice of bank, investments, and pension funds. Socially Responsible Investing or SRI is becoming an increasingly familiar concept. In 2005, one out of every ten dollars under professional financial management in the United States was in some form of SRI. This amounted to $2.9 trillion.[5] The top ten US banks controlled almost half of the nation's bank assets.[6] We normally think of the returns we receive on our investments, but we are, in truth, lending our money to banks and others to loan to companies, utilities, and individuals. Whether we have a small amount of money or great assets, we can influence how that money is spent.

Socially responsible or ethical investing usually involves one of the three following approaches: screening, community investing, or shareholder advocacy. Screening is the process of evaluating mutual funds or investment strategies based on social, environmental, or other criteria. "Socially responsible or ethical" can, of course, mean different things, with different "ethical investors" adopting different approaches to how they do business. Military hardware, pornography, tobacco, gambling, General Motors technology, and animal welfare are the areas most commonly avoided. Increasingly, screens are being used to seek out companies that are leaders in adopting clean technologies. Box 7.4 highlights organizations that specialize in evaluating funds and companies or provide useful information for socially responsible investors.

Some banks focus on providing services and funds to local or underserved communities, the basis for the growing area of community investing. But banks in a given area may also specialize in funding environmental projects and other actions on climate change. The best way to search this out is to ask your bank what types of loans they approve. Large banks often provide the financing for construction of new electricity generating power plants. In early 2008, three major US banks developed "the Carbon Principles," guidelines designed to help these banks address the carbon risk in their transactions with power plants.[7] This is another indication of the social change in the United States. Lending institutions such as banks are beginning to recognize the reality and risk of climate change and starting the process of planning how they will address these issues. Changes such as these have been brought about by the threat of legislation at a national level, campaigns by non-profits who understand the relationship between what banks finance and any movement towards a sustainable society, and the final type of SRI—shareholder advocacy.

Even small shareholders have potent power, because they are part owners of a company. They are entitled to submit shareholder resolutions, statements which call a company to action on a particular issue. For example, in 2005 Exxon Mobil was forced to place two shareholder resolutions on the proxy ballot for the upcoming annual meeting. The first dealt with how the company planned to reduce its emissions in countries that had signed the Kyoto Proto-col and where Exxon had operations. The second required Exxon Mobil to release the research data it had been using to dispute the reality of climate change. As a result of these resolutions, Exxon Mobil was publicly berated by two US senators and asked to stop funding the anti-climate change organizations it supported.[8] In-creasingly shareholders are asking their companies how they are planning for the risks of climate change—how management is going to maximize their profits and maintain something of inesti-mable value—the company's public reputation.

Box 7.4 Resources on Ethical Investment

- Social Funds.com: www.socialfunds.com provides a wealth of information on SRI funds and socially responsible investing in general.

- ResponsibleInvesting.org: www.responsibleinvesting.org is an extensive database of funds and screening categories.

- Social Investment Forum: www.socialinvest.org is affiliated with Co-op America and provides information on trends in social in-vesting as well as the opportunity to participate in shareholder advocacy campaigns.

- FTSE4Good Index: www.ftse4good.com provides statistical tools designed especially for socially responsible investors.

The cost of such measures is primarily in financial terms (and not all have a cost: research shows that ethical investments per-form as well as the overall market). The moral complexity of such personal responses amounts to little more than a trade-off between financial cost and environmental benefit. But when we move into the area of consumerism and lifestyle choices, the decisions become fraught with a bit more moral and practical complexity.

In the United States, consumption patterns affect climate change by the amount of waste we generate through the products we buy and throw away, the amount of energy that is invested in manufacturing these products, and the distances they travel. On top of this, as we saw in chapter 2, our own well-being is affected. We may give mental assent to saving energy, but when it comes to

such decisions as buying a new car, other priorities, such as perceived safety, social pressure, or financial costs, must be considered.
And when we think about choices that emphasize a sense of place as
means of building social capital (and reducing carbon emissions),
we discover more subtle trade-offs. Again, we may ask, "Do our
personal choices make a difference?"

In a recent discussion on new vehicle fuel efficiency standards,
Charles Territo, a spokesman for the Alliance of Automobile Manufacturers said: "On the one hand, Congress is saying that consumers
want more fuel-efficient vehicles, and we don't disagree. But we also
see in a large part of the country—where there are available more
than 200 models that achieve fuel economy rations more than 30
mpg on the highway—consumers purchased more minivans, vans,
SUVs and pickup trucks."[9] A *Wall Street Journal* article in 2007
investigating toxic lead in children's jewelry imported from China,
quoted one jewelry merchant: "We do what our customers want. If
they ask for no lead, we can do it. But a lot of Americans see the
cost of lowering the lead content and say: 'forget it.'" And another
merchant remarked: "It is too costly to make lead-free products.
Chinese products have to be sold cheaply in foreign markets, or
they are not competitive."[10]

The latter example is ironic in the light of transportation's contribution to climate change. Many electronic products, including
computers, are manufactured in China and shipped to the West
for sale. These electronic components utilize materials that become
toxic if not disposed of properly. The lifespan of modern electronics is about two years and then most of these items are discarded in
favor of the newest and fastest equipment. In 2005, Americans threw
away about 2.63 million tons of e-waste of which approximately 12.5
percent were recycled. The rest went into our landfills (contributing 40 percent of the heavy metals found there) or were burned.
Of those that were recycled, 50 to 80 percent were shipped abroad,
usually to China, Pakistan, or India. In some areas of China where
e-waste is "recycled," the lead in local rivers is 190 times higher than
World Health Organization safety standards. Lead, including toxic
lead, once extracted from old computers, is then sold to jewelry
manufactures and incorporated into products they then ship back
to America. So, that inexpensive piece of jewelry has, in one form
or another, made at least one and a half circles around the world.[11]

There is a budding movement in North America towards "critical," "ethical," or "conscientious" consuming. For some the goal is to live simply. But others aim to use their lifestyles and the power of being a consumer to influence what is being produced, and how and where it is manufactured. The effects of this can be seen in such things as the growing availability of organic produce and the "greening" of advertising.

Box 7.5 (see next page) provides some ideas for living purposefully. Unlike the recommendations of earlier boxes, these can present us with rather more awkward choices and challenges but the reward is a step towards sustainability. Thus, the emphasis on pedestrian shopping and the use of local retailers and producers will challenge existing shopping habits, which for most people involve supermarkets. That will demand thought, organization, time, effort, and perhaps (although not necessarily) more money. The challenge is not *never* to use a supermarket (all but impossible in the modern West), but to support local butchers, bakers, and farmstands where they still exist.

The moral complexity of the issue does not end with this trade-off, however, and gives an indication of the questions faced by those who want to become ethical consumers. For all the millions of food miles that supermarket supply chains rack up each year, supermarkets are, at least, open about their sourcing, and it is often easier to tell whether their fruit comes from California, Mexico, or New Zealand than it is for fruit bought at a local greengrocer or on a market stall. The advantages accrued by shopping locally in terms of building social capital and not using an extended United States or Canadian supply chain, in which goods travel hundreds of miles to and from regional depots, may be outweighed by local shops and markets that source their products internationally but don't tell their customers.

To complicate matters still further, many of the low-income countries most severely threatened by climate change are also dependent on such international trade. To boycott food grown abroad might reduce carbon dioxide levels but it would also damage the economies of many low-income nations dependent on the international food trade. This problem is not necessarily insuperable. Food that is shipped by surface rather than flown accrues the same "mileage" but at a considerably lower environmental cost. Similarly,

Box 7.5 Local Responses

- Walk (or cycle) rather than drive whenever you can. Use local stores (if you still have any!) and walk to them if you are able.

- Be aware of food miles! Buy local and seasonal food when you can.

- Try out your local farmer's market. Become part of a Food Co-op. Grow your own vegetables or participate in a local Community Supported Agriculture program (CSA). For local resources see: www.localharvest.org.

- Car-share and/or use public transport. For city dwellers, explore the ZipCar—renting a car only when you need one: www.zipcar.com.

- Drive a "green" car or at least one with a high mileage per gallon. For vehicle comparisons see: www.eere.energy.gov/afdc.

- Live closer to (or think twice about moving away from) relatives, friends, church, and your place of work.

- Cut down on waste going to landfills by recycling or reusing items. Shop in thrift stores and other outlets for used items. For recycling e-waste see: www.computertakeback.com; for recycling cell phones and donating the proceeds to charity see: www.collectivegood.com. To give away other items to charities see: www.throwplace.com.

- Become an informed and "critical" shopper. See: www.responsibleshopper.org and www.coopamerica.org. There are many good books on sustainable living. Two suggestions are: *The Rough Guide to Shopping with a Conscience,* by Duncan Clark and Ritchie Unterberger (Rough Guides, 2007), and *Green Living: The E Magazine Handbook for Living Lightly on the Earth,* by the editors of E Magazine (Plume, 2005).

food that is processed as well as just grown in low-income countries is not only more readily shippable but can strengthen such economies by giving them a greater share in the total food chain. In such ways international food trade can minimize carbon dioxide emissions without decimating low-income economies. But the issues are far from simple and remain hotly debated. Box 7.5 also includes some suggestions for organizations who research these issues.

If there is moral complexity over where we buy our fruit from, there is even more over the question of how close we live to our parents, siblings, children, church, or place of work. Few people are likely to elect to live somewhere on the basis of potential future carbon emissions—too many other consideration are (rightly) deemed more pressing. Nevertheless, living close to relatives, friends, and church family on whom we can depend, or to a place of work that permits us to get home quickly is not only environmentally kinder but practically sensible and liable to improve our quality of life.

As with where and what food we buy, however, the moral complexity does not end with that decision. In reality, all decisions we make are taken in the context of choices that have already been made. Thus, the question "How should we travel?" is, in actual fact, "How should we travel *given that* we (and others) already live and work where we do?" When our relatives and friends live abroad or at the other end of the country, should we value the relational benefits of seeing one another frequently over the environmental impact of regular short or even long-haul flights?

One apparent way out of this conundrum is to offset the unavoidable carbon emissions of our travel. A number of organizations (see Box 7.6) help travelers calculate and compensate for their carbon emissions (and some for domestic carbon emissions). Many do this by planting trees to absorb the carbon dioxide emitted by travel. Some also work with communities to reduce deforestation, currently responsible for 20 percent of emissions worldwide. An increasing number offer other offset options, such as purchasing and not using credits from carbon-trading schemes, investing in sustainable technology development, or supplying energy efficient technologies to low-income countries. Each option has its place. Those that attempt to reduce emissions before they reach the atmosphere may be more effective.

Offsetting carbon emissions is certainly better than not doing so, but it is only one part of a long-term solution to the problem. There is a real danger that carbon-offset schemes become a guilt-payment, legitimizing irresponsible behavior by encouraging people to think that once they have made their payment, they can do pretty much what they like; in other words, a modern form of medieval "indulgences."

So what do we do as individuals? The guidelines to sustainability from chapter 6 might provide good questions to ask as we make our decisions. Will this action value and protect the creation, reflecting the close bond between society and the natural world? Will these decisions promote justice for the vulnerable and marginalized, foster relational health, and take account of natural, human, and social capital? Do our actions demonstrate a commitment to our immediate environment and favor local solutions? Are we responding to the challenges of our lives with seriousness and hope?

Box 7.6 Carbon Offset Schemes

The following are only a few of the many opportunities to calculate and offset your carbon footprint. Each offers a slightly different approach and a variety of helpful information. For more on carbon offsets read "Carbon Offsets Demystified" www.coop america.org/pubs/realmoney/articles/carbonoffsets.cfm March/April 2007.

- Climate Stewards: www.climatestewards.net

- Carbonfund.org: www.carbonfund.org

- Climate Care: www.climatecare.org

- Terrapass: www.terrapass.com

- Tearfund: www.tearfund.org/share

- My Climate: www.myclimate.org

- The Climate, Community and Biodiversity Alliance: www.climatestandards.org. Establishes standards for land-based carbon offset projects.

Communal Response

We fall into a peculiarly modern error if we understand a personal response to mean solely an individual one. Our culture of freedom, autonomy, and individual sovereignty means that the individual or perhaps household response is the one most obviously available to us. Yet we are all members of wider networks that, in themselves, can impact the problem of climate change. For Christians this will include many different organizations, foremost among which is the local church.

It will hardly need saying that this means more than church buildings. Churches are—or should be—rather more: outposts of the coming kingdom of God that live out the sustainable communal life that is part of that kingdom. They should be opportunities to showcase how sustainable living is not only possible but is also beneficial and joyful.

Unfortunately, sustainable living and climate change have not been on the radar screen for many Christians or churches in North America. This is changing but not without a struggle. We often derive our worldview from our churches as well as from our own reading of Scriptures. For the more liberal and mainline denominations in America, with a history of concern for social justice, engagement in environmental issues has been easier than for conservative groups, who have tended to emphasize personal holiness and salvation or focused mainly on issues involving sexuality and family concerns. However, there is a growing desire among conservative Christians to apply their thirst for holiness more widely and to develop a more holistic view of Christianity which includes actions related to poverty, Darfur, and the impacts of climate change around the world.[12]

American Christians face four unique challenges as they encourage their churches to become serious on issues such as climate change. First, environmental problems have become extremely politicized in the United States. Often conversations regarding environmental concerns, such as climate change, turn into conversations about political parties or political action. One church member said: "When I saw that *An Inconvenient Truth* was produced by Al Gore, I did not watch it because I don't like him, politically." Many church members do not want to see "politics" invade their churches. At the same time, evangelicals are seen, by politicians, as powerful voting blocks, shapers of national elections. The leadership of some evangelical groups has begun to use this possible influence to engage in supporting public policy initiatives, including those on climate change, which they perceive as reflecting a biblical imperative. To church members it can be confusing to understand the role they play in what has become a political issue in a country that has not always welcomed (but often ridiculed) religion in the public square.

Secondly, a popular theological interpretation of the end times interprets environmental problems, whether climate change, pollution, or species extinction, as part of God's plan for the earth and not to be challenged. Another "theology" considers the world and all it contains as existing only for human use. Neither of these beliefs provides a genuine foundation for action on climate change (chapter 3 addresses this).

A third issue is the suspicion many Christians have of science. This largely stems from the creation/evolution debates or the battles over abortion. So a Christian scientist might be more "trustworthy" to this audience than someone who is an expert but holds a different world view. And the strategy to highlight the "uncertainties" of science finds a ready audience among this group.

The final challenge is the economic view that sees the American way of life as the ultimate outgrowth of biblical faith and God's blessing. Peter Harris, the founder of the international conservation organization, A Rocha, and a British pastor, observes: "Commitments of that kind have left the church throughout the USA particularly vulnerable to attempts to baptize a particular national culture, and even to understand the especially privileged lifestyle that many enjoy, but from which many other millions in the country are excluded, as an expression of the Kingdom of God. It then becomes particularly difficult to challenge the hold that materialism and individualism, each so fundamental to common American thinking about wealth, has on the church."[13] In other words, culture is confused with Christianity and actions to mitigate climate change become attacks on a "Christian" way of life.

It is important to understand these challenges because what happens in churches in America has the potential to impact the wider world. Peter Harris goes on to say: "Popular American spirituality and thinking have become a global export of enormous proportions. . . . While a biblical faith can be a powerful agent for conservation and renewal of a degraded environment, a sub-biblical one that baptizes consumerism and individualism is literally dangerous. We had seen in the rapid deforestation, soil depletion and polluted water sources of several places where Christians were in the majority that it could even be a significant driver of unsustainable living conditions for both believers and others alike."[14]

The growing involvement of the church within America is part of the cultural shift that may move us towards a sustainable lifestyle and genuine action on climate change. Ultimately, it will take more than policy recommendations. The proof will be in concrete actions, such as implementing many of the energy saving measures outlined in the boxes above. But it should extend beyond such measures. In the first instance it will involve helping people understand the problem and the appropriate Christian response. Adopting the practices of this chapter without rooting them in the theology of Part 2 is to allow the tail to wag the dog. Worse, they may encourage people to think that recycling rather than repentance is what makes them right with God. Sermon series, Bible studies, discussion groups, sung worship, and corporate excursions can all play a role in inculcating the awareness that the gospel actively invites us to "live sustainably," albeit in its own terms. It is in addition to rather than instead of such activities that energy saving and efficiency measures should be implemented.

Beyond such obvious communal responses, however, there is enormous scope for positive action in the way in which a congregation lives and cooperates. Carpooling, sharing household or garden products, exchanging energy efficiency tips, doing school-runs or shopping trips for each other: these can all make a difference to a congregation's total energy consumption, not to mention standing as a powerful testimony of practical love, support, and co-operation. Personal and communal measures such as these and those outlined in the previous section *could* solve the problem. We could all switch to a renewable energy supplier while making our houses as energy efficient as possible. We could all invest more in our localities, choosing to live close to relatives and places of work, to shop locally, and to travel by foot, bicycle, or public transport whenever possible. We could all pay more attention to the mechanisms by means of which our food reaches our tables, buying locally sourced products wherever possible. We could all refuse to invest in those companies that fail to acknowledge a duty of care for creation. We could all live counter-cultural lives, reducing, reusing, and recycling wherever possible, placing people and principles above price in our purchase decisions. We could all, in other words, spend time, money, and energy, to make personal sacrifices, to repent of our ultimately unsustainable ways of life. And if we did, not only would we dramatically reduce our carbon emissions, but we would also reinvigorate local communities, reclaim public space for the public, and pry ourselves from the grip of a consumer culture. Few other changes in behavior would signal so powerfully the Christian determination to live according to God's ordering of creation, rather than our present notions of unrestricted personal freedom. In addition, some churches have begun to recognize that helping local groups adapt to climate change may become an integral part of their foreign missions ministry. Box 7.7 provides resources for those congregations ready to embark on this adventure.

Box 7.7 Resources for Congregations

The following churches provide broad resources for other groups as well as insights from their own experiences.

- Vineyard Boise: www.letstendthegarden.org. Tri Robinson's book documents how one congregation put the call to care for creation into practice. Provides practical tips on forming an environmental action committee, which is key to helping engage the wider congregation. Provides connections with other organization engaged in Christian creation care.

- Northland—A Church Distributed: www.creationicare.net is actively involved in climate change efforts, nationally and through local projects such as a total energy audit (including waste). Provides information for pastors as well as general green consumer reports and actions.

- Churches in Hamilton Committed to Caring for Creation: http://truecityenvironment.wordpress.com actively seeks to equip churches to care for creation and tackle environmental injustice. Focuses on Canada.

Technical resources and links

- The Regeneration Project: www.theregenerationproject.org. The portal to local state Interfaith Power and Light organizations. Resources include climate change education, helping congregations with energy audits, and an online store for energy efficiency products for faith communities and their members (www.ShopIPL.org).

- Energy Star site for congregations: www.energystar.gov/index
  .cfm?c=small_business.sb_congregations includes technical
  resources for planning and calculating energy savings.

- Christians for the Mountains: www.christiansforthemountains
  .org works primarily to engage Christians to stop mountain top
  removal for coal in Appalachia, but their Web site includes biblical, theological, and church resources covering the breadth and
  history of faith-based involvement in creation care (Christian
  and Jewish). For other organizations see their links—"National
  Christian Ministries working on Sustainability with Annotated
  Notes."

Another community that has grown vibrantly active over the past few years has been college student groups. Wheaton College's President, Dr. Duane Litfin, took a bold step and signed the Evangelical Climate Initiative because of the challenge and example of one such student group, A Rocha Wheaton. Students are helping their campuses become "carbon neutral," generating student summits on climate change and creating ways that alumni can support "green" or energy efficient efforts on college campuses. As of early 2009, at least 8 Christian colleges had signed the American College and University President's Climate Commitment, committing their campuses to reducing greenhouse gas emissions and incorporating sustainability studies throughout their curriculum. For information on key student initiatives see Box 7.8.

Box 7.8 Resources for Student Groups

Web sites frequently change, however some of the most active groups are:

- Focus the Nation: www.focusthenation.org

- Energy Action Coalition: www.climatechallenge.org

- American College and University Presidents' Climate Commitment: www.presidentsclimatecommitment.org

Other efforts include: the Evangelical Youth Climate Initiative, the Sierra Student Coalition: www.ssc.org and the Campus Ecology Program: www.nwf.org/campusEcology

The following organizations sponsor student environmental groups on Christian college campuses: Restoring Eden: www .restoringeden.org/campus, and A Rocha USA: http://daisy.arocha .org/us-en/work/students.html or www.arocha.org. Other exciting opportunities for students include: The AuSable Institute for Environmental Studies: www.ausable.org and the Creation Care Study Program: www.creationcsp.org/index.html.

Two helpful books for student groups and others are: *Ignition: What You Can Do To Fight Global Warming and Spark A Movement*, edited by Jonathan Isham and Sissel Waage (Island Press, 2007), and *Green Revolution: Coming Together to Care for Creation*, by Ben Lowe (InterVarsity Press, 2009).

Of course we know that not everyone will pursue personal or communal efforts to fight climate change. Many people are overwhelmed with their own lives, or would not take action unless forced by circumstances or pressure from government. Others would like to make changes but find the costs prohibitive. And without government participation, these actions are likely to remain disconnected, piecemeal, and insufficient—a start, but not a complete solution. As a nation that changes from the bottom up, our political representatives respond to pressure from their constituents. Organizations often make this easier by combining the power of many individuals to make a point with politicians. But whether you participate in a "campaign for climate change" sponsored by one of the organizations mentioned in this section or work towards change on your own, you may find a responsive ear at the local, state, and regional level. This is where climate change action begins and is happening right now.

Governmental Response

It has become fashionable over recent years to "bash" the United States for inaction on climate change, largely because of the nation's failure to ratify the Kyoto Protocol. Usually the United States cites impacts on the economy and the need to include China, India, and Brazil as the reason for its reluctance to undertake mandatory international agreements to limit greenhouse gas emissions. But other countries do not accept these as valid reasons. In fact, the US delegation to the 2007 climate change conference in Bali was booed by representatives from 180 nations for what they perceived as obstructionism. Finally, Kevin Conrad, a delegate from New Guinea, challenged the United States by saying: "I would ask the United States, we ask for your leadership, but if for some reason you're not willing to lead, leave it to the rest of us. Please get out of the way."[15] The assembly applauded. The United States delegation backed away from their objection. Later one of the UK's church development organizations wrote that the UK and its European partners should "name and shame" the United States for standing in the way of governments acting together to prevent catastrophic climate change.[16] These statements reflect a growing bitterness towards the United States from those who only see the international face of the country or who equate agreements such as these as automatic solutions to the problem.

In an interview with *The New York Times* after the Bali Conference, Kevin Conrad went on to say that the United States was "'set up' by other countries to take the blame." "There was a certain feeling that maybe the United States could be the fall guy for this whole thing, that if the G-77 (low-income countries) couldn't resolve its own issues, if it just held the line on a position they already knew the United States rejected, that the United States would be the one that stepped up and had to take the flak for collapsing the whole thing." He went on to say that emissions need to be cut from all sources wherever they come from. "The climate doesn't know whether it came from a factory or from Papua New Guinea's deforestation. We've really got to get all hands on deck and tackle all of the issues."[17]

Canada has not escaped international condemnation either. They, along with the United States and Saudi Arabia, received the "Fossil of the Day Awards" from youth groups attending the Bali Climate Change Conference. The award was meant to signify that they were the world's worst polluters and was accompanied by boos and laughter.[18] In 1998, Canada became one of the first signers of the Kyoto Protocol on climate change pledging to reduce greenhouse gas emission by 6 percent below 1990 levels between 2008–2012. But in 2007, the Canadian government backed away from Kyoto saying that they could not meet their commitments by the timeframe set under the treaty. Canada's emissions have grown to 27 percent above 1990 levels, 33 percent more than the Kyoto targets.[19]

Tackling climate change is difficult for national governments. It takes more than good intentions to transform society. And what might seem to be a solution may prove less effective in actual practice. In the United States the "laboratories" for climate change efforts are the actions of local governments, whether city, county, or state. The US national policy on climate change will emerge from the lessons learned at this level and these are growing in depth, width and intensity. It is also here that sustainability is being discussed and tested. While the United States has not signed the Kyoto Protocol, the requirements of the treaty are being used as targets for local action. The absence of national leadership on climate change has been a challenge and a stimulus inspiring genuine local government leadership.

Cities

On February 16, 2005, the day the Kyoto Protocol went into effect, Greg Nichols, the mayor of Seattle, Washington, launched the US Mayor's Climate Agreement by inviting other US cities to join him in three goals: a) striving to meet or exceed the Kyoto Protocol emissions limits in their own communities; b) urging their state governments and the federal government to enact policies and legislation to beat the 7 percent emissions reductions from 1990 levels suggested for the United States by 2012; and c) encouraging the US Congress to establish a national carbon emissions trading program. Two years later the US Conference of Mayors formed the Mayor's Climate Protection Center to not only increase the number of cities involved in the Agreement but also to provide them with the information to fulfill their commitment. By early 2008, 810 US cities, representing 78 million people or approximately one quarter of the US population, had signed the agreement. Lessons learned in one city have been shared with others through such venues as the "Climate Protections Strategies and Best Practices Guide."[20] In November 2007, the US Conference of Mayors hosted the "Seattle Summit," "the largest meeting of American mayors devoted solely to climate protection."[21]

These mayors see themselves as "leading the way" on climate protection—the "first responders" according to Mayor Doug Palmer of Trenton, N.J., President of the US Conference of Mayors.[22] Seattle's Mayor Nichols became involved in climate action because lack of snow in 2004–5 had a huge negative affect on the ski industry and the local economy, and also threatened the city's water and hydroelectric power supply. By 2007 Seattle had managed to beat the goals of the Kyoto Protocol for reducing their emissions, a feat that required conservation efforts by citizens, businesses, and the city-owned power company—plus a transition to more renewable energy and natural gas. Other cities have focused on a more fuel efficient vehicle fleet, energy-saving lights and appliances in government facilities, or even urban forestry as a form of carbon offset.

Cities may also be "first responders" in the move to a more sustainable lifestyle. Among the tools at a city's disposal are building codes and city planning. By 2015, the city's energy code will require all new single family homes in Austin, Texas, will have to be "zero-energy capable," meaning that each home must be able to produce as much energy as it consumes over the year.[23] Minneapolis Mayor R. T. Rybak believes that, "No other single thing we do can have as big an impact on climate change as our local role in the land use planning. . . . As mayors we can have a major impact on the use of cars."[24] Mixed use developments, along transportation corridors, with safe biking or pedestrian trails can create more sustainable communities and can also reduce vehicle miles traveled. According to Todd Litman, Executive Director of the Victoria Transportation Policy Institute, "A gallon of gas saved by reducing driving is worth an order of magnitude more in terms of consumer savings . . . community savings . . . savings to your business, in terms of economic development than that same gallon of gasoline used to get someone to drive a more fuel efficient car."[25] In other words, the actions of these and other mayors are helping to shape the society in which we live, and have the possibility of addressing some of the lifestyle concerns highlighted in chapter 2. However, these mayors also recognize that while their efforts have great impact on their local environment and citizenry, it will not be enough to lessen the global effects of climate change. Thus, they are actively pushing for an aggressive national response as well.

The state governments are also beginning to act, instead of waiting for the national government to act.

States

While one of the principles on sustainability in chapter 6 encourages us to reflect the close bond between society and the environment in our decisions, it is actually this close bond that is driving many US states to undertake their own plans and actions on climate change. The IPCC's evaluations do not seem so distant when you are watching your city's water supply wither away, as has been happening with Lake Mead, the fresh water source for such southwestern cities as Las Vegas, Nevada, or Los Angeles and San Diego, California.[26] They seem particularly relevant when your state has 28,793 miles of roadway in the 100-year floodplain, which are at very high risk from sea level rise and have sustained $42 *billion* in property damage in the 2004 hurricane season, as is the case of Florida. Many states depend on their natural resources, whether from agriculture, fisheries, or forestry, for their economic health. In addition to recognizing their risk from climate change, state governments have also been attracted to economic opportunities that tackling this issue might provide—whether through new uses of their natural resources such as renewable energy, or by attracting jobs in the green technology fields.

State governments have the power to regulate energy that is consumed or generated within their jurisdictions, and they have the responsibility to ensure the health and economic well-being of their citizens as well as the preservation of their natural resources. By early 2008, 36 of the 50 US states had either developed or were in the process of finalizing their own climate action plans. Work on almost 70 percent of these plans began after 2005. Seventeen states have established state-wide greenhouse gas emission targets. For many, these targets are the ones suggested by the Kyoto Protocol or derived from the recommendations by the IPCC reports of 2007, interim goals to slow emissions by 2015 and to achieve 80 percent reductions by 2050. In 2005, New Mexico became the first major oil, coal, and gas producing state to set specific targets for cutting emissions. In 2006, California enacted the first legislation in the United States designed to cap all greenhouse gas emission by industries within the state and also included penalties for noncompliance.

States are also involved in encouraging the development of green energy technology. Twenty-six states and the District of

Columbia have established renewable portfolio standards, requiring their electric utility companies to generate a specific amount of electricity from renewable sources by target dates. As noted earlier, the opportunity for consumers to buy green energy or sell energy back to the grid varies state to state.

States have begun requiring new or existing power plants to offset a portion of their emissions through emissions reductions or mitigation projects. After the US Supreme Court ruled in April 2007 that carbon dioxide could be considered a pollutant under the Clean Air Act, the Secretary of the Kansas Department of Health and Environment refused an air permit for a proposed coal-fired power plant.[27] By January 2008 more than 50 proposed coal-fired power plants in 20 states had either been cancelled or postponed. The resistance by state regulators has been one factor in these decisions, as has the uncertainty of global warming legislation at the national level, transportation issues, and rising costs.[28]

States have strengthened their efforts by joining regional initiatives with the goal of reducing greenhouse gas emissions or promoting green technology. The Regional Greenhouse Gas Initiative (RGGI), which includes ten New England and Mid-Atlantic States, is the first cap-and-trade system in the United States to cover carbon dioxide emissions. Other examples of regional initiatives include the Midwestern Regional Greenhouse Gas Reduction Accord (six states as full partners, three additional observer states, and one Canadian province); the Western Climate Initiative (six states and three Canadian provinces); and Western Governors' Association Clean and Diversified Energy Initiative (eighteen states). By 2008, more than thirty states, seven Canadian provinces, two Mexican states, plus Tribal nations had joined the Climate Registry—a collaboration to provide a common greenhouse emissions reporting system. In October 2007, representatives of the Western Climate Initiative and the Regional Greenhouse Gas Initiative joined with European Union members and other countries in the International Carbon Action Partnership, a mechanism to ensure that emerging cap and trade programs will be well designed and globally compatible.

States are pressuring changes in the transportation sector. Because of a special provision in the Clean Air Act, California has the authority to set vehicle emission standards, with the approval of the

US Environmental Protection Agency (EPA). Other states have the option of following federal standards or adopting California's. By late 2007, fourteen states had announced their intention to follow California's lead. Also in 2007, the US EPA rejected California's request to implement these standards, citing the newly passed Energy Bill which included less restrictive fuel efficiency standards. At that time, the Agency was reluctant to consider carbon dioxide as a pollutant in spite of the 2007 Supreme Court ruling directing them to do so. However, a new Federal Administration presented an opportunity for change. In early 2009, the Environmental Protection Agency prepared a new report linking greenhouse gases to dangers in human health and welfare. If approved, this proposal would provide EPA with the authority to regulate carbon dioxide and other greenhouse gases as "pollutants" under the Clean Air Act.[29] Eventually, this authority could be used to regulate emissions from such sources as coal-fired power plants as well as the transportation sector. This struggle illustrates the dynamic and emerging nature of U.S. policy to address greenhouse gas emissions and the important role states play in shaping Federal policy.

A common theme for these state plans and actions is to "demonstrate leadership." For example, Maryland is one of the smallest states but counts their risk from sea level rise and other aspects of climate change significant enough to push for aggressive reduction goals.

> While Maryland can certainly not by its actions alone constrain global warming, as a prosperous, knowledge-rich society with per capita emissions that are more than five times the global average, it has a responsibility to lead in addressing the global challenge. . . . Maryland's goals not only set reduction targets to drive State programs and reductions, they are also intended to send a message about the kind of reductions that Maryland believes other states, the Federal government and the international community need to be pursuing to combat climate change.[30]

When you consider that emissions from the states involved in the Regional Greenhouse Gas Initiative are equivalent to the entire emission from Canada, it is plain that these efforts can make a global difference.[31] If Texas, California, Pennsylvania, Ohio, Illinois, and Florida were individual countries, they would rank among the top thirty GHG emitters globally. State actions have been critical for laying the foundation for future energy and climate policy in the United States, and for establishing the basis for any future national cap-and-trade program. But states, as well as cities, have limited funding to devote to climate action and are susceptible to changes in the political arena. State action also presents business with a patchwork of regulations, and businesses themselves are beginning to push for national standards in both energy and transportation.

The same is happening in Canada. Canadian provinces, like US states, have authority over energy generation, transportation, and building codes within their jurisdictions. "In the absence of federal leadership," some of the provinces are designing their own innovative approaches to climate change, including participation in a future cap-and-trade program with regional initiatives in the United States. In February 2008, British Columbia announced specific greenhouse gas emission reduction targets plus a proposed "carbon tax," the first in North America. A tax on all greenhouse gases emitted from burning of any fossil fuel, whether gasoline, diesel, natural gas, coal, or heavy fuel oil: its goal is to help spur a broad cultural shift to a cleaner fuel economy. According to BC Finance Minister Carole Taylor, "The principle is simple. Tax carbon emitting fuels to discourage their use, and give the money back to people, back to business, so they have control. They can make their own choices about how the tax affects them. At the same time, by making greener choices more commercially viable, it will stimulate innovation and open up new economic opportunities across British Columbia." BC's proposed budget includes a one time dividend to all BC citizens before the tax takes effect in order to help them prepare for the new taxes, plus funding to encourage energy efficiency and other measures to support effective climate action.[32] Whether this will work or not remains to be seen, but it illustrates the dynamic, changing, aggressive, and experimental responses to the climate change challenge happening across North America.

National Governments

Both Canada and the United States have faced a lack of "federal leadership" on climate change. Canada signed the Kyoto Protocol and proposed various plans over the years, but without substantive action and, as noted above, publicly backed away from their international commitment in 2007. Canada's situation illustrates the challenges confronting governments that try to change their national energy policies towards sustainability.

Historically, Canada's energy policy has focused on developing its nonrenewable natural resources, such as oil, coal, and natural gas, for export. Canada's main sources of GHG emissions are its industrial and transportation sectors, especially in its lucrative oil and gas industries. Government support, whether in the form of fiscal incentives, such as tax benefits, or the technical, scientific, and organizational expertise of federal agencies has created an infrastructure that favors the non-renewable energy industries. The national climate change strategies Canada has implemented have been overshadowed or overwhelmed by the prior investment and commitment to the non-renewable energy development and export path.[33] Canada's challenge cannot be resolved simply by putting emissions controls on their large industries, but requires a reorientation—a change of energy policy direction towards clean, renewable energy sources, and/or the creation of tools that will allow for the development of these natural resources without the climate impacts, if possible. Canada continues to desire to be a "leader" in confronting climate change. Their task is to show how this can be accomplished as an energy producing nation.

The US did not sign the Kyoto Protocol and, at least through 2008, has had no national policies relative to climate change. Over the past few years, energy discussions have focused primarily on "energy security" or how to provide an economical, steady supply of energy for a growing population. As state and regional climate change initiatives have become more widespread and vibrant, the pressure for a national policy on climate change has also grown. The 2007–2008 US Congress introduced more bills and resolutions dealing with climate change than any previous session. In 2007, for the first time, legislation to set caps for GHG emissions and establish a cap-and-trade program made it out of the committee for discussion before the entire Senate. President Obama included a request for a cap and trade bill when he sent his first budget to Congress in early 2009. Increasingly energy studies and proposals are citing national security, energy security and climate change as interrelated challenges that must and will be addressed within the next five years.

Whatever the climate change history of these two countries, there is a definite role and need for national government involvement if there is to be a viable solution to this problem. Perhaps a good question would be—what is the responsibility of government, at any level, to respond to climate change and to move towards a sustainable society? According to the Center for Public Justice, a policy research and civic education organization, "Government's purpose is to uphold a healthy public commons in which the great diversity of human activities—as well as complex social and ecological balances—is maintained for the long-term well-being of everyone. As government concentrates on upholding public justice, there may, as a consequence, be advances of human freedom, economic prosperity, environmental safeguards, and international peace."[34] One of government's responsibilities is to "clarify the dangers and call the whole society to work on this problem because we will all be endangered."[35]

Increasingly, climate change is becoming recognized as more than scientific speculation of an impending environmental catastrophe. States, provinces, and local jurisdictions are treating climate change as a genuine danger to the social and economic fabric of life. Government has been entrusted with ensuring the safety, health, and well-being of its citizens. In dealing with climate change, the federal government has a role only they can fulfill—setting national fuel and product efficiency standards, creating national mandatory renewable energy standards and caps on emissions, and creating the market environment where solutions such as a cap-and-trade program are viable. Many state plans are depending on energy efficiency to help them meet their reduction targets in the short term but are relying on technological advances to create new solutions in the long term. The federal government has the power to create incentives to stimulate research and development on a scale unavailable to states and provinces. Finally, the federal government is the entity best able, through international negotiations and cooperation, to address the global challenges inherent in climate change.

Obviously, every level of government as well as individuals and communities need to be engaged if solutions to climate change are to be found. Government has some unique tools to apply to the problem, often expressed as "sticks" and "carrots." "Sticks" are meant to restrain deleterious actions and take the form of taxes or regulations. "Carrots" are incentives to spur change in a positive direction. Cap and trade is an example of sticks and carrots. A "cap" is put on the amount of emissions an industry or facility is allowed, and efficient companies are allowed to sell their "credits" to more polluting organizations, thus being "greener" or "more efficient" becomes enticing and profitable. A carbon tax is a stick approach. A fee is levied on fossil fuel use based on the amount of greenhouse gases the fuels emit. The fee can be imposed where fossil fuel is used, or at the point of extraction—the mine or well head. To lessen the impact on consumers, revenues can be returned to businesses and consumers through changes in the income tax or business tax code, rebates, or dividends.[36] Cap and trade, a carbon tax, or cap and dividends are all forms of "putting a price on carbon" to limit emissions and spur a move towards a lower carbon society.

As government initiatives increase across North America, how do we know what we should support? One way is to examine them in light of their potential to encourage sustainability by using some of the guidelines in chapter 6. How will a new regulation or tax affect the vulnerable and marginalized? Does a new proposal have the potential to create more positive relationships among families and communities? Will an incentive encourage new ideas that will move us towards sustainability?

Clearly, tools that provide measurable goals or definite standards have been of great value in developing policy initiatives across North America. States have made use of targets defined by the IPCC and Kyoto to set their own goals without having to reinvent them. Cities have utilized the Leadership in Energy and Environmental Design (LEED) building standards to help redefine their building codes. The principles expressed in chapter 6 are a foundation for a framework to enable policy makers to include sustainability in the process as they shape their own proposals. These principles can also be applied to government efforts, not only to policy options. Across North America there are people—whether inside government, as part of a non-profit, or as individuals—who have been attempting to set policy and directions to press for an effective response to the difficult issue at hand. Where many citizens have withdrawn from public life, we can encourage reengagement by supporting those local efforts that may be "weak and vulnerable," but also reflect a commitment to the spirit of Jer 29:7—to seek the welfare of the city where we have been placed because in its welfare we also have welfare.

Technological Response

One of the most popular ideas in debates over climate change and sustainability is that there is a techno-fix. Somehow someone, somewhere will develop some cleaner fuel or more efficient technology that will allow us to carry on as before, to maintain our current lifestyles and habits, *and* to "save" the world in the process.

It has been a contention of this book that a techno-fix is not sufficient because social and environmental problems cannot be divorced, either in biblical understanding or in modern societies. An authentically Christian response insists that we should understand the problems presented to us by our unsustainable energy consumption not simply as a technical problem that needs fixing, but as a warning that we are not living the way we should. Formulating a Christian response should be seen as an opportunity to reorient ourselves both morally and socially.

Even ignoring this point, the fact is that techno-fixes rarely *solve* problems. In reality, their effect is often cancelled out by the "rebound effect" of modified human behavior. Seat belts, against all intuition, do not decrease the number of road deaths because, by making drivers feel safer, they simply "redistribute the burden of risk from those who [are] already the best protected inside vehicles to those who [are] the most vulnerable outside vehicles." [37] Better-insulated homes can, paradoxically, increase heating bills because lower gas bills encourage people to turn up the heat and thus increase their fuel bills. In a free market, greater energy efficiency can result in *increased* energy use.[38] In the words of the UK's House of Commons Environmental Action Committee, "while energy efficiency improvements may lead to energy savings at a micro-economic level, they [can] result in additional demand in the economy as a whole . . . by making the effective cost of energy cheaper, they promote the development of additional energy-consuming products or services."[39] Scott Lang, CEO of an energy efficiency company, believes that, "For years the world considered the light bulb to be the killer application for electricity that drove the modernization of our economy. Over time it became clear that the killer app was actually the wall socket and plug enabling millions of devices to access power from the grid."[40] Technology is not an alternative to changed human behavior.

This does not mean, however, that it cannot be a *supplement* to changed human behavior or that modifications in energy sources or improvements in energy efficiency have no role to play in addressing climate change. Broadly speaking the technological options fall into four categories: alternative sources of electricity (e.g., nuclear, renewables), alternative sources of fuel (e.g., biofuel, hydrogen), improvements in efficiency (e.g., micro-generation, building regulations and planning), and new forms of carbon usage (e.g., sequestration). This section addresses each of these, assessing which are more or less consonant with the principles outlined in chapter 6.

Alternative Sources of Electricity

Fossil fuels currently account for about 70 percent of the electricity generated in the United States, followed by nuclear power (20 percent) and renewable sources (9 percent) (Figure 7.1). Coal is the foundational fuel for electricity generation for many nations in the world including the United States and China. The US Energy Information Administration's Annual Energy Outlook for 2007 predicted that without significant policy changes, use of coal would continue to grow through 2030, eventually forming 57 percent of the fuel mix to create electricity in the United States.[41] Since coal is the dirtiest of fuels by climate change standards, we badly need to find alternative sources of electricity.

One of these alternatives is nuclear power itself, although few topics are more highly charged.[42] Its potential danger and its association with nuclear weaponry lend it a sinister shadow that colors the whole debate. The difficulty in securing accurate and well-established data further obscures the issue.[43]

Nuclear power has gained advocates as the pressure to reduce carbon emissions and provide a secure energy source mounts. According to the Electric Power Research Institute, "Nuclear power is currently the only technologically mature non-emitting generation technology that is proven and already deployed on a large scale."[44] Many of the 104 existing nuclear power plants in the United States

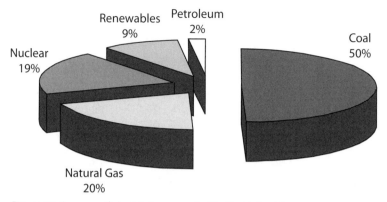

Figure 7.1 Sources of electricity generated in the United States

Source: Energy Information Agency. www.eia.doe.gov

have the potential to accommodate multiple units, so expansion on those sites would be fairly easy. Nuclear power's share of electricity production could grow from the current 20 percent to 25 percent by 2030 and 40 percent by the next century.

As with all the options to be discussed in this section, the merits of nuclear power can be evaluated on a balance sheet. On the positive side, and in spite of our instinctive reactions, it has historically, in the West at least, proved safe. Given the developments in design and security the well-known accidents at Chernobyl, in the former Soviet Union, and Three Mile Island, in the United States, are not reasonable precedents. Even George Monbiot, an environmental campaigner with little sympathy for nuclear power, admits that "the grim moral accountancy which must inform all the decisions we make obliges me to state that nuclear power is likely so far to have killed a much smaller number of people than climate change,"[45] not to mention far fewer than coal-mining accidents.

Nuclear power has a minimal life-cycle carbon footprint. Operational carbon dioxide emissions are extremely low, and even those resulting from uranium extraction and plant decommissioning are comparatively small.[46] Although technically unsustainable (all but renewable sources are finite), and despite widely differing opinions about its long-term availability,[47] there are, in the words of the UK's Sustainable Development Commission (which opposes nuclear power) "no major concerns over the long-term availability of uranium."[48]

Against this positive column of historic safety, low carbon emissions, long-term resources, potential expansion, and year-round reliability, there are the negative points of cost, waste, and risk. Virtually every nuclear power station in the world relies on subsidies in some form, not least for insurance, as no commercial insurer is willing to take on the risk. The utility incurs massive construction and equipment costs long before it begins to produce electricity. New laws in several US states are making it easier for utility companies to pass these costs along to ratepayers as they occur, whether the facility is actually completed or not. In early 2008, Florida approved construction of two new nuclear plants— the first in decades—at a proposed construction cost of $24 billion. The cost of nuclear power becoming a long-term option for the United States will include not only construction of approximately sixty new plants, but also research and technology to insure that the current fleet remains safe and productive for an additional twenty to forty years.[49]

Nuclear power also includes environmental costs, especially in the need for large amounts of clean water for cooling and condensing steam. Currently, power plants are regulated to insure that the water they use and release back into the environment is adequate, safe, and cool enough to protect the lives of local plant and animal species. But a guaranteed fresh water supply, either for the fish or the power plant, is partly dependent upon climate. In 2006, the heat wave in Europe produced low water levels and forced some French, German, and Spanish power plants to either shut down or reduce power. In 2008, twenty four of the power plants in the United States were located in the southeast—an area of widespread drought. If the plants have to reduce production, it would mean purchasing power from an alternative source—at a greater cost than nuclear power.[50] The Idaho National Laboratory/Nuclear Power Industry's 2007 Strategic Plan stated: "Most nuclear plants built in the future will be unable to access enough clean water to use the current technology of natural draft evaporative cooling towers." The cost of these structures would be too expensive; the facility may face using reclaimed water with associated equipment problems; new technology would be needed; and ultimately the Department of Energy "needs to strike a balance between the competing environmental goals of species protection and water conservation."[51]

In other words, will we be so pressed for energy and mitigating climate change that we forgo other priorities?

Waste is another significant problem. Although many maintain that it *can* be dealt with safely, to do so is costly. So far, in the United States, the proposed nuclear waste repository at Yucca Mountain, Nevada, has been in process for over a decade, but still does not have a firm opening date. In addition to the technical questions of isolating radioactive materials, there are social issues. How can we insure that the waste will be safe for thousands of years? In essence, are we transferring the stewardship of our waste to future generations? For some, the thought of nuclear waste traveling across the country within a mile of 60 million people is unnerving. Ultimately, in order for nuclear power to become a long-term method of combating climate change, a cost effective, integrated, safe, national waste management and transport system would have to be in place.[52]

Finally, there is the question of risk. Put simply, although the track record of nuclear power in the West is generally good, the effect of a major accident or a terrorist attack, no matter how remote, is almost inestimable. Nuclear power also carries with it the risk of proliferation—or the misuse of civilian nuclear capability for military purposes.

The other alternative source of electricity, renewables, is less controversial but no less complex. "Renewables" is something of a catch-all category, which includes solar photovoltaics, wind, hydroelectric, tide, wave, and geothermal heat. This is a diverse group with advantages and disadvantages that are particular to each source. There are, however, some general points that can be made.

Renewables are the archetype of a sustainable technology. They harness naturally occurring processes. They go on pretty much forever. They can't be switched off. They emit very low levels of carbon dioxide over their lifetime. The fuel source is free, not the property of any particular nation or organization.

North America has abundant potential renewable resources. Theoretically, the following could provide:

- Wave action off Canada's Pacific Coast—55 percent of national electricity

- Waves on the Atlantic Coast—Twice Canada's electrical needs[53]

- Geothermal—2,000 times our annual consumption of primary energy[54]

- Wind energy, especially in the plains states—Three times the total electricity needs of the United States.

- The abundant sunshine of the American Southwest is already helping to spur such programs as California's Million Solar Roofs Initiatives—an attempt to enable solar power to become competitive with conventional electricity.[55]

Renewables have captured the imagination of those who foresee a carbon constrained world and are looking for business opportunities for the future. Investment in clean technology by venture capitalists has grown from 3 percent to over 17 percent since 2004.[56] Many types of renewable technology can be deployed rapidly and make an immediate difference in greenhouse gas emissions, a clear appeal to investors, when compared to the long construction time of traditional generating sources. Use of renewable energy is growing worldwide. Globally, in 2007, over $100 billion was invested in renewables.[57] Forty percent of existing renewable power capacity is used in low-income countries, as is more than 70 percent of existing solar hot-water heating. In 2006, renewable energy, not including large hydroelectric power, generated as much electric power globally as one quarter of all the nuclear power plants. By 2007, grid connected solar photovoltaics (PV) was the fastest growing power generating technology worldwide.[58]

Nevertheless, many policy experts or energy analysts do not consider renewable energy as the prime solution to climate change and energy use. Why? First, some technologies such as harnessing wave energy are not yet sufficiently mature; others, as is the case of solar power, are still expensive relative to traditional energy generation. But a more serious issue is renewable energy's intermittent nature. A utility cannot control the Sun or wind in the same way they do coal, natural gas, or nuclear power. Modern society depends on access to a base load of reliable energy at the flick of a switch. As long as a renewable source, such as wind, supplies between 10 and 20 percent of the energy mix for a day, the utility will likely have enough flexibility among its resources to provide a consistent stream of electricity. But above 20 percent, the utility will have to purchase or guarantee back-up power—fossil fuel generated—to use if the wind fails.[59]

In essence, increasing renewable supply does not permit you to decrease fossil fuel supply at the same rate. The more renewable installations we build, the greater is the impact on the grid of the wind ceasing to blow or the Sun being obscured. So each additional gigawatt of renewable power we install displaces a smaller proportion from a conventional plant.[60] Needing to maintain a conventional base load supply does not necessitate *using* it, and this means that it is likely that an increase in renewable resources *would* have a significant impact on carbon emissions. Yet, this strange inverse economy of scale from which renewables suffer—the more we have, the greater the total generating capacity we need to maintain—means that most estimates of the amount of the total electricity of the United States that renewables could *practically* supply range from 20 to 30 percent.

Currently, renewable energy provides 9 percent of electricity generation, the majority from hydroelectric power, so there is vast room for growth in this field. Wind power, the least expensive technology, could realistically meet the 20 percent goal, by itself, over the next decades. The development and availability of transmission lines able to accept intermittent energy will be a key to how quickly wind power develops. In the long term, a viable storage and recovery system will be needed to transform renewable energy into a consistent, dependable supply. Geothermal offers another possibility. It is the only renewable that is not intermittent or variable. With investments in new facilities, research, and technology, geothermal plants could potentially provide 10 percent of the base load power for the United States by 2050.

Beyond these closely linked issues, different renewables suffer from different problems. Onshore wind farms disfigure landscapes and are, not surprisingly, unpopular with local residents. Land base wind farms have been criticized as hazards to migratory birds, though proper siting can limit these impacts. Studies have shown that more birds have been killed by collisions with tall building, or encounters with neighborhood cats than by wind farms. Tidal barriers can harm ecosystems, though they may also provide enhanced albeit different, ecological habitats. Solar photovoltaic power uses considerable energy to make the crystalline silicon that, with present technology, is its key constituent.

Overall, renewables would be the perfect solution to our energy problems—relatively clean, endlessly sustainable, and reasonably priced (although estimates vary)—were it not for their practical problems. As we shall see, however, none of the technological options available is without difficulties. How we should gauge the relative seriousness of each will be left to the conclusion of this section.

Alternative Sources of Fuel

Green electricity, however derived, could only ever be part of the solution. Natural gas is used to heat millions of houses, and almost all our road vehicles are powered by gasoline or diesel. We need alternatives to these fossil fuels.

No technology illustrates our connection with the natural world and each other as well as the quest for energy from biomass and biofuels. Both biomass and biofuels utilize organic matter, theoretically plentiful and renewable. Humankind has been burning plant matter for energy and heat since the discovery of fire. Biomass, usually in the form of wood or agricultural waste, is the major source of energy in many parts of the world. For instance, in sub-Saharan Africa, biomass supplies energy to 94 percent of rural households and 41 percent of city dwellers. In low-income countries, more energy efficient biomass stoves and other small scale biomass technologies can not only reduce the amount of fuel needed, but improve indoor air quality, human health, the livelihood of women, encourage small business ventures, and lower greenhouse gas emissions.[61]

In the United States, wood may be an alternative fuel source for heating some homes, but the main use of biomass is by industry and communities through the reclamation of energy stored in "waste." Approximately 100 biomass plants use methane gas from landfills for energy generation. Industries such as lumber, paper, and pulp manufacturers are able to supply 60 percent of their energy needs through use of the wood "refuse" from their industrial processes. Municipal solid waste, construction wood waste, and forestry residues are other forms of biomass. Biomass has many advantages. It does not have the same polluting qualities of coal and can be used by power plants, along with coal, to reduce some types of air pollution. In 2006, biomass was the second largest supplier of energy from the renewable sector, after hydroelectric. Certainly the use of "waste" in a more effective manner is a valuable tool in our attempt to resolve climate change, but the expansion of biomass through planting and harvesting "dedicated energy crops" would encounter the same issues faced by biofuels.

Biofuels have demonstrated both the promises and challenge of an emerging technology. They have also illustrated the danger of focusing on solutions of one problem without consideration of the effects on another. In 2007, biofuels were thought to be almost carbon neutral—or at least much less a threat than petroleum. The greenhouse gases they emitted would be removed from the atmosphere by the next crop planting. Raising crops for fuel was also seen as a way to regenerate rural economies or restore degraded land. Technology was readily available to produce ethanol from either plant starches (such as those derived from grains such as corn) or sugars (from sugar cane and sugar beets). Various seed crops were good sources of biodiesel fuel. In each instance, animal feed or electricity was a potential by-product of the production process. Future technology promised the ability to utilize the entire plant in the production of ethanol (cellulosic) enabling the use of other, more productive plants such as native perennials and switchgrass. Ethanol from biofuels had the potential to reduce both the dependence on foreign oil and greenhouse gas emissions. Both the European Union and the United States set renewable fuel standards mandating specific target amounts and dates for biofuel production. However, by early 2008 biofuels were being challenged for their effects on greenhouse gas emissions, biodiversity, and human hunger. According to the Institute for Agriculture and Trade Policy, "The issue is that growing demand for agricultural commodities changes the behavior of farmers and the agribusiness industry. Skyrocketing prices, whether induced by a new demand like biofuel, weather-related crop losses or government policies, can lead to reckless clearing of native vegetation to take advantage of increasing profit potential."[62]

Eighty percent of Brazil's greenhouse gas emissions are the result of deforestation, partly due to the expansion of sugar cane fields for ethanol into the forest. Indonesia has become the third largest emitter of carbon dioxide. While palm oil plantations may supply one of the best sources of biodiesel, their expansion into the forest not only changes the land's ability to act as a carbon sink, but threatens some of the richest areas of biodiversity on earth.

This trend is not unique to low-income countries. Over the past decades, the United States has made progress in wildlife conservation by placing marginal agricultural land into conservation reserves. But these gains may disappear as much of this land is expected to be returned to farming. The biofuel mandates have greatly increased the profitability of corn. The world has become increasingly interconnected. Decisions by US farmers to plant more corn than soybeans led to the conversion of portions of Brazilian ranchland and savanna, unique ecosystems, into monoculture soybean fields. While the global hunger crisis of 2008 was caused by such issues as drought in Australia and lower global harvests, higher corn prices did contribute to higher meat prices and led to the accusation that wealthy countries were growing fuel for their cars rather than food for the poor and hungry.

Does this mean that biofuels should no longer be considered an option? Not necessarily. It isn't biofuels, per se, that is the problem but the methods of production. Several organizations, as diverse as the Union of Concerned Scientists and the Institute of Agriculture and Trade Policy, have recommended imposing standards for biofuels. These include protecting native ecosystems, concentrating biofuel production on degraded and abandoned lands, utilizing the best feedstocks (such as mixed crops of perennial prairie grasses that can produce 238 percent more energy than a monoculture crop without the necessity of petroleum based inputs such as fertilizer), and requiring that all biofuel production be sustainable. These standards may provide the guidance needed as we continue to explore biofuels.

A final option for transportation fuel may be hydrogen. Hydrogen is an energy "carrier" rather than an energy source itself, meaning it transfers usable energy from one place to another, similar to the function of electricity.[63] Hydrogen can be produced from nuclear power stations, hydroelectricity, coal, gas, biomass, algae, or via electrolysis (splitting water). It can then be burnt, like a fossil fuel, at the point of use. Hydrogen can also be used to store energy in the form of fuel cells, akin to efficient, rechargeable batteries, in a way that is otherwise very difficult. Moreover, the heat generated in fuel cells can be used in Combined Heat and Power systems (see below). Hydrogen's main advantages are that hydrogen itself is clean, producing only water vapor when burnt.

These advantages have led many to talk of the future hydrogen economy, in which clean, efficient hydrogen fuel cells replaces internal combustion engines. Iceland, for example, has announced its intention to become the world's first hydrogen economy.[64] There are, however, several major problems. First, hydrogen production is (currently) extremely expensive and its real effect on greenhouse gas emissions depends on the fuel used in its production. Second, transporting hydrogen, in either liquefied or compressed forms, is difficult, expensive, and potentially dangerous (although not significantly more dangerous than petroleum). Fuel cells are currently heavy, costly, and inefficient, and they are considerably more expensive than an internal combustion engine in producing the same amount of energy.[65] Finally, hydrogen vehicles would also require an infrastructure of hydrogen refueling stations. Hydrogen technology has potential but remains in its infancy and seems unlikely to revolutionize economies, at least in the short term.

Efficiency

New sources of energy might be the most obvious (and exciting) technological response to the problem, but they are not necessarily the best. Amory Lovins of the Rocky Mountain Institute believes that "Increased energy end-use efficiency—technologically providing more desired service per unit of delivered energy consumed—is generally the largest, least expensive, most benign, most quickly deployable, least visible, least understood, and most neglected way to provide energy services."[66]

In this case, efficiency means more than the consumer choices, behavioral changes, and conservation efforts suggested in the personal section. Efficiency is not a retreat but a bold venture into a new way of doing things—whether lighting or cooling spaces, providing communications and entertainment devices, running an industrial plant, or operating a public utility. The burden is on industry, manufacturing, builders, architects, and public officials to provide the goods and services society requires, using the least amount of energy and eliminating waste in the process. Efficiency decreases greenhouse gas emissions by lowering the *demand* for energy, reducing the need for *supplying* energy through burning fossil fuels. For instance, California's per capita electric use has remained flat since 1974, mainly through aggressive pursuit of efficiency, building and appliance standards, and utility conservation programs.

Some states are using Energy Resource Efficiency Standards to set energy saving goals for their utilities, but allowing the company to determine the best methods to meet those goals. This requires a new way of thinking—rewarding a utility for decreasing the demand for energy, or "decoupling" the utilities profits from its energy sales. California requires its utilities to pursue efficiency first, even before purchasing renewables for new generation needs. Conventional generation becomes a third option.[67]

One of these efficiency measures is known variously as micro-CHP (Combined Heat and Power), cogeneration, micro-generation, distributed generation, the local grid, or the energy internet. CHP covers a multitude of complex ideas but is based on one simple one: the current, heavily centralized model of energy production, subsequently distributed by the national grid, is inefficient, partly because power stations lose over half of total potential energy in waste heat[68] and partly because the national grid loses about 7 percent of energy in transmission.[69]

Micro-generation seeks to address both of these problems. First, it decentralizes electricity generation. Instead of electricity being generated from fossil fuels at a handful of large, isolated, industrial-scale plants, it advocates distributed generation, "islands of generation" related to city districts, towns, industries, or even individual homes. Smaller power stations generate electricity close to the point of consumption, hence minimizing energy loss in transmission, and can be supplemented by renewables and other local sources such as landfill methane. These islands are connected to one another in such a way as to transmit energy to each other, if and as necessary.[70]

Second, these localized power stations *use* the heat that is otherwise lost in large-scale, centralized electricity generation. The fact that power stations lose over half of total potential energy in waste heat is not as shocking as it sounds. "There are limits on the levels of efficiency that can be achieved in converting primary fuels into delivered energy," and although even the most efficient devices for generating electricity from fossil fuel currently operate at efficiencies of less than 50 percent, even that efficiency "takes one close to the thermodynamic limit, which represents an absolute constraint."[71]

If, however, plants could use the heat that they, by necessity, produce in electricity generation, efficiency levels could, in theory, rise to over 90 percent. The potential energy and carbon dioxide savings are enormous. CHP's Internet-style decentralization also makes it robust against local failures. Its openness to an energy mix (i.e., energy input from other sources) should encourage micro-generation from renewables and, in theory, permit excess energy produced in this way to be "sold back" to the local micro-grid. More generally, "distributed generation offers opportunities to engage local communities and to develop a sense of ownership of, and responsibility for, localized energy production."[72]

New homes are one of the major factors in energy demand growth. As noted before, states and cities can use their planning and zoning codes to shape the energy use of new construction, many through standards set by the US Green Building Council (Leadership in Energy and Environmental Design-LEED) as guides. However, by combining whole house efficiency with renewable micro-generation, it is possible to construct near zero energy buildings, using 30 to 90 percent less energy than standard models.

The Beddington Zero Energy Development (more popularly known as BedZED) is an example from the UK of what can be done in an entire community. A carbon-neutral neighborhood, in Wallington, Surrey, BedZED consists of 99 homes and 100 "workspaces," arranged in five south-facing terraces, all with triple-story conservatories to maximize light and the Sun's warmth. The houses' outer walls and roofs are super-insulated, which, when combined with triple-glazed windows, obviate the need for a central heating system. Numerous photovoltaic panels and a CHP plant, fuelled by woodchips from waste timber, meet most of the neighborhood's remaining energy demands, which are, in any case, reduced by the use of energy saving and smart appliances. The buildings are constructed primarily from recycled, reclaimed, environmentally accredited, local materials, and the neighborhood itself is built around a "green transport plan," which includes a car club, and promotes walking, cycling, and the use of public transport.[73] Cost is still a major barrier for homes in the United States, but a number of projects have begun to incorporate efficiency, wise use of resources, and a sense of community.[74]

On a larger scale, the combination of micro-generation of renewables and efficiency can have direct impact on greenhouse gas emission. San Francisco had committed to reduce the city's greenhouse gas emissions by 20 percent below the 1990 levels by 2012. In 2002, San Francisco began to upgrade its conference venue, the Moscone Center, using state of the art energy efficiency techniques, natural lighting, high performance windows, and a 60,000 foot solar rooftop array. The solar array and energy efficiency measures in the Moscone Center alone will reduce carbon emissions by 35,000 tons over the next 30 years. To put this in perspective, the amount of energy the system saves and generates would be enough to power 8,500 homes.[75]

According to a study by the Union for Concerned Scientists and the American Council for an Energy-Efficient Economy, aggressively pursuing efficiency and cogeneration, plus the growth in renewables, could reduce the electricity generation of the United States from conventional sources by more than 60 percent by 2020. This would result in a reduction of greenhouse gas emissions to a level 47 percent below those in 1990.[76] But it would take consistent, persistent, and focused efforts.

New Ways of Using Carbon

A fourth technological response to the problem is to find new ways of using or, at least, disposing of carbon dioxide. In some instances, this is already occurring. In the Netherlands, carbon dioxide from Shell's refinery outside Rotterdam is being used in thousands of Amsterdam's greenhouses, which grow much of Europe's fresh fruit, vegetables, and flowers. Pumped along an unused gas pipeline, the carbon dioxide doubles the normal concentration in the greenhouses, speeding plant growth and reducing the level of gas previously burnt in the greenhouses.[77]

This seems an ideal way of using "waste" carbon dioxide. The project saves 95 million cubic meters of natural gas each year and reduces carbon dioxide emissions by 170,000 tons. However, it was only made possible because the Dutch Government built the original pipeline, supported the project with a $6 million innovation grant and then $25 million tax relief. Such projects are admirable and useful but ultimately small scale, heavily subsidized, and unlikely to make a big impact on national carbon emissions.

A larger-scale and more promising venture is carbon capture and storage (CCS) or sequestration. It involves catching the carbon dioxide emitted by burning fossil fuels and storing it, preferably in deep geological formations, old oil and gas fields or saline aquifers (underground pockets of salt water). Ideally, CCS would be combined with a new generation of highly efficient coal-fired power plants. Rather than burning "pulverized coal," the current model for most power plants, these new designs heat coal under pressure to form a methane-rich gas, which is then used to generate energy in a combined cycle of gas and steam turbines (IGCC, Integrated Gasification Combined Cycle). Theoretically, an IGCC plant combined with CCS could capture 85 to 95 percent of emissions which would then be injected and stored underground indefinitely.[78]

The process has much to recommend it. Coal is found on every continent, in over 70 countries. The World Coal Institute estimates that the world's reserves could last for 155 years.[79] Some of the fastest industrializing nations, such as China and India, depend heavily on coal for both industry and power generation. According to the Electric Power and Research Institute, coal's viability as a fuel source in a carbon constrained world will depend on "increasing the efficiency and reducing the capital costs of pulverized coal (PC) and integrated gasification combined cycle (IGCC) technologies, and bringing CO2 carbon capture and storage to the point of cost-effective commercialization by 2020."[80]

This will be a challenge. Currently, "there is a lack of experience in integrating the component technologies in single projects at the scale required."[81] China will begin construction of their first power plant equipped with CCS technology, GreenGen, in 2009.[82] The demonstration plant of the United States—FutureGen—has been struggling with escalating costs and government funding that ebbs and flows with each election. Carbon capture technology is difficult and expensive to bolt onto existing "pulverized" coal power stations. It is easier to install on advanced coal, IGCC plants, but the plants themselves are more expensive to construct than the older designs.

Construction on most new advanced coal power plants was halted in the United States in 2007 and 2008 due to growing concern for coal's effects on climate change, the environment, human health, rising costs, and the uncertainly about future carbon restrictions. However, the pressure to provide a baseline energy supply, at a time of rising oil and gas prices, inspired Italy and other European countries to resurrect plans for 50 coal-fired power plants over the next five years.[83] Since power stations have a life of about 40 years, the design decisions made today will impact greenhouse gas emissions for decades.

According to the International Energy Agency: "Large-scale carbon capture and storage is probably ten years off, with real potential as an emission mitigation tool from 2030 in developed countries."[84] One nation may move away from coal, but in this interconnected world, it is almost certain that coal will remain a basic source of energy somewhere for years to come. Whether coal continues to be a large contributor to climate change or part of the solution will depend on the development, effectiveness, and widespread implementation of technologies such as CCS.

Evaluating the Options

How might we evaluate this diverse range of technological responses? On one level, we might wish to let a thousand flowers bloom. If we are to avoid the worst consequences of climate change, we need to be open to using each and every one of these technological responses.

We need to go beyond this, however. Practical open-mindedness will not help us answer the question that underlies this book: how should we *as Christians* respond to the issue at hand?

This question might be reframed in the light of the principles outlined in chapter 6 to read: how should our principles—of valuing and protecting creation, reflecting the bond between society and environment, pursuing justice for the vulnerable, disentangling wealth and value, favoring regulated market solutions, favoring local solutions, assuring just and equitable access to natural resources, and responding seriously—shape our attitude to these technological responses? To answer this question we also need to identify our goal, consider the timescale of our challenges, and understand the nature of technology.

A serious commitment to valuing and protecting creation as well as pursuing justice for the vulnerable requires that we move towards a low-carbon future. The negative impact on species, the land, and human well-being from climate change brought on by burning fossil fuels are becoming more and more evident. Scientists tell us that we might have a few decades to respond in order to avert the most serious effects of climate change, but the longer we delay the fewer options we will have. At the same time, because of the nature of greenhouse gases in the atmosphere, responding to climate change could be considered a long-term war rather than a short-term battle. Some technologies, such as renewables, which might get us to the low carbon future, face significant challenges, a viable storage system for instance, which will take time to develop. Other options, such as a new system of nuclear power plants will also take at least a decade for permit review and facilities construction. Technology, when new, presents its promise, but reveals its flaws as it is tested through time. We need a long-term view if we are to weather the uncertainties of the new technologies we hope to enlist in the fight against climate change.

Several of the options stand out as impossible to reject from any perspective. Improved efficiency is an obvious one, whether efficiency in power plants, home appliances, or motor vehicles. Efficiency buys time. By reducing the amount of energy required it lowers the pressure to build new power plants, reduces fossil fuel use, and allows other technologies the time to mature.

Planning and building regulations, plus green building technology, are other valuable tools against climate change. Building homes more efficiently and designing "sustainable" neighborhoods not only reflects the close bond between society and the environment but also improves our quality of life. Along with these is the potential of micro, or distributed generation (CHP). In addition to increasing efficiency, the decentralized character that CHP provides reflects a commitment to local solutions and, because of significant carbon dioxide savings, is consonant with the principle of valuing and protection creation.

What of longer-term measures? How might our principles shape our engagement with these? How are we to generate our "base load" energy supply? These questions invariably direct us towards the vexed nuclear versus renewables question. As noted

above, this is not a simple question, with a complex and often uncertain set of factors balancing the scales in each case. In one respect, the answer is obvious. Renewable resources are the epitome
of sustainability—clean, safe, and naturally occurring. In this, they
more than satisfy the principle of valuing and protecting creation.
Renewable energy also has the potential for reinvigorating rural
communities. Wind power is a good example. Ninety-five percent
of the best exploitable wind reserves in the United States are located
in the sparsely populated Great Plains. Wind turbines have a small
ecological footprint, not affecting the use of land below. A farmer
is typically paid a royalty for use of the land, which then supple-
ments his income. Potentially, the land could be restored to prairie,
supporting native buffalo, a high protein food source becoming
increasingly popular in our health-conscious society, and providing an additional source of income to a region that has been losing
population for many years.[85]

That said, if we are serious about averting the problems with
which we began this book, we need to be serious about renewables'
deficiencies: unpredictability, and the peculiar inverse economy of
scale from which they suffer. If we make a commitment to renewables, it also has to be to a redesigned transmission grid, a quest for
adequate storage techniques, and policy measures to lower renewable energy costs.

Given the difficulty in fitting carbon capture and storage technology onto existing fossil fuel power stations (and, therefore, the
long time we will have to wait before we can produce a low-carbon
base load from fossil fuels), it is difficult to see how we can avoid
nuclear as a low-carbon means of supplying the base load. In fact,
by 2010 the US Nuclear Regulatory Commission expects to receive
34 applications for licenses to build and operate new nuclear power
plants in 16 US states.[86]

This will alarm some, not least because of the unsolved waste
problems and the risk, no matter how theoretical, associated with
all nuclear energy. The licensing process involves a public comment
period. A commitment to valuing and protecting creation might
mean that we would become involved in insuring that the siting
and operation of these plants would not adversely impact water
supplies, as well as the habitat and survival of other species. More
particularly, it would be a mistake if a government's decision to

support a major new program of nuclear power stations were to negatively affect investment in other areas, in particular efficiency, renewables, and carbon capture and storage.

> The potential of these various technologies over the next 20 to 30 years is immense, and any public subsidies for nuclear must be weighed against the substantial progress towards reducing carbon emissions and ensuring a greater degree of security of supply which these alternatives, such as renewables, could achieve with similar subsidies.[87]

Biofuels/biomass illustrates a technology that may benefit from a long-term perspective. While in 2007, biofuels seemed to be the answer to a lower carbon vehicle fuel, by 2008, flaws in this technology became apparent. It would be hard to support biofuels where their production degrades and imperils creation or compromises human health and survival. Yet sustainability standards, land use regulations, and alternative feedstocks might provide a viable way forward for this technology.

In summary, therefore, while no technological response to the problems we face should be proscribed, we believe that those which are particularly resonant with the principle of valuing and protecting creation (like renewables and improved efficiency), or with the principle of addressing social and environmental problems (like improved planning and building regulations and renewables), or with the principle of localization (like micro-CHP), deserve our particular attention. Technology will change and may present its flaws, but basing our decisions on values or principles, remembering our goal, understanding the role of time and the nature of technology will help us focus on those tools we think can best meet the challenge of climate change.

International Response

We return to the point with which we started: the international perspective. Climate change is a global issue. It has worldwide causes and worldwide consequences, albeit consequences that are most intensely felt by those least able to defend themselves against them. No matter what we do personally, or as individual cities, states, or nations, our efforts will be insufficient without the engagement of the international community.

The premise of this book is that relationships matter and that environmental and social sustainability are intertwined. In no sphere is this more apparent than in the international arena. Action on climate change must be negotiated between sovereign states. Cooperation is the only way forward. While nations might agree on the ideal of combating climate change jointly, they are also concerned for their own interests. As a result, achieving substantive, effective agreements has been difficult. Nevertheless, three significant foundations have been established—access to solid scientific information, a framework to negotiate political agreements, and tools to reduce greenhouse gas emissions. The international community also responds to social changes similar to those going on in the United States. As a result, in 2007 an opportunity to use these foundations to pursue a new international agreement became possible.

In 1988, climate change was just beginning to become an international concern. The World Meteorological Organization and the UN Environmental Programme established the Intergovernmental Panel on Climate Change (IPCC) to provide independent scientific advice and insights on all aspects of climate change. The IPCC was not to conduct its own research, monitor climate data, or recommend policies. Instead it was charged with gathering, assessing, and synthesizing the scientific, technical, and socio-economic research being done around the world on human induced climate change, its potential impacts, and possibilities for adaptation and mitigation. In this way, the IPCC could provide an objective basis for decision-making.[88]

The IPCC's first report in 1990 spurred the UN to develop an international climate treaty, the United Nations Framework Convention on Climate Change (UNFCCC), introduced at the Rio Summit in 1992, signed by 192 countries and becoming effective in 1994. The UNFCCC set the overarching objective of stabilizing atmospheric concentrations of greenhouse gases at a safe level and established key principles for achieving this.

> Countries should act consistently with their responsibility for climate change as well as their capacity to do so. Developed or industrialized nations would take the lead, given their historical contribution to greenhouse gas emissions, whilst developing ones would recognize an "unquantified" commitment to emissions reduction that would be linked to assistance received from developed countries.[89]

Emissions reductions under the UNFCCC were voluntary. However, the IPCC's second assessment led the UNFCCC to create an addition to the treaty, the Kyoto Protocol. Kyoto maintained the separation of countries into two categories: "developed" or industrialized nations, which accepted legally binding emission reduction targets, and "developing" ones, which had no obligations placed on them. The Kyoto Protocol was negotiated in December 1997, subsequently ratified by over 150 countries, and entered into force in February 2005. The targets placed on industrialized nations were not ambitious: a commitment to reduce combined emissions by 5 percent on the 1990 level by 2008–12.

Kyoto also created a mechanism for carbon emissions trading. Carbon trading works by allowing industrialized countries to buy carbon "units" or "credits" from other sources in such a way as to result in an overall reduction of greenhouse gas emissions. Thus, a low-income nation (with no reduction target) that chooses to implement a (certified) emissions reduction project, such as carbon sequestration, methane extraction, or reforestation, can sell credits, relating to the greenhouse gases they have saved, to industrialized nations who do have reduction targets to meet. This sounds complex but has proved a promising way of reducing total global carbon emissions and of transferring funds to low-income countries.

In reality, these agreements have proved to be only the beginning of what will be needed to address climate change on a global level. They have been politically hampered because the world's largest greenhouse gas emitters, such as the United States, have not signed the Kyoto Protocol. The fast industrializing nations, such as China, which surpassed the United States in greenhouse gas emissions by 2007, India, Brazil, and others were not required to have binding targets.

High-income countries have felt that any efforts they took would be overwhelmed by nations such as India and China who had no restrictions. Low-income countries, many of whom already are experiencing some of the predicted consequences of climate change such as famine, drought, and disease, have primarily been concerned with economic growth to raise their citizens out of poverty and have resisted any emissions restrictions that might hamper that growth. In order to grow their economy without climate impacts, low-income countries want open access to clean technology from the West. But Western nations perceive clean technology as business opportunities and want to protect their intellectual property rights.

Nations also have been wary of undertaking aggressive action on climate change unilaterally for fear that they will lose their "competitive edge." Nations without emissions restrictions might "out-compete" them in the marketplace and industries might relocate "offshore" where they would not face emissions controls. Island countries and other poor nations who are most impacted by climate change have felt helpless—they are not responsible for emissions but they suffer the consequences. Low-income countries reject emissions restrictions when major industrialized countries fail to participate, as with the United States, or to fail to meet their commitments, as with Canada, whose emissions are predicted to be 31 percent higher than their Kyoto target by 2012. According to the UN, the industrialized nations in general are unlikely to meet the 5 percent lower emission target agreed to under Kyoto; rather their combined emissions in 2010 is expected to be 10 percent *above* the 1990 level.

The failure of nations to take climate change and their international commitments sufficiently seriously has led to frustration and acrimony. As one editorial in the *Bangkok Post* put it after the G8 summit in 2008, "The entire world must accept the fact that it is being presented with a long overdue bill for a lifestyle that, it must be admitted, originated in the world's richest countries, and has been perpetuated and exported by these countries. It is high time to stop balking and start making payments."[90]

Throughout 2007, the IPCC released a series of reports that formed its 4th Assessment. Later that year, the IPCC was awarded the Nobel Peace Prize "for their efforts to build up and disseminate greater knowledge about man-made climate change, and to lay the foundations for the measures that are needed to counteract such change." The seriousness of the IPCC's findings and the rising concern for climate change around the world helped create the opportunity for a possible new political direction as well. At the end of 2007, the signers of the UN Framework Convention on Climate Change approved the Bali Roadmap—a call to negotiate a new climate agreement by the end of 2009 to take effect in 2012. Low-income countries played a key role in making this opportunity possible. Not only did they push for action, but agreed to take on "nationally appropriate mitigation actions by developing country Parties, supported and enabled by technology, financing and capacity building, in a measurable, reportable and verifiable manner."[91] For the first time, there was an opportunity to engage all nations.

The Bali Roadmap actually follows two tracts. Those nations that signed the Kyoto Protocol are charged with drafting new emission reduction commitments to begin after 2012. All Parties to the Convention are involved in the second tract, the Bali Action Plan, which seeks to negotiate a new agreement on long-term climate cooperation. The ultimate goal would be to bring the two groups together into one overall climate action plan. Yvo de Boer, executive secretary of the United Nations Framework Convention on Climate Change, said: "We have less than two years to craft what may well be one of the most complex international agreements that history has ever seen. If we fail, we'll all be losers."[92] The Roadmap has delineated the five key points that need to be addressed if any future climate agreement is to succeed.

The first point, "a shared vision (including a long-term global goal for emissions reductions)" and this forms the basis for the other four points—enhanced action on mitigation, adaptation, technology, and finance. What is the safe level of CO2 concentrations in the atmosphere? Given the projected growth in energy use, the world is on track for long-term greenhouse gas concentrations at 550 ppm or a 3–4°C rise in temperatures. In order to prevent the most severe climate impacts, the IPCC has recommended stabilizing these CO2 equivalents at 445–490 ppm (holding temperature rise at 2–2.4°C). To accomplish this, emissions would have to peak before 2015 and decline to 50 percent of current levels by 2050. Delaying either the peak or reductions would limit options and raise the risk of severe, sudden impacts. Some scientists have called for an even more strident goal, getting emissions to zero by 2050 and beginning removing CO2 from the atmosphere in order to bring concentrations down to 385 ppm, or the range in the mid 1980s.[93] In one of the follow up conferences to the Bali Action Plan, Elliot Diringer of the Pew Center on Global Climate Change said: "There's a huge gap between what the scientists say is necessary (to hit the 2-degree mark) and what the political process can deliver. The challenge is to narrow that gap, even if it isn't slammed shut."[94]

The question of how to narrow that gap includes the four other key issues: mitigation, adaptation, technology, and finance. Some skeptics have charged that mitigating climate change will be too expensive—just fund adaptation. The IPCC sought to quantify their confidence levels to make their point. They said: "Unmitigated climate change would, in the long term, be *likely* (66 to 90 percent chance) to exceed the capacity of natural, managed and human systems to adapt. Reliance on adaptation alone could eventually lead to a magnitude of climate change to which effective adaptation is not possible, or will only be available at very high social, environmental and economic costs."[95] But mitigation and adaptation combined could significantly reduce these risks.

If the voluntary actions under the UNFCCC and the binding targets under the Kyoto Protocol have not been sufficient to meet the global challenge of mitigating climate change, what might we do? Contraction and Convergence, a model devised by Aubrey Meyer of the Global Commons Institute illustrates the goal (see Figure 7.2). The theory is that no nation has a disproportionate right to pollute the atmosphere, emissions need to decrease, and nations should converge on equitable and sustainable emissions levels. The explorations under the Bali Action Plan are beginning to look beyond the economy wide emissions targets of Kyoto to a flexible approach that might produce such appropriate actions and commitments by all nations.

The Pew Center for Climate Change proposed such a plan based on input from policy experts and stakeholders from 15 countries.[96] This multi-track approach would require binding commitments, but those commitments might vary in nature and timing. Economy wide emissions reduction targets would still be appropriate for industrialized nations. Many low-income countries, however, do not have the technological expertise or capacity to monitor and predict emissions. Policy or sectoral commitments might be a significant first step. For instance, they might want to set a target to improve their energy intensity—the rate at which energy is used compared to their Gross Domestic Product. While this would not reduce their emissions, it would slow their emissions growth—all that might be needed for some nations. For others, such as China, their own policy initiatives for fuel economy standards, increases in energy efficiency, and renewable energy might be developed

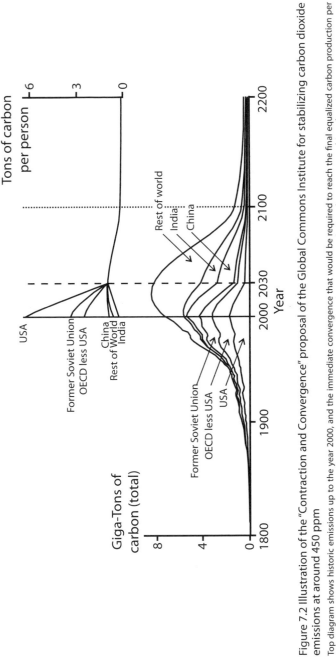

Figure 7.2 Illustration of the "Contraction and Convergence" proposal of the Global Commons Institute for stabilizing carbon dioxide emissions at around 450 ppm

Top diagram shows historic emissions up to the year 2000, and the immediate convergence that would be required to reach the final equalized carbon production per person by 2030. Bottom diagram shows total global carbon in atmosphere if the carbon production rates in the top diagram were achieved.

Note: Top diagram describes tonnes of carbon, not of carbon dioxide. For approximate conversion multiply figures by 3.2

Source: Organization for Economic Cooperation and Development (OECD)

into international commitments. Other nations might undertake policies to reduce deforestation. Each of these policy commitments would be measurable and binding, but appropriate to that nation's circumstances.

Sectoral agreements provide an additional opportunity for wide engagement. Since emission restrictions threaten the competiveness of certain industries more than the entire economy, a sectoral approach would enable nations to undertake agreements to reduce emissions in certain sectors, such as aluminum or cement manufacturing, electricity production, or the automotive industry. If these sectoral agreements are global, industries can be assured that their counterparts face the same restrains as they do. These connections also provide opportunities for shared knowledge and technology.

A nation might make commitments on several tracks—overall emissions reductions and sectoral agreements as an example. But these decisions cannot be left up to each individual country. According to the Pew Report, to be effective "countries must agree up-front on terms of engagement specifying the different commitment types and to which countries they will apply. Second, all tracks must be agreed as a single comprehensive package. This allows countries the flexibility of different commitment types while promoting a balanced and therefore more ambitious outcome."[97] The Bali Action Plan does not specify a goal of binding emissions reduction targets, but international climate cooperation history has demonstrated that targets, even small ones, produce more results than none at all.

Reducing vulnerability to climate change and funding adaptation is the third major building block of any new post-2012 framework. Unlike mitigation, which focuses on the causes of climate change, adaptation tackles its effects, in particular its effects on those least able to withstand them. Adaptation recognizes that whatever we do to prevent climate change some long-term impact is inevitable and must be moderated. Changing farming, water management, and building practices, improving coastal and flood plain protection, establishing early warning systems, investing in public health resources: all such measures stand to limit the damage of climate change, although how effectively and, in particular, how cost-effectively is far from certain. Such uncertainty is invariably an obstacle to long-term investment: no one likes to waste money. That said, while there is room for debate over the most effective forms of adaptation, there is none over the *need* for adaptation nor over the fact that it is high-income nations that face the moral imperative to fund adaptation since it is they that have historically benefited most from the large-scale burning of fossil fuels.

One of the goals of the new set of negotiations is to speed up research, development, and deployment of key clean technologies. Globally, demand for energy is expected to double by 2050. Two thirds of that energy is predicted to be supplied by fossil fuels. Even with a move to renewable energy, ways must be found to manage emissions from petroleum and coal. Yvo de Boer urged the World Petroleum Congress to become part of the input to the new negotiations, to "transform yourselves into modern energy companies, providing climate-friendly energy."[98] He challenged them to perfect and demonstrate carbon capture and storage, which, according to the IPCC, is "the most promising technology for the rapid reduction of global emissions: up to 55 percent by 2100."[99] Access to clean technology, both for climate mitigation and adaptation, is a major concern for low-income nations. Many other nations are worried about energy security, which then affects their mitigation efforts. Poland, for example, supplies 90 percent of its energy from coal. Switching from coal might mean greater reliance on natural gas from Russia, a move Poland would prefer not to take.[100]

Finally, in order to enable low-income nations to make a meaningful contribution to climate change action, mechanisms need to be devised that enable and spur investments in appropriate technologies and mitigation or adaptation efforts. Over the coming decades, the major growth in power plants and other energy generating facilities will be in low-income countries. Shifting these facilities to renewables or more climate friendly plants will take outside financial assistance. By 2030, if about 46 percent of the global total of international investments in climate change goes to low-income countries, the result would be a 68 percent drop in global emissions. Eighty-six percent of investments and financing comes from the private sector. A long-term international agreement on policy change would not only provide a level of policy certainty important to investors, but might also open up new investment opportunities.[101]

Carbon markets, such as the one under Kyoto, have been major sources of transferring funds for climate mitigation and adaptation to low-income countries. At the same time, these markets should not be a means for Western industries to avoid the task of reducing their carbon emissions by buying credits from low-income nations that are implementing carbon-friendly policies. Environmental issues are intrinsically linked to social ones, and environmental pressures can and should be read as signs that we should morally and socially reorient ourselves. The poor should not be made to bear the effect of the way of life of the rich.

Many experts believe that the success or failure of the Bali negotiations will depend on the actions of the United States. Other nations, including Canada, have failed in their own commitments to climate change. But the United States has a global role. Historically, it has been the world's largest economy and the largest emitter of greenhouse gases. The United States signed the UNFCCC and was among the first to promote binding emissions targets but then became the only major economy that did not sign the Kyoto Protocol. Whether for good reasons or not, this act was symbolic. To many nations, the United States has even failed to live up to its voluntary obligations under the UNFCCC. To date, the United States has tried every argument to avoid undertaking any type of binding international commitments relative to climate change; it has denied that climate change is real, questioned the science behind emissions reduction targets or timing, claimed that dealing with climate change will disrupt the economy, complained that technology has to mature before we have binding targets, required that others have to be involved before we take action. Over time many of these objections have proved groundless or less significant than the threats posed by climate change.

At the end of chapter 6 we envisioned a future North America would take the challenge of climate change and the ideals of sustainability seriously. As a result we would become world leaders in climate policies and technology. In our vision, we would adopt carbon control policies, implement energy saving measures, and promote the innovative growth of the renewable industry. We would drastically reduce greenhouse gas emissions without damaging the economy. We would grow our social well-being. We would become models of modern sustainable societies.

This is not an impossible vision, for either the United States or Canada. As this chapter has shown, the seeds needed to bring this vision about are already sprouting in individual, city, state, and provincial actions. Nations are responsible to insure a sound economy for its people. Yet they have other responsibilities as well, including social well-being, which we examined in chapter 2. Herman Daly, an ecological economist with a focus on sustainable development, wrote: "There is a lot of evidence that GDP growth at the current margin in the United States is in fact uneconomic growth—that is, growth that increases social and environmental costs faster than it increases production benefits, growth that accumulates 'illth' faster than it accumulates wealth."[102] As one recent college graduate observed, "It seems that my generation is really looking for something to live for. Many devote their lives to drinking, romance, video games, or whatever the latest obsession is—only to be consistently disappointed at the end of the day. We claim that we have something worth living (even dying) for here: we believe in a God who created this world, loves it, and calls us to take care of it; and the world today is in a mess."[103] Might not creating a sustainable society be a worthy goal for a nation, as well as for individuals?

UN Secretary General Ban Ki-Moon expressed hope that the United States would take on its leadership role in the new round of negotiations. "This is what the whole international community expects of the United States."[104] That hope is expressed in another way by Herman Ott of Germany's Wuppertal Institute: "The U.S. often takes a long time to act, but when it does, it does it full-scale. That gung-ho, 'we can do it' mentality would be helpful."[105]

The multi-track plan being considered by both the Bali Roadmap and proposed by the Pew Center has many aspects that resonate with the principles of sustainability from chapter 6—valuing and protecting creation by including an emphasis on combating deforestation; adapting commitments to local contexts even at a national level; pursuing adaptation, technology, and financial mechanisms which strengthen the vulnerable, and market-based mechanisms for emissions reductions. Negotiating an agreement that is just and equitable will not be easy. Nevertheless, it is an opportunity to move the world in a sustainable direction. Ultimately, the outcome will be the result of the quality of international relationships and are matters of "trust and credibility," or put another way, faith and faithfulness.

Given the global character of climate change, the principles of sustainability impel us to be engaged internationally. How else can we seek justice for the vulnerable and marginalized, especially those that are affected by the close connection between the environment and society that climate change presents? We are a pragmatic society, concerned for what will work, what will be achievable. This quality can be a great gift in tackling an issue of this magnitude. The United States has an important role to play in whatever negotiations take place in the future. In order to be able to take a leadership role and be persuasive to other nations, the United States must demonstrate that it is serious and willing to take action itself. The Pew Center outlined four key steps the United States must take to rebuild trust. The United States should (1) set its own national "ambitious, achievable, mandatory targets to reduce greenhouse gas emissions." Then, when the United States has credibility it should (2) seek fair, effective, and binding agreements for all major economies. Then the United States should (3) provide emerging economies with positive incentives in order to enable and encourage them to participate in a binding agreement. And finally, the United States needs to (4) establish interim goals to minimize potential impacts on business and industry.

The international community is more likely to act if prominent national governments have already done so, and national governments will only act if their populations have created for them the space of public permission. The social changes in the United States and Canada have already begun this process. Will we use these changes to prod ourselves, our nations, and the world towards sustainability? This chapter has affirmed that our actions, lifestyles, and beliefs can make a meaningful difference, even on an issue as large and complex as climate change. Reflecting on the message of the Revelation of St. John and God's purposes for creation, Herman Daly said,

> Christianity affirms the hope and faith in God's promise that neither the world while it exists, nor its ultimate demise, are purposeless. Our main task is to reflect more deeply on our purposes and to align them with our best understanding of God's purposes. To end the world prematurely by our own actions, I submit, is to usurp God's prerogative

as much as if we insisted on trying to make the world everlasting. To despair of making the world last as long as possible, because it will all end someday no matter what we do, is to lose faith both in God's promise and in our direct intimate experience of purpose as part of ourselves and therefore of the cosmos to which we belong. It is analogous to an individual committing suicide rather than living life.[106]

8

A NEW CREATION

I F ANYONE IS IN Christ, he is a new creation; the old has gone, the new has come!" (2 Cor 5:17).

Christ came to fulfill God's plan: not to "rapture the faithful," not just save a few souls, but to renew all creation.

Newness is a recurrent theme in the Gospels: new wine, new treasures, a new garment, a new teaching, a new command, a new covenant. The kingdom of God is more or less continually described as "news."

Paul repeatedly emphasizes the newness of life in Christ. "Just as Christ was raised from the dead . . . [his followers] too may live a new life" (Rom 6:4). Accordingly, he urged them to "be transformed by the renewing of [their] mind" (Rom 12:2), and "to put on the new self, which is being renewed in knowledge in the image of its Creator" (Col 3:10). "What counts," he told the Galatians, "is a new creation" (Gal 6:15).

Paul is not alone. The writer of the letter to the Hebrews recognizes that the coming of Jesus heralds "the time of the new order" (Heb 9:10). Peter writes of how "we are looking forward to a new heaven and a new earth" (2 Pet 3:13). John has the same vision (Rev 21:1–5).

We must hold this in mind as we stand back from the details of chapter 7 and attempt to gain some perspective on how we should respond to the challenges of climate change and sustainable living. The New Testament is infused with a sense of "now and not yet," the belief that the kingdom of God has come in Jesus but is not yet fully here, that Christ came to "make all things new" but, as yet, all things are not made new.

The Christian response to climate change and the ideal of sustainable living needs to be embedded in this realization. We are not called to conceive, design, build, and maintain a better version of the old world but rather to participate in the new one that has been inaugurated on the cross. We are expected not to haul ourselves up by our moral bootstraps but to discover the people we already are in God's sight. We are summoned not simply to surrender those pleasures that make life worthwhile but to rediscover what in fact does make life worthwhile.

Properly understood this tension guards against the twin pitfalls of moral burnout—"this task is too big for us"—and complacency—"things will inevitably improve." It asks serious questions of us—are we willing to make a difference, to step forward in faith, to make personal sacrifices, even when others are reluctant to do so?—but removes from us the guilt and shame that would otherwise accompany our (inevitable) failure to do what we really should.

This book has argued that we *should* care about climate change. We should care about those who stand to lose their homes, possessions, livelihoods, even their lives for entirely avoidable reasons. We should care about the creeping sense of disenchantment and disillusionment that accompanies the consumerism of the West and is the flip side of unsustainable living. We should care about the way in which careless or selfish behavior disfigures us. We should care about disfiguring the Earth. And we should care because none of it belongs to us, because the one to whom it does belong loves it and is concerned for his handiwork, and because we have a duty of love to our neighbors, no matter how far they are from us in space or time.

But we should not be worn out by our cares. Instead we should understand, not least from the vision of Isa 40–66 and the events recorded in the New Testament, that God has not given up on this creation but has chosen to recreate it from within, that God invites us to participate in that recreation of all things and promises that he will one day finish the job himself.

In this regard, climate change is not significantly different from many other challenges we face. "All things" is not a biblical euphemism for "the environment" but really does mean *all things*. Our personal lives, the cultures in which we live, the systems that structure our society—all of these require renewal. Climate change is, of course, marked by its particular scope and potential severity, but we are all participants in many other big systems: economic, social, and political. Our response to the challenge of climate change is part of our wider response to God's renewing activity on the cross.

The same narrative that records this promise of renewal has much to say about how we should participate in that re-creation.

It urges us to see creation as a whole and issues of environmental and social sustainability as inextricably linked, to grasp the fact that living sustainably should be a cause for joy and not mourning, and to understand that participation in the "re-creation" may also mean participating in the supreme act of divine self-sacrifice that made it possible.

Moreover, it offers us a model, in the checkered history of the people of God, of how we might participate in what God is doing: ideas, laws, practices, criticism, stories, visions of what the people did (and often failed to do) in response to God's call—all of which should inform our own response.

Whatever else it demands, that response demands faith, even if that faith is not obviously "religious." Facing the consequences outlined in chapter 1 or the forecasts for global fossil fuel consumption mentioned in chapter 7, and not throwing up one's hands in desperation or defeat demands faith—faith that things can be different. For Christians, however, their faith is that ultimately things *will* be different.

But that faith, inspiring as it is, must not stand alone. "Faith by itself, if it is not accompanied by action, is dead" (Jas 2:17). Christians around the world are in a distinct and key position to turn their faith into collective action. Sir Nicholas Stern remarked in his report on the economics of climate changes that "shared notions of responsible and collaborative behavior, within and outside governments, create the conditions in which countries honor international commitments."[1]

Christians are in a unique position to live and promote such "responsible and collaborative behavior." We need to do so now.

FURTHER ENGAGING

A Rocha is an international conservation organization working to show God's love for all creation through community based conservation projects. Founded in 1983 in Portugal, A Rocha means "the rock." Now working in 18 countries, A Rocha conducts scientific research, hands-on conservation projects and environmental education. A Rocha is engaged in mitigating climate change through its Climate Stewards Program (www.climatestewards.org) and in facilitating adaptation through research projects. All of A Rocha's efforts provide opportunities for Christians and others to work side by side in caring for creation and are characterized by five core commitments: Christian, Conservation, Community, Cross-cultural, and Cooperation. A Rocha welcomes participation in local groups and chapters in the United States, Canada, and the UK as they strive to respond to environmental and human needs in ways appropriate to the local context. A Rocha is the only faith-based organization admitted as a member of the World Conservation Union (IUCN). More information on the organization's scientific research, conservation projects, accomplishments, and specific ways to become involved with their work are chronicled on the Web site: www .arocha.org.

The Au Sable Institute of Environmental Studies is a Christian institute whose mission is to bring healing to the biosphere and the whole of Creation. Au Sable's activities fall into five main areas: a teaching institute with academic programs for college and university students, research projects, academic forums, environmental education for local school children, and information services for churches and community. Au Sable was founded upon the conviction that followers of Christ should be careful and thoughtful stewards of God's creation. For over three decades this foundational purpose has taken root in the Au Sable Institute's programs and activities, which underscore their abiding respect for the ongoing handiwork of their Creator and their desire to do all they can to bring healing and wholeness to the biosphere for the glory of God, the well-being of humanity, and the flourishing of all of Creation. For more information go to www.ausable.org.

Center for Public Justice is a public policy think tank and civic education organization in the Washington, D.C., area working to develop a full-blown Christian approach to the responsibilities of government and citizenship. Its mission is to equip citizens, develop leaders, and shape policy. Among its concerns has been government's responsibility to uphold a healthy and sustainable commons, including the ecological commons. A basic statement on environmental justice has been articulated in the Center's *Guidelines* on that subject (www.cpjustice.org/guidelines). The Center is attempting to refine and deepen a Christian-democratic approach to public life with an eye especially to our global commons. Many of the Center's books and other publications, as well as additional *Guidelines,* can be found on its Web site: www.cpjustice.org.

The Faraday Institute for Science and Religion is an academic research enterprise based at St. Edmund's College, Cambridge, England. It was founded in 2006 by Denis Alexander and Robert White. The Institute has four main activities:

- Scholarly research and publication on science and religion, including the organization of invited groups of experts to write joint publications.

- Provision of short-term courses in science and religion.

- Organization of seminars and lectures on science and religion.

- Provision of accurate information on science and religion for the international media and wider public.

The group of scholars based at St. Edmund's College is linked informally to a cohort of Faraday Associates, based mainly within the scientific community, who are actively involved in science-religion interactions through publishing and lecturing. The Faraday Institute derives its name from Michael Faraday, one of Britain's best-known scientists, who saw his faith as integral to his scientific research. The Faraday Institute has a Christian ethos, but encourages engagement with a wide diversity of opinions concerning interactions between science and religion. It aims to provide accurate information in order to facilitate informed debate. For further information about the Faraday Institute, to access an extensive free multimedia library of lectures and seminars, learn about forthcoming events, or join the free mailing list, please visit www.faraday-institute.org.

The John Ray Initiative (JRI) brings together scientific and Christian understanding of the environment to promote the twin themes of sustainable living and environmental stewardship. It is named after the Essex-born naturalist and theologian John Ray (1627–1705). It was set up in 1997 by a group of scientists, and Robert White is a director. JRI believes in a strong and open scientific base to counter misunderstanding and prejudice, because God has set us in a world where we need to understand what is there. It is a world where the discoveries of science (within their limits) are as much a part of God's world as is the revealed word of God. JRI has responded to a hunger among Christian believers to integrate their concern for the environment with their faith, or their scientific profession with their beliefs, and considers education through courses, seminars, and publications an important aspect of its work. See www.jri.org.uk.

The Jubilee Centre was founded in 1983 in England. It believes the Bible describes a coherent vision for society that has enduring relevance for the world in the twenty-first century. At the heart of this social vision is a concern for right relationships, rooted in Matt 22:37–40. The relevance of this relational agenda for modern society is evident from the wide range of topics that the Jubilee Centre has explored over the years, including criminal justice, care for the elderly, asylum and immigration, and sexual ethics. Among its publications is the ground-breaking Jubilee Manifesto. It also produces the quarterly Cambridge Papers, an influential collection of peer-reviewed studies on contemporary issues.

The vision of social engagement based on careful research, inspired by the example of Christian reformers such as William Wilberforce, initially led to the well-known and now independent campaign on Sunday trading (Keep Sunday Special). Its work later gave rise to a number of other organizations involved in British social reform, including Credit Action, the Relationships Foundation, and the international peace-building charity Concordis International. A number of groups are now drawing upon the experience and expertise of the Jubilee Centre to establish similar organizations internationally in countries as diverse as Singapore, Kenya, and the USA.

An archive of the Jubilee Centre's research and a blog discussing the application of the biblical social vision to issues in the news can be found on its Web site. For further information about the Jubilee Centre, to order or download its publications, or to join the free mailing list, please visit: www.jubilee-centre.org.

The National Religious Partnership for the Environment was formed in the US in 1993 in response to an appeal by Dr. Carl Sagan and 32 other prominent scientists and nobel laureates for religious organizations to become more engaged in the environmental issues facing all of mankind. The Partnership's Web site provides an entry-way into environmental efforts of four faith communities—Jewish, Catholic, mainline Protestant, and evangelicals. Each group has approached challenges such as endangered species or climate change through their own denominational traditions. Actions can range from practical efforts in energy efficiency, concerns for poverty, justice, and refugees, to political engagement. See www.nrpe.org.

Plant With Purpose, an initiative of Floresta, is an international Christian organization that transforms lives in rural areas where poverty is caused by deforestation. For 25 years, Plant With Purpose has worked to heal the relationship between people and their environment by planting trees, revitalizing farms, and offering loans to create economic opportunity. Working specifically in areas where environmental degradation and poverty intersect, Plant With Purpose's programs are comprised of interlocking elements designed to promote self-sufficiency and responsible environmental stewardship. Through community development, sustainable agriculture and reforestation efforts, microenterprise credit, and discipleship, Plant With Purpose is bringing hope and dignity to the rural poor. Plant With Purpose farmers have planted over 4 million trees in nearly 200 communities worldwide. Additionally, over 5,000 low-interest loans have allowed farmers to invest in their land and start sustainable businesses. Plant With Purpose's highly qualified indigenous staff is committed to sharing the love of Jesus both in word and deed. They have helped empower tens of thousands of rural farmers to transform their communities and break free from a cycle of poverty and environmental destruction. Plant With Purpose currently operates programs in the Dominican Republic, Mexico, Haiti, Tanzania, Burundi, and Thailand. To find out more, visit their Web site: www.PlantWithPurpose.org.

Tearfund is an evangelical Christian relief and development charity, passionate about seeing God's justice here on earth. Its vision is to transform the lives of millions of the world's poorest people in a positive and sustainable way, by providing practical help alongside hope. It works with a vast network of Christian partners, made up of local churches and Christian organizations, which extends around the world. Together they are combining their efforts to focus on: families affected by HIV and AIDS; partnering poor communities; children at risk; communities torn apart by disaster; people affected by climate change. Tearfund's focus on climate change is driven by the fact that climate change hits the poorest hardest. As well as working to help communities cope practically with the inevitable effects of climate change, it is also lobbying and campaigning for more urgent action to reduce global greenhouse gas emissions, and encouraging individuals to play their part by making lifestyle changes. See www.tearfund.org.

World Vision is a Christian relief, development, and advocacy organization dedicated to working with children, families, and communities to overcome poverty and injustice. It has more than 22,000 staff in 100 countries. In most of its projects, World Vision works through local staff who are connected to the community they serve. To make a real impact, it also partners with governments, nongovernment organizations, and others who share the commitment to fighting poverty. World Vision works to make a serious and sustainable impact on poverty and the causes of poverty, especially as they affect children. It is committed to long-term change, which means connecting people. Whether it's enabling people in developing communities to support each other, or linking donors to those in need through child sponsorship, or creating networks to campaign for justice with its supporters, World Vision believes that getting people connected is the best way to make a difference. See www.worldvision.org.

Especially for Students

This is a challenging and exciting time for Christian college students. There is a growing student movement on many college campuses to openly and actively demonstrate their care for creation. Students want to connect their faith, their lives, and their studies in seeking to solve some of the generation's great issues—climate change, care for the poor, and biodiversity conservation as examples.

The Au Sable Institute of Environmental Studies (www.au sable.org) helps to foster and lay the foundations for this movement. Many of the leaders in today's student movement, or the teachers at the colleges themselves, have studied at Au Sable.

The Creation Care Study Program (www.creationcsp.org) provides an opportunity for students to gain a global perspective by offering a semester abroad program at its campuses in either Belize or New Zealand/Samoa. Students study topics such as tropical ecosystems and sustainable development.

Renewal: Students Caring for Creation (www.renewing creation.org) has drawn together many of the groups and programs working among students for creation care into a network to demonstrate the power of working together. In essence, Renewal is engaged in mobilizing and equipping the student creation care movement across all college campuses. At their website, students can find information on other student groups, ideas for campus service or advocacy, participation in a campus day of prayer, news and opportunities with a wide variety of environmental organizations.

Restoring Eden helps students and the church grow in their appreciation of the natural world and their understanding of stewardship, and they also equip students to participate in public policy discussions and advocacy efforts (www.restoringeden.org).

Web sites

The response to climate change is emerging so rapidly that on-line resources are some of the best places for current information. The following sites are especially useful:

The Faraday Institute for Science and Religion's Web site at www. faraday-institute.org

The Pew Center on Global Climate Change in the United States: www.pewclimate.org

The Pembina Institute in Canada: http://climate.pembina.org

World Watch Institute: www.worldwatch.org

World Resources Institute: www.wri.org

FURTHER READING

Resources

The following is a beginning list of resources and books for those who want to delve more deeply into the topics addressed in this book.

Jubilee Centre and Tearfund. *Christianity, Climate Change, and Sustainable Living: Five Bible Studies* (2009) Hendrickson Publishers. These Bible studies were created to be used with *Christianity, Climate Change, and Sustainable Living,* by N. Spencer, R. White, and V. Vroblesky. They are available as a free PDF download at www.hendrickson.com on the book detail page.

Climate Change

Hensen, Robert. *Climate Change: The Symptoms, the Science, the Solutions* (2006) Rough Guides. Easily accessible guide to the basic issues surrounding climate change, including insights into the causes of skepticism and the debates over proposed solutions.

Houghton, John. *Global Warming: the complete briefing (Fourth edition)* (2009) Cambridge University Press. An excellent and accessible book on the science of global climate change, its impacts on the world and what we might do about it. Written by Sir John Houghton, a Christian who worked for many years with the IPCC and shared the Nobel Peace Prize with Al Gore and others.

Isham, Jonathan and Sissel Waage (eds). *Ignition. What you can do to Fight Global Warming and Spark a Movement.* (2007) Island Press. With an introduction by Bill McKibben, this book examines how organizations and cultures change, provides insights into how values, climate justice and health concerns contribute to the need for action, and equips readers with tools to enable them to become part of transforming our culture into a more sustainable society. Using experts from academia, business, politics and general life it asks the question: "What works?"

Kolbert, Elizabeth. *Field Notes From a Catastrophe* (2007), Bloomsbury Publishing. Climate change can seem to be only a theory, but the author brings it close and real through her exploration of its impacts in the Artic and her quest to understand the political response.

Linden, Eugene. *The Winds of Change. Climate, Weather, and the Destruction of Civilizations.* (2006) Simon and Schuster Publishing. Describes the effects of rapid climate change on past cultures and how this could happen again. The book includes an excellent chronology tracing the accelerating pace of climate change and its corresponding science and politics from 1950 through 2005.

Mooney, Chris. *Storm World: Hurricanes, Politics, and the Battle over Global Warming.* (2007) Harcourt. By examining the specific question of "Are hurricanes increasing in strength and what can we do about them?" the author unravels the relationship between competing scientific theories, media pressure and political debate, all within the context of climate change.

Northcott, Michael. *A Moral Climate: The Ethics of Global Warming.* (2007) Orbis Books. Northcott is the author of *The Environment and Christian Ethics* and other books dealing specifically with Christian ethics. Here he examines climate change, energy, economics and social responses from the perspectives of ethics and Christian thinking.

Sustainable Living

Clark, Duncan and Richie Unterberger. *Shopping with a Conscience.* (2007) Rough Guides. Explores the broad issues of "ethical consumption" such as the positive and negative effects of boycotts, the role of fair trade products and the power of companies to affect public policy. Provides specific resources for shopping "ethically" for food, energy, household products, travel, etc.

Editors of E Magazine. *Green Living: The E Magazine Handbook for Living Lightly on the Earth.* (2005) Plume. An excellent evaluation of many products and solutions for green living.

Hartsfield, Susan. *The Complete Guide to Energy Conservation for Smarties.* (2008) Green Being Publishing Company.

Compilation of tips and ideas garnered from Web sites and non-profits. Everything from the speed when it is more economical to open your car windows rather than use the air conditioner to getting off of junk mail lists.

White, Robert S. (editor) *Creation in Crisis: Christian Perspectives on Sustainability,* (2009) SPCK Publishing. A follow up to this book with essays by 14 leading scientists and theologians addressing the root causes of unsustainabilty and what changes might be needed to address them.

World Watch Institute: (www.worldwatch.org) Several of the titles in the *State of the World* Series have dealt with sustainability and climate change. These books examine global trends and proposed actions. *State of the World 2009: Into a Warming World; State of the World 2008: Innovations for a Sustainable Economy; State of the World 2004: Special Focus—the Consumer Society.*

Christian World View

Alexander, Denis, and Robert S. White. *Science, Faith and Ethics: Grid or Gridlock?* (2006) Hendrickson Publishers. A good general introduction to science and Christianity with chapters on topical issues facing Christians today, including one on "Spaceship Earth" which is a wider view of some of the issues discussed in this book.

Bouma-Prediger, Stephen. *For the Beauty of the Earth: A Christian Vision for Creation Care.* (2001) Baker Academic. Written by a theologian and ecologist, this widely used book examines the role Christian theology has played in our relationship to nature in the past and how theology can establish an ethical Christian approach to creation care as we face the challenges of our era.

Brown, Edward. *Our Father's World: Mobilizing the Church to Care for Creation.* (2008) InterVarsity. Examines the Biblical foundations for a Christian's care of creation, provides practical steps for individuals and organizations, and offers a model for a new form of "missions"—that the way Christian organizations respond to the environmental crisis has the potential to transform people and the land that supports them.

Harris, Peter. *Kingfisher's Fire: A story of hope for God's earth.* (2008) Monarch Books. The story of a Christian conservation organization's growth from a small center in Portugal to projects in 18 countries around the world. The chapter on the United States illustrates the cultural challenges confronting American Christians as they try to put a belief in creation care into practice.

Koetje, David S., ed. *Living the Good Life on God's Good Earth.* (2006) Faith Alive Resources. This eighty-three-page, ten-chapter study guide includes questions for discussion, review, and action.

Lowe, Ben. *Green Revolution: Coming Together to Care for Creation.* (2009) InterVarsity. Using stories of community organizing on college campuses, Ben Lowe challenges this generation to demonstrate what Christian care of creation would look like. Each section contains articles by some of the leading thinkers and activists within the Christian environmental movement.

Robinson, Tri. *Saving God's Green Earth.* (2006) Ampelon Publishing. Tells how a pastor and a church transformed their belief in care of creation into practical action that affected their community. Provides ideas and the key steps to effectively integrate care of creation into church life.

Schulter, Michael et al., *Jubilee Manifesto.* (2005) Not specifically on the environment, this book develops a Biblical vision of society, as explored by the Jubilee Centre for over 25 years. It presents an alternative to capitalism, socialism and other ideologies by identifying relationships as the foundation stone of any society. For this and resources on other social topics, see www.jubilee-centre.org.

Van Dyke, Fred, David Mahan, Joseph Sheldon, Raymond Brand. *Redeeming Creation: The Biblical Basis for Environmental Stewardship.* (1996) InterVarsity. Written by four biologists, *Redeeming Creation* examines issues such as the role of God as creator, the value of creation, the consequences of our actions, the Christian response of restoration and redemption, and ecology and the Christian mind. Though a decade old, this book is still relevant and widely used.

ENDNOTES

Note to Preface to the American Edition

1. First Chronicles 12:32: "And of the sons of Issachar, men who understood the times, with knowledge of what Israel should do" (NASB).

Notes to Introduction

1. Dr. Margaret Chan, "Climate Change and Health: Preparing for Unprecedented Challenges." The 2007 David E. Barmes Global Health Lecture, 10 December, 2007. Bethesda, Maryland. www.who.int/dg/speeches/2007/20071211_maryland/en/print.html.

2. "Key Messages from the Congress," 12 March 2009. "Climate Change: Global Risks, Challenges and Decisions," 10-12 March 2009 in Copenhagen, Denmark. Hosted by the University of Copenhagen. http://climatecongress.ku.dk/newsroom/congress_key_messages/.

3. For the first time, in February 2007, the IPCC used the term "unequivocal," citing evidence from observations of increases in global average air and ocean temperatures, widespread melting of snow and ice, and rising global mean sea level. See Intergovernmental Panel on Climate Change, *Climate Change 2007: The Physical Science Basis, Summary for Policymakers*, available for free download at www.ipcc.ch.

4. In 2005, the Academies of Science of Brazil, Canada, China, France, Germany, India, Italy, Japan, Russia, UK, and the US issued an unprecedented statement endorsing the conclusions of the Intergovernmental Panel on Climate Change (www.royalsoc.ac.uk/document.asp?id=3222).

5. M. S. Northcott, *The Environment and Christian Ethics* (Cambridge University Press, 1996).

6. R. J. Berry, ed., *The Care of Creation* (InterVarsity Press, 2000).

7. See M. Schluter, and J. Ashcroft, eds., *Jubilee Manifesto: A Framework, Agenda and Strategy for Christian Social Reform* (InterVarsity Press, 2005).

8. J. Lovelock, *The Revenge of Gaia: Why the Earth Is Fighting Back— and How We Can Still Save Humanity* (Allen Lane, 2006).

9. *Sunday Times* (23 July 2006). The Bishop of London said, "Sin is not just a restricted list of moral mistakes. It is living a life turned in on itself where people ignore the consequences of their actions." He also said there was now an "overriding imperative" to "walk more lightly upon the earth," adding that people needed to make decisions in their daily lives with a greater consideration of the environmental consequences.

10. Lord Rees, Kt, *Anniversary Address 2006,* The Royal Society (30 November 2006) www.royalsoc.ac.uk.

Notes to Chapter 1, Global Warming, Local Causes

1. See Al Gore, *An Inconvenient Truth,* Rodale Press, 2006, and a DVD with the same title for an accessible and well-illustrated account of global climate change.

2. C. D. Thomas, A. Cameron, et al., "Extinction Risk from Climate Change," *Nature* 427 (2004), pp. 145–48.

3. This chapter draws on an excellent summary in J. Houghton, "Global Warming," *Reports on Progress in Physics* 68 (2005), pp. 1343–1403; and on a briefing from the Hadley Centre for Climate Prediction and Research, *Climate Change and the Greenhouse Effect,* 2005, at www.ukcip .org.uk/index.php?option=com_content&task=view&id=345&Itemid=9. See also J. Houghton, *Global Warming: The Complete Briefing* (Cambridge University Press, 2004).

4. Details of the history can be found in F. B. Mudge, "The Development of Greenhouse Theory of Global Climate Change from Victorian Times," *Weather* 52 (1997), pp. 13–16.

5. See H. Steinfeld, et al., *Livestock's Long Shadow: Environmental Issues and Options* (Livestock, Environment and Development [LEAD] Initiative, Food and Agriculture Organisation of the United Nations, 2006). Available free from www.virtual-centre.org/.

6. The purpose of this book is not to debate the age of the Earth, an issue for some, but rather to examine the evidence that has led to the conclusion that human activity has been a major faction driving current climate change. For further details on dating the Earth see R. S. White, *The Age of the Earth,* Faraday Paper, 8 (2007), available from www.faraday-institute.org and discussion in D. A. Alexander and R. S. White, *Science, Faith, and Ethics: Grid or Gridlock?* (Hendrickson Publishers, 2006).

7. L. A. Hinnov, "Earth's Orbital Parameters and Cycle Stratigraphy," in F. I. Gradstein, J. Ogg, and A. Smith, eds., *A Geologic Time Scale 2004* (Cambridge University Press, 2004), pp. 55–62.

8. North Greenland Ice Core Project Members, "High-resolution Record of Northern Hemisphere Climate Extending into the Last Interglacial Period," *Nature* 431 (2004), pp. 147–51; EPICA (European Community for Ice Coring in Antarctica) Community Members, "Eight Glacial Cycles from an Antarctic Ice Core," *Nature* 429 (2004), pp. 623–28.

9. See IPCC, *Climate Change 2007*.

10. The IPCC Fourth Assessment Report in 2007 reports that warming of the climate system is "unequivocal" and that it is "very likely" (more than 90 percent certain) to be caused by the observed increase in anthropogenic greenhouse gas concentrations. See IPCC, *Climate Change 2007*.

11. C. B. Field, L. D. Mortsch, M. Brklacich, D. L. Forbes, P. Kovacs, J. A. Patz, S. W. Running and M. J. Scott, 2007: North America. *Climate Change 2007: Impacts, Adaptation and Vulnerability. Contribution of Working Group II to the Fourth Assessment Report of the Intergovernmental Panel on Climate Change, M. L. Parry, O. F. Canziani, J. P. Palutikof, P. J. van der Linden and C. E. Hanson, Eds., Cambridge University Press, Cambridge, UK, 617–652* see also: David Ertischek. "Global Warming Seen in the Parkway." *Gatehouse News Service*, May 30, 2007. www.townonline.com/roslindale/news. Richard Primack has used the observations recorded by Henry David Thoreau in the 1850s to investigate changes in plant flowering dates and bird arrivals at Arnold Arboretum in Boston, Mass.

12. J. M. Gregory, et al., "Recent and Future Changes in Arctic Sea Ice Simulated by the HadCM3 AOGCM," *Geophysical Research Letters*, 29 (2002), p. 2175; see also *One Planet, Many People: Atlas of Our Changing Environment* (United Nations Environment Programme, 2005), for an excellent pictorial account of changes to the Earth's environment over the past 30 years. Also available free online at http://na.unep.net/OnePlanetManyPeople/.

13. Deborah Williams, and Howard Hanson. "Impacts of Global Warming in Alaska." in *Encyclopedia of Earth*. Eds. Cutler J. Cleveland (Washington, D.C.: Environmental Information Coalition, National Council for Science and the Environment). Published February 16, 2007. www.eoearth.org/article/Impacts_of_global_warming_in_Alaska.

14. "Canada Country Studies: A Window on Climate Change in Canada," *The Green Lane*, Environment Canada's Web site. www.ec.gc.ca/default.asp?lang=En&n=FD9B0E51-1.

15. www.royalsoc.ac.uk/document.asp?id=3222.

16. See www.ipcc.ch for details.

17. See, for example, chapter 2 of G. Monbiot, *Heat: How to Stop the Planet Burning* (Allen Lane, 2006).

18. R. A. Wod, M. Vellinga, and R. Thorpe, "Global Warming and Thermohaline Circulation Stability," *Philosophical Transactions of the Royal Society (A)*, 361 (2003), pp. 1961–75.

19. N. Stern, *The Economics of Climate Change: The Stern Review* (Cambridge University Press, 2007).

20. IPCC 2001, *Climate Change 2001: The Scientific Basis*, Contribution of Working Group 1 to the Third Assessment Report of the Intergovernmental Panel on Climate Change, J. T. Houghton, et al., eds. (Cambridge University Press, 2001); and IPCC, *Climate Change 2007*, both available free at www.ipcc.ch.

21. See J. Leggett, *Half Gone: Oil, Gas, Hot Air and the Global Energy Crisis* (Portobello Books, 2005), and A. Witze, "That's Oil, Folks . . . ," *Nature* 445 (2007), pp. 14–17.

22. An up-to-date source of energy estimate is the annual BP statistical review of world energy at www.bp.com.

23. See: Crystal Davis, "Oil Sands Become Canada's Fastest Growing Source of CO2 Emissions." *World Resources Institute EarthTrends.* January 15, 2008. http://earthtrends.wri.org/updates/node/276; and the Alberta Government Energy Web site on Oil Sands at www.energy.gov.ab.ca/OurBusiness/oilsands.asp.

24. Field, pp. 620–21.

25. Field, p. 632.

26. http://droughtsheatwaves.suite101.com/article.cfm/north_america_heat_wave_2006.

27. P. A. Stott, D. A. Stone, and M. R. Allen, "Human Contribution to the European Heat Wave of 2003," *Nature* 423 (2004), pp. 610–14.

28. P. Ciais, et al., "Europe-wide Reduction in Primary Productivity Caused by the Heat and Drought in 2003," *Nature* 437 (2005), pp. 529–33.

29. C. Schär, et al., "The Role of Increasing Temperature Variability in European Summer Heatwaves," *Nature* 427 (2004), pp. 332–36.

30. See Knutson, et al., "Simulated reduction in Atlantic hurricane frequency under twenty-first-century warming conditions." *Geoscience* (May 2008); Wang & Lee, "Global Warming and United States landfalling hurricanes." *Geophysical Research Letters* (January 2008); and Donnelly & Woodruff. "Intense hurricane activity over the past 5,000 years controlled by El Niño and the West African monsoon." *Nature* (May 2007).

31. K. Emmanuel, "Increasing Destructiveness of Tropical Cyclones over the Past 30 Years," *Nature* 436 (2005), pp. 686–88.

32. Chris Mooney, *Storm World, Hurricanes, Politics, and the Battle over Global Warming* (New York: Harcourt, Inc., 2007), 165.

33. James G. Titus, "Rising Seas, Coastal Erosion and the Takings Clause: How to Save Wetlands and Beaches Without Hurting Property Owners." *Maryland Law Review* 57 No. 4 (1998).

34. Titus, p. 1306.

35. Lesley Ewing, "Considering Sea Level Rise as a Coastal Hazard." *Proceeding of Coastal Zone 07*, Portland Oregon, July 22–26, 2007 www. csc.noaa.gov/cz/2007.

36. N. Myers, and J. Kent, *Environmental Exodus: An Emergent Crisis in the Global Arena* (Washington, D.C.: Climate Institute, 1995).

37. *One Planet, Many People.*

38. Field, p. 633.

39. Myrna H. P. Hall and Daniel B. Fagre, "Modeled Climate-Induced Glacider Change in Glacier National Park, 1850–2100," *BioScience* 53: 131–40.

40. Field, p. 629.

41. J. A. Patz, D. Campbell-Lendrum, T. Holloway, and J. A. Foley, "Impact of Regional Climate Change on Human Health," *Nature* 438 (2005), pp. 310–17.

42. Human Development Report 2006, *Beyond Scarcity—Power, Poverty and the Global Water Crisis* (United Nations Development Programme). Available for download from http://hdr.undp.org.

Notes to Chapter 2, Sustainability and Well-Being

1. Which is not to say that societies necessarily lived sustainably. Entire societies—from the Greenland Norse to the Easter Islanders—have committed "ecocide." See J. Diamond, *Collapse: How Societies Choose to Fail or Succeed* (Allen Lane, 2005), for details.

2. In 1909 President Roosevelt asked world powers to meet in the Hague to discuss conservation of the world's natural resources. Twenty years later the economic theorist, Harold Hotelling, was writing openly about the economics of exhaustible resources. We are indebted to John Ashcroft for these references.

3. World Commission on Environment and Development: the Brundtland Report, *Our Common Future* (Oxford University Press, 1987).

4. Maurie J. Cohen, "Sustainable consumption in national context: an introduction to the symposium." *Sustainability: Science, Practice and Policy*, 2005. http://ejournal.nbii.org.

5. For further details, see J. Porritt, *Capitalism as if the World Matters* (Earthscan, 2005), ch. 2.

6. Dinah A. Koehler and Alan D. Hecht, "Sustainability, well being, and environmental protection: perspectives and recommendations from an Environmental Protection Agency forum." *Sustainability: Science, Practice and Policy,* 2006. http://ejournal.nbii.org.

7. Porritt, *Capitalism as if the World Matters,* p. 27.

8. See www.eia.doe.gov and www.iea.org.

9. Other parts of the world use "final energy" for this concept. In the US the energy that is used to generate and distribute electricity is divided between the four sectors based on electricity sales. This figure is combined with the "primary" or direct fossil fuel energy use in each sector to equal the "total energy" for that sector.

10. In the UK, for example, energy consumtion is divided roughly equally across three sectors: transport, domestic, and industrial/services. In France, by comparison, industry and the residential sector each consume around a third of the total energy, with the remaining third being shared predominantly between transport and "commerce and other public services."

11. Energy Information Administration, "Consumption by Sector." *Annual Energy Review 2007. Table 7.3* Accessible at www.eia.doe.gov.

12. "National Inventory Report, 1990–2005: Greenhouse Gas Sources and Sinks in Canada." www.ec.gc.ca/pdb/ghg/inventory_report/2005_report/som-sum_eng.cfm.

13. These emissions grew by 48 percent. "National Inventory Report, 1990–2005: Greenhouse Gas Sources and Sinks in Canada." www.ec.gc.ca/pdb/ghg/inventory_report/2005_report/som-sum_eng.cfm.

14. "Energy Profile of Canada–the Encyclopedia of Earth." www.eoearth.org/article/Energy_profile_of_Canada.

15. There are several other countries with higher per capita energy consumption than the US and Canada, such as Kuwait (9 tons), UAE (13 tons), Bahrain (14 tons), the Virgin Islands (25 tons), and Qatar (30 tons), but these tend to be small and/or hot and/or islands and/or major oil producers. See http://globalis.gvu.unu.edu/indicator.cfm?IndicatorID=146&country=FR#rowFR.

16. In this instance, household emissions figures were derived by dividing the total national greenhouse gas emissions by number of households. This brings the whole of the national economy onto a personal level, not just those actions normally related to life at home.

17. For more information on standby power or "phantom loads" see: US Department of Energy-Energy Efficiency and Renewable Energy. "Home Office and Home Electronics." www1.eere.energy.gov/consumer/tips/ (accessed July 1, 2008) and Lawrence Berkley National Laboratory. "Standby Power FAQ" by Alan Meier. http://standby.lbl.gov/faq.html. (accessed July 1, 2008)

18. US Census Bureau. "Food and Beverage Sales, 1990–2004" in *Statistical Abstracts.*

19. Figures come from US Environmental Protection Agency reports, "Greenhouse Gas Emissions from U.S. Transportation Sector, 1990–2003" and "Inventory of U.S. Greenhouse Gas Emissions and Sinks: 1990–2005," available at www.epa.gov/climatechange. Also from the Energy Information Agency, "Annual Energy Outlook 2007 with Projections to 2030" www.eia.doe.gov/oiaf/aeo/demand.html, and Energy Information Agency, "Petroleum Reports."

20. Of this 40 percent came from OPEC countries, predominantly Saudi Arabia, Venezuela, Nigeria, and Iraq. Twenty-nine percent was imported from Canada and Mexico.

21. Table 2.8, "Motor Vehicle Mileage, Fuel Consumption and Fuel Rates, Selected Years, 1949–2005" in Department of Energy's *Annual Energy Review.* www.eia.doe.gov.

22. Three of these sectors—public transport, air transport, and household transport—are explored in this section, with the fourth, freight transport, examined in the following section on consumption.

23. American Public Transportation Association. "Public Transportation's Contribution to US Greenhouse Gas Reduction." September 2007, www.apta.com. See also Janet Sawin, "Making Better Energy Choices" in *State of the World 2004* (World Watch Institute; New York: W.W. Norton & Company, 2004), p. 30.

24. Federal Aviation Administration. "Aviation and Emissions: A Primer," January 2005, www.faa.gov; and EPA. "Inventory of US Greenhouse Gas Emissions and Sinks: 1990–2005."

25. Energy Information Agency. "Household Vehicles Energy Use: Latest Data and Trends." www.eia.doe.gov.

26. Gross Domestic Product is defined as the value of the total final output of durable and nondurable goods and services produced within a country.

27. Total resources are the sum of gross household disposable income and the adjustment for the change in net equity of households in pension funds.

28. Julie Schor, "US Consumers, Cheap Manufacturers and the Global Sweatshop" in *State of the World, 2004* (WorldWatch Institute; W.W. Norton & Company, 2004), pp. 117–18.

29. www.epa.gov/climatechange.

30. See N. Ahmad, N. and A. Wyckoff, "Carbon Dioxide Emissions Embodied in International Trade of Goods," OECD Science, Technology and Industry Working Papers, 2003/15 (OECD Publishing, 2003), which concludes: "emissions associated with imports or exports are usually above 10% of *domestic production,* and often above 20%" (p. 8).

31. T. Garnett, *Wise Moves: Exploring the Relationship between Food, Transport and CO2* (Transport 2000 Trust, 2003), p. 8.

32. Friends of the Earth, *Checking Out the Environment? Environmental Impacts of Supermarkets* (June 2005), p. 2.

33. Rich Pirog and Andrew Benjamin. "Checking the Food Odometer: Comparing food miles for local versus conventional produce sales to Iowa institutions." Leopold Center for Sustainable Agriculture. July 2003. www.leopold.iastate.edu.

34. Maurie J. Cohen, Aaron Comrov, and Brian Hoffner, "The new politics of consumption: promoting sustainability in the American Marketplace." *Sustainability: Science, Practice, & Policy*. http://ejournal.nbii.org/.

35. US Center for Disease Control. "Eliminate Disparities in Infant Mortality." www.cdc.gov/omhd/AMH/factsheets/infant.htm.

36. Institute for Innovation in Social Policy, Vassar College. "Index of Social Health," http://iisp.vassar.edu/ish.html.

37. Eduardo Porter, "Marc L. Miringoff, 58, Dies; Measurer of Social Health" *The New York Times* (March 6, 2004).

38. Information for this section gathered from: "Study: U.S. employees put in most hours" by Porter Anderson, August 31, 2001, *CNN.com*; "Longer Work Hours Stress Families" from Monster Career Advice, by John Rossheim, http://career-advice.monster.com, "Lights Out for Long Hours" by Silja J. A. Talvi, *The Christian Science Monitor*, December 17, 2001; "Are Shorter Work Hours Good for the Environment? A Comparison of U.S. and European Energy Consumption" by David Rosnick and Mark Weisbrot, Center for Economic and Policy Research (Washington, D.C.), December 2006, www.cepr.net.

39. Such surveys have obvious problems, such as being susceptible to moods and circumstances, but are conducted and analysed so as to address such problems. See R. Layard, *Happiness: Lessons from the New Science* (Allen Lane, 2005), and C. Hamilton, *Growth Fetish* (Pluto Books, 2003).

40. Pew Research Center. "Are We Happy Yet?" Pew Reseach Center Publications (February 13, 2006), http://pewresearch.org/pubs/301/are-we-happy-yet.

41. N. Donovan and D. Halpern, *Life Satisfaction: The State of Knowledge and Implications for Government* ([Cabinet Office] Strategy Unit, 2002), para. 3.

42. Health is a complex factor. Self-reported health is strongly correlated to life-satisfaction but more objective measures of health are not. People become habituated to some forms of ill-health but not to others. Mental health is strongly correlated with low levels of well-being.

43. For a discussion of relationships and happiness see Layard, *Happiness: Lessons from the New Science*, pp. 59–73.

44. Data from: EPA: "Greenhouse Gas Emissions from US Transportation Sector, 1990–2003," www.epa.gov and Larry Copeland, El Nasser and Paul Overberg. "As commutes begin earlier, new daily routines emerge" *USA Today*, September 12, 2007; US Census Press Release. "Labor Day 2007: Sept. 3," www.census.gov.

45. US Census Bureau, "Summary of Travel Trends: 1977–2001," *Statistical Abstracts* (2006).

46. Joseph Carroll, "Worker's Average Commute Round-Trip is 46 Minutes in a Typical Day." *Gallup News Service*. August 24, 2007, www.gallup.com.

47. EPA, "Greenhouse Gas," p. 12.

48. Robert Putnam, *Bowling Alone* (Simon & Schuster, 2000). We are indebted to John Ashcroft for bringing this information to our attention.

49. John Adams, *The Social Implications of Hypermobility*, www.oecd .org/publications/0,3353,en_2649_201185_1_1_1_1_1,00.html, p. 126.

50. Adams, *Social Implications of Hypermobility*, p. 127.

51. The following has been taken from *Last Child in the Woods* by Richard Louv, Algonquin Books of Chapel Hill.

52. Louv, p. 122.

53. See N. Spencer, *The Measure of All Things? A Biblical Perspective on Money and Value in Britain Today* (Jubilee Centre, 2003).

54. Commendation on Clive Hamilton's *Growth Fetish* (Pluto Press, 2004).

55. Much of the data for this portion is drawn from *SuperCapitalism: The Transformation of Business, Democracy & Everyday Life* by Robert B. Reich (Alfred A. Knopf, 2007) and *State of the World 2004* (WorldWatch Institute).

56. Cohen, p. 61.

57. Cohen, p. 61.

58. Data derived from the Center for the New American Dream www .newdream.org: "Just the Facts: Junk Mail Facts and Figures." "Facts about Marketing to Children."

59. Richard Harwood, *Hope Unraveled: The People's Retreat and Our Way Back* (Kettering Foundation Press, 2005).

Notes to Chapter 3, The Biblical Vision of Care for the Environment

1. R. Attfield, *Environmental Philosophy: Principles and Prospects* (Avebury, 1994), contains a good historical summary of Judeo-Christian attitudes to the environment. R. B. Fowler, *The Greening of Protestant Thought* (The University of North Carolina Press, 1995), provides a contemporary history of the rise of Christian environmental stewardship.

2. M. S. Northcott, *The Environment and Christian Ethics* (Cambridge University Press, 1996).

3. Translation from Calvin's *Commentary on Genesis 2:15* (Christian Classics Ethereal Library), at www.ccel.org/c/calvin.

4. Matthew Hale, *The Primitive Origination of Mankind* (London, 1677), quoted by Attfield, *Environmental Philosophy.*

5. S. Sivasundaram, *Nature and the Godly Empire: Science and Evangelical Mission in the Pacific, 1795–1850* (Cambridge University Press, 1995).

6. The view that many of the world's environmental ills are due to exploitation as a result of abusing the command in Genesis that mankind should have dominion over the world was propounded by Lynn White Jr., "The Historical Roots of Our Ecological Crisis," *Science,* 155 (1967), pp. 1203–7. This historical interpretation has been thoroughly refuted by many authors, including those in R. J. Berry, ed., *The Care of Creation—Focusing Concern and Action* (InterVarsity, 2000). See P. Harrison, "Having Dominion: Genesis and the Mastery of Nature," in R. J. Berry, ed., *Environmental Stewardship: Critical Perspectives—Past and Present* (T&T Clark, 2006), pp. 17–31.

7. The prominent secular humanist E. O. Wilson of Harvard University has written an open letter to the evangelical Christian community asking precisely that they should make care of the environment a higher priority and pointing out the strong reasons for doing so (E. O. Wilson, *The Creation: An Appeal to Save Life on Earth* [W.W. Norton, 2006]). It is ironic that a humanist should have to plead with evangelicals to join in a common cause when it should really have been the other way round.

8. See J. Jones, *Jesus and the Earth* (SPCK, 2003), for a discussion of Jesus as the savior not only of humanity but also of the planet and the whole cosmos.

9. Ps 104; 147:8, 16–19; Eccl 12:1; Isa 40:28; 43:15; Rom 1:25; Eph 3:9; 1 Pet 4:19; Rev 4:11.

10. Example from Stephen Rand, quoted by R. Bauckham, "Stewardship and Relationship," in Berry, ed., *Care of Creation,* p. 142. Available from www.jubilee-centre.org/engage/cambridge_papers.

11. www.jri.org.uk.

12. See Berry, ed., *Care of Creation.*

13. The full text of the declaration is at www.christiansandclimate.org.

14. www.nrpe.org.

15. Interfaith Power and Light is part of the Regeneration Project www.theregenerationproject.org; or chapters can be accessed through the Greater Washington Interfaith Power and Light Web site, www.gwipl.org.

16. http://en.arocha.org/home.

17. J. Coffey, *The Abolition of the Slave Trade: Christian Conscience and Political Action*, Cambridge Paper, 15 no. 2 (Jubilee Centre, 2006); available for free download from www.jubilee-centre.org/engage/cambridge_papers.

18. See G. Goldsworthy, *The Goldsworthy Trilogy* (Paternoster Press, 2000).

19. For an overview of Old Testament views on ecology and the Earth see C. Wright, *Old Testament Ethics for the People of God* (InterVarsity Press, 2004), ch. 4.

20. Gen 1:30; 2:7; 6:17; Ps 104:29.

21. For example, see White, "Historical Roots," and the series of essays which analyse and refute Lynn White's conjectures in Berry, ed., *Care of Creation*.

22. See Harrison, "Having Dominion," and other essays in the same book.

23. I. Hore-Lacy uses the term "responsible dominion" as the title of his book: *Responsible Dominion: A Christian Approach to Sustainable Development* (Regent College Publishing, 2006).

24. 1 Kgs 12:7; Ezek 34.

25. D. Wilkinson, *The Message of Creation* (InterVarsity Press, 2002), p. 38.

26. Speech to Conservative Party Conference 14 October 1988, www .margaretthatcher.org/speeches/displaydocument.asp?docid=107352

27. See John Stott, *The Message of Romans* (InterVarsity Press, 1994).

28. C. Ash, "On the Dangers of Christian Shorthand: "Going to Heaven,"" *Briefing*, 327 (Dec. 2005), pp. 14–16.

29. N. T. Wright, *New Heavens, New Earth: The Biblical Picture of the Christian Hope* (Grove Books, 1999). See also 1 Pet 1:4–5; 1 Cor 13:12.

30. D. Russell, *The "New Heavens and New Earth": Hope for Creation in Jewish Apocalyptic and the New Testament* (Studies in Biblical Apocalyptic Literature 1; Visionary, 1996), pp. 206–9.

31. This heading comes from the title of a book by D. Cosden, *The Heavenly Good of Earthly Work* (Hendrickson, 2006).

Notes to Chapter 4, The Biblical Vision of Sustainable Living

1. Matt 3:3; Mark 1:3; Luke 3:4–6; John 1:23.

2. See Matt 21:13; Mark 11:17; Luke 19:46.

3. Specifically Rev 1:17; 2:8; and 22:13; and Isa 44:6; and 48:12.

4. Specifically Isa 54:11–12.

5. See, for example, Ps 45:17; 71:18; 78:4; 89:1.

6. Unlike other "create" verbs that are variously translated "do," "make," "form," or "mold," which are also used of humans.

7. See, for example, Hos 4:1–3; Jer 31.

8. See, for example, Deut 29:22–28; Lam 1:9; 5:4–14.

9. Compare Ps 96, 98, and 148.

10. See, for example, 2 Cor 8:2; 1 Thess 1:6; Jas 1:2; Heb 10:34.

11. We are indebted to Marika Rose for this observation, as well as for her forensic and extremely helpful comments on this entire chapter.

Notes to Chapter 5 , The Biblical Practice of Sustainable Living

1. Attributed, translated by Isaiah Berlin.

2. For more details on this, see Schluter and Ashcroft, eds., *Jubilee Manifesto,* on which this chapter draws heavily.

3. N. T. Wright, *Jesus and the Victory of God* (SPCK, 1996), pp. 294–96. Italics original.

4. For more details see W. Brueggemann, *The Land* (SPCK, 1978); also N. Spencer, *Where Do We Go from Here? A Christian Perspective on Roots and Mobility Today* (Jubilee Centre, 2003).

5. See Hore-Lacy, *Responsible Dominion,* for further reflection on this idea.

6. Neither biblical nor extra-biblical texts record it ever happening, although neither do they record the Day of Atonement. The corruption of most of Israel and Judah's kings, and the protests of the prophets suggest that, in this instance, absence of evidence can be equated with evidence of absence. Chris Wright suggests that it was an early law that was quickly neglected because it became ineffectual against the scale of social disruption (*Old Testament Ethics for the People of God,* p. 205, n. 12).

7. The "robbers" of Mark 11:17, etc., derives from Jer 7:11 which uses the word "parisim," meaning not so much "swindlers" as "brigands," "those who rob with violence," or even "revolutionaries."

8. See M. Schluter, "What Charter for Humanity? Defining the Destination for Development," *Cambridge Papers,* 15, 3 (September 2006). Available from www.jubilee-centre.org/engage/cambridge_papers.

9. This section relies on the work of Paul Mills, particularly as it appears in his sections on economy and finance in Schluter and Ashcroft, eds., *Jubilee Manifesto,* for which the author would like to register his thanks.

10. The parallel story of how the king in question "went to a distant country to have himself appointed king" but was followed by "a delegation" of "his subjects [who] hated him" and didn't "want [him] to be [their] king"

sounds odd to modern ears but was almost certainly a reference to the story of Archelaus, son of Herod the Great, "who went to Rome in 4 BC to petition Augustus for the kingdom of his father, was followed by a deputation of Jews protesting against him, and was given half the kingdom." See Wright, *Jesus and the Victory of God*, pp. 632–39 (633), for this and for an interpretation of the parable as a whole and the corresponding one in Matthew.

11. So the master says in Luke 19:22–23: "You knew, did you, that I am a hard man, taking out what I did not put in, and reaping what I did not sow? Why then didn't you put my money on deposit, so that when I came back, I could have collected it with interest?"

12. Indeed his remarks about giving in Matt 5:42 and Luke 6:34–35 suggest quite the opposite.

13. For further details see Wright, *Old Testament Ethics for the People of God*, pp. 146–81.

14. Lev 19:35–36; Deut 25:13–16.

15. Mills, Paul, "Economy," in Schluter and Ashcroft, eds., *Jubilee Manifesto*, pp. 225–26.

16. See, for example, Deut 24:10 or Ezek 18:10–16.

17. Paul Mills, "Finance," in Schluter and Ashcroft, eds., *Jubilee Manifesto*, p. 204.

18. For more on the topic of slavery, see Schluter and Ashcroft, eds., *Jubilee Manifesto*, pp. 193–95.

19. C. Wright, *Living as the People of God* (InterVarsity, 1983), p. 92.

20. Wright, *Old Testament Ethics for the People of God*, p. 190.

21. W. D. Davies, *Gospel and the Land: Early Christianity and Jewish Territorial Doctrine* (University of California Press, 1974), p. 368.

22. Graham Tomlin, *The Provocative Church* (SPCK, 2002), p. 78.

23. Wright, *Old Testament Ethics for the People of God*, p. 118. For thoughts on new media and communities of interest, see N. Spencer, "Forever Engaged?" *Third Way* (May 2002), pp. 12–15.

24. T. J. Gorringe, *A Theology of the Built Environment: Justice, Empowerment, Redemption* (Cambridge University Press, 2002), p. 1.

25. Flora Thompson, *Lark Rise* (Oxford University Press, 1939), p. 69.

26. Oliver O'Donovan, "Where Were You . . . ?" in Berry, ed., *Care of Creation*, pp. 90–93 (90).

27. See Mark 2:23–28/Matt 12:1–8/Luke 6:1–5; Mark 3:1–6/Matt 12:9–14/Luke 6:6–11; 13:10–17; 14:1–6; John 5:2–18; 9:1–41.

28. Wright, *Jesus and the Victory of God*, pp. 390–96.

29. N. Lohfink, *Options for the Poor: The Basic Principle of Liberation Theology in the Light of the Bible* (BIBAL, 1987), quoted in Wright, *Old Testament Ethics for the People of God*, pp. 172–80.

30. "The First Epistle of Clement to the Corinthians," in A. Louth, ed., *Early Christian Writings: The Apostolic Fathers* (Penguin, 1968; rev. 1987), p. 23.

31. "Letter to Diognetus," in Louth, ed., *Early Christian Writings*, pp. 144–45.

32. I am indebted to my coauthor Bob White for making this point to me—*Nick Spencer.*

Notes to Chapter 6, A Vision of Sustainable Living Today

1. See the Preface for a description of the work of the Jubilee Centre, in England.

2. Schluter and Ashcroft, eds., *Jubilee Manifesto.*

3. See M. Schluter, "What Charter for Humanity? Defining the Destination for Development," *Cambridge Papers*, 15, 3 (September 2006).

4. The example of post-communist Ukraine is instructive here. See Nick Spencer, *Asylum and Immigration: A Christian Perspective on a Polarised Debate* (Paternoster, 2004), pp. 92–93.

5. "Economists have moved steadily away from seeing location as a determinant of human experience. Indeed, economic progress is seen as a release from location's grip on our lives . . . Modern theories of economic development dismiss geography as a negligible factor in progress." See "Bottlenecks," Partha Dasgupta's review of Jared Diamond's *Collapse: How Societies Choose to Fail or Succeed* (Allen Lane, 2005), *London Review of Books*, 10, 27.

Notes to Chapter 7, The Practice of Sustainable Living Today

1. Ginny Vroblesky, "Robin Pie and Egret Feathers." *A Rocha USA Newsletter Summer 2005*, www.arocha.org, USANews–Issue 9.

2. Tom Tiger, "Birdwatchers Must Be Protected from Chainsaw Huggers." www.purewatergazette.net/ttbirdwatching.htm.

3. Richard Harwood, *Hope Unraveled: The People's Retreat and the Our Way Back* (Ohio: Kettering Foundation Press, 2005).

4. Maggie Eldridge, Neal Elliott, William Prindle, Katie Ackerly, Shon "Skip" Laitner, Vanessa McKinney, Steve Nadel, and Max Neubauer. "Energy Efficiency: The First Fuel for a Clean Energy Future Resources for

Meeting Maryland's Electricity Needs." February 2008, American Council for an Energy Efficient Economy, www.aceee.org/pubs/e082.htm.

5. "Socially Responsible Investing Facts." Social Investment Forum: www.socialinvest.org.

6. Duncan Clark and Richie Unterberger. "Money Matters," in *Shopping With a Conscience* (New York: Rough Guides, 2007), p. 207.

7. Anne Moore Odell, "Three Major Banks Sign the Carbon Principles." February 13, 2008. www.socialfunds.com/news.

8. Eileen Claussen, "Climate Change and the Business Challenge, in *Ignition,* eds. Jonathan Isham and Sissel Waage (Island Press, 2007), p. 220.

9. Elizabeth Wasserman, "Running on Energy. Legislative analysis as of September 24, 2007." CQ Public Affairs Collection. http://library.cqpress.com.

10. Gordon Faircloth, "E-Waste from Computers Discarded in West Turns Up in China's Exported Trinkets," *Wall Street Journal* (July 12, 2007), p. B 1.

11. Sarah Tarver-Wahlquist, "The Perils of E-waste." *Co-op America Quarterly* 73 (Fall 2007), p. 28.

12. See such articles as: "More evangelicals say God is green" by Alex Johnson. MSNB. November 6, 2007. www.msnbc.msn.com or "Evangelicals a Liberal Can Love." Nicholas D. Kristof. *The New York Times* (February 2, 2008) www.nytimes.com.

13. Peter Harris, *Kingfisher's Fire: A Story of Hope for God's Earth.* (Oxford, UK and Grand Rapids, Mich.: Monarch, 2008), p. 165. See pages 161–65 for a more in-depth look at these issues from a non-American perspective.

14. Harris, p. 159.

15. Andrew C. Revkin, "Issuing a Bold Challenge to the U.S. Over Climate," *The New York Times* (January 22, 2008) www.nytimes.com.

16. "UK should name and shame USA on climate change says churches' agency." *Ekklesia,* December 18, 2007. www.ekklesia.co.uk/node/6477.

17. For further information see the *New York Times* interview with Kevin Conrad. www.nytimes.com/dotearth.

18. "Canada flounders on issue of climate change." Canada Abroad. December 4, 2004. www.cbc.ca/news/viewpoint/vp_burman/2007/12/canada_flounders_on_issue_of_c.html.

19. "In Depth: Kyoto and Beyond. Canada-Kyoto Timeline." *CBC News In Depth,* February 14, 2007. www.cbc.ca/news/background/kyoto/timeline.html.

20. "Climate Protection Strategies and Best Practices Guide. November 2007." US Conference of Mayors Web site. www.usmayors.org/climateprotection.

21. Seattle Office of the Mayor. "US Conference of Mayors Climate Protection Summit." www.seattle.gov/mayor/climate.

22. Lisa Stiffler, "U.S. mayors meet in Seattle to push for a green revolution." Thursday, November 1, 2007. http://seattlepi.nwsource.com.

23. Debra DeHaney-Howard, "Blueprints for Building a Green City." November 19, 2007. US Mayors Conference of Mayors Climate Protection Center, Conference Articles. www.usmayors.org.

24. Judy Sheahan, "Panel Explores How Land Use Strategies Can Reduce a Communities Carbon Footprint," November 19, 2007. US Conference of Mayors Climate Protection Center, Conference Articles.www.usmayors.org.

25. Brett Rosenberg, "Growing Transit and Expanding Infrastructure." November 19, 2007 US Conference of Mayors Climate Protection Center Conference Articles. www.usmayors.org.

26. "Lake Mead Water Could Dry Up by 2021." *Environment News Service:* San Diego, California, February 12, 2008. www.ens-newswire.com. See also Bryan Walsh. "Postcard: Lake Mead," *Time* (March 31, 2008), p. 14.

27. Much of the information in this section taken from: "Learning from State Action, December 2007 Update." Pew Center on Global Climate Change. www.pewclimate.org.

28. Judy Pasternak, "Coal is no longer on front burner." *Los Angeles Times* (January 18, 2008) www.latimes.com/news.

29. Barringer, Felicity. "US report ties human risk to climate change." *International Herald Tribune,* Monday, March 23, 2009. http://www.iht.com/bin/printfriedly.php?id=21012446.

30. Maryland Commission on Climate Change. *Climate Action Plan, Interim Report to the Governor and the Maryland General Assembly* (January 14, 2008), pp. 3, 14.

31. "How U.S. State GHG Emissions Compare Internationally," report by the World Resources Institute. October 2, 2006. www.wri.org/stories/2006/10/how-u-s-state-ghg-emissions-compare-internationally#

32. See "Greener Future, Stronger Economy," February 19, 2008, www.gov.bc.ca/bcbudget; "Oh, Canada!" by Alan Durning, March 13, 2008, http://gristmill.grist.org/; and "Provinces free to tackle climate, Ottawa says" by Justine Hunter, *Globe and Mail,* February 21, 2008, www.theglobeandmail.com.

33. Mark S. Winfield, "Climate Change and Canadian Energy Policy: Policy Contradiction and Policy Failure." *Behind the Headlines.* Canadian International Council, Vol. 65 Number 1 (January 2008), p. 6, www.pembina.org.

34. Center for Public Justice. "Government." *Guidelines for Government and Citizenship.* www.cpjustice.org/content/government.

35. Jim Skillen, President of Center for Public Justice, personal communication March 2008.

36. For a further discussion on carbon taxes see: "The Bottom Line on Carbon Taxes." World Resources Institute. June 2008, www.wri.org/climate/usclimate). And Herman E. Daly, "Climate Policy: from 'know how' to 'do now.'" Presentation to American Meteorological Society, November 13, 2007, available at www.commondreams.org/archive/2008/05/13/8925/.

37. See John Adams, "The Failure of Seat Belt Legislation," in M. Verweij and M. Thompson, eds., *Clumsy Solutions for a Complex World: Governance, Politics and Plural Perceptions* (Palgrave Macmillan, 2006). This has led Adams elsewhere (*Risk* [UCL Press, 1995]) to suggest, somewhat tongue-in-cheek, that one of the best means of improving total road safety would be to affix to the steering wheel of every car a giant spike pointing directly at the driver's heart!

38. This line of reasoning, known as the Khazzoom-Brookes Postulate, argues that "cheaper energy has two effects: the substitution of energy for other factors of production, which are now relatively more expensive, and the release of income which can then be reinvested in new production capacity, and so on. As a result . . . developed countries have, since the Industrial Revolution, seen 'rising energy productivity outstripped by rising total factor productivity, hence *rising* energy consumption alongside rising energy productivity.'" See House of Lords Science and Technology Committee 2nd Report of Session 2005–2006, *Energy Efficiency,* Vol. 1, ch. 3, for further details. The Khazzoom-Brookes Postulate is, however, hotly contested.

39. House of Commons EAC, *Keeping the Lights On: Nuclear, Renewables and Climate Change,* Sixth Report of Session 2005–2006, Vol. 1, para. 31.

40. "Electricity Solutions for a Carbon Constrained World." 2007 Summer Seminar, 11, *EPRI Journal.* http://my.epri.com/portal/server.pt?

41. Energy Information Administration. "Energy Trends to 2030." *Annual Energy Outlook 2007,* p. 9, www.eia.doe.gov.

42. By which we mean nuclear fission. If and when nuclear fusion becomes an economically viable option, the picture would change significantly, with an effectively unlimited, although by no means risk free, supply of electricity.

43. For information on nuclear power in the UK see www.world-nuclear.org/info/inf84.htm.

44. Energy Technology Assessment Center. "The Power to Reduce CO_2 Emissions: The Full Portfolio." Discussion Paper prepared for the EPRI 2007 Summer Institute, pp. 3–7.

45. George Monbiot, *Heat: How to Stop the Planet Burning* (Allen Lane, 2006), p. 91.

46. See Parliamentary Office of Science and Technology, Postnote no. 268, "Carbon Footprint of Electricity Generation," October 2006.

47. See House of Commons EAC, *Keeping the Lights On,* Vol. 1, para. 82.

48. Sustainable Development Commission, *The Role of Nuclear Power in a Low Carbon Economy* (March 2006), p. 10.

49. Greg Allen, "U.S. Gives Nuclear Power a Second Look," *NPR,* April 15, 2008, www.npr.org.

50. Mitch Weiss, "Drought Could Force Nuke-Plant Shutdowns," January 24, 2008, www.sfgate.com.

51. Idaho National Laboratory/Nuclear Power Industry, 14.

52. Energy Technology Assessment Center, 3–9.

53. "Oceans of Energy." Natural Resources Canada, www.nrc-cnrc.gc.ca/eng/news/nrc/2008/04/08/cornett.html.

54. Massachusetts Institute of Technology, "The Future of Geothermal Energy: Impact of Enhanced Geothermal Systems (EGS) on the United States in the 21st Century." http://geothermal.inel.gov.

55. Environment California, "Making Solar Power Mainstream," www.environmentcalifornia.org/energy/million-solar-roofs/fact-sheet2.

56. Jonathan Lash, "Environmental Stories to Watch in 2008." World Resources Institute. Remarks on December 18, 2007 at the National Press Club Briefing for Journalists, p. 8, www.wri.org.

57. Ibid., 16.

58. "Renewables 2007: Global Status Report." REN21 (Renewable Energy Policy Network for the 21st Century) 2008, p. 6, www.ren21.net.

59. American Wind Energy Association, "Wind Energy Potential." www.awea.org/faq/wwt_potential.html.

60. Monbiot, *Heat,* p. 108.

61. Renewables 2007, 32–34.

62. Dennis Keeney and Claudia Nanninga. "Biofuel and Global Bio-diversity," Institute for Agriculture and Trade Policy, April 2008, p. 5, www.iatp.org.

63. For more information on hydrogen research see the Energy Efficiency and Renewable Energy Web site: www1.eere.energy.gov/hydrogenandfuelcells.

64. See, for example, http://news.bbc.co.uk/1/hi/programmes/newsnight/archive/2208013.stm.

65. National Academy of Engineering, "The Hydrogen Economy: Opportunities, Costs, Barriers, and R&D Needs" (2004), quoted in Monbiot, *Heat,* p. 164.

66. Amory B. Lovins, "Energy End-Use Efficiency." Commissioned by Inter Academy Council, Amersterdam, as part of its 2005–2006 study "Transitions to Sustainable Energy Systems," Rocky Mountain Institute, www.rmi.org.

67. Bill Prindle and Maggie Eldridge, American Council for an Energy-Efficient Economy, and Mike Eckhardt and Alyssa Frederick, American Council on Renewable Energy, "The Twin Pillars of Sustainable Energy: Synergies between Energy Efficiency and Renewable Energy Technology and Policy," May 2007, ACEEE Report Number E074, www.aceee.org, 33.

68. Monbiot, *Heat,* p. 82; House of Lords Science and Technology Committee, 2nd Report of Session 2005–2006, *Energy Efficiency,* Vol. 1: Report, para. 2.14.

69. House of Lords Science and Technology Committee, 2nd Report of Session 2005–2006, *Energy Efficiency,* Vol. 1: Report, para. 2.14.

70. House of Lords Science and Technology Committee, 4th Report of Session 2003–2004, *Renewable Energy: Practicalities,* Appendix 11: "An Energy Internet?"

71. House of Lords Science and Technology Committee, 2nd Report of Session 2005–2006, *Energy Efficiency,* Vol. 1: Report, para. 2.14.

72. House of Lords Science and Technology Committee, 4th Report of Session 2003–2004, *Renewable Energy: Practicalities,* Appendix 11.

73. For more information see www.sd-commission.org.uk/communities summit/show_case_study.php/00035.html.

74. For example see Civano, Arizona. www.terrain.org/unsprawl/5/ and www.smartcommunities.ncat.org/success/civano.shtml (accesssed July 11, 2008).

75. "The Twin Pillars of Sustainable Energy," p. 24.

76. "The Twin Pillars of Sustainable Energy," p. 5.

77. "Gas for the Greenhouse," *Nature* 442 (2006), p. 499.

78. World Resources Institute. "A Snapshot of U.S. Energy Options Today: Climate Change and Energy Security Impacts and Tradeoffs in 2025," 13A. www.wri.org.

79. World Coal Institute, "Where is Coal Found," www.worldcoal.org.

80. "The Power to Reduce CO2 Emissions," 3–10.

81. House of Commons Science and Technology Committee, *Meeting UK Energy and Climate Needs,* Vol. 1, Summary, p. 3.

82. "Waiting on the Climate to Change: It's Time To Take the Opportunity to Invest in Carbon Capture and Sequestration," Center for American Progress, www.americanprogress.org.

83. Elizabeth Rosenthal, "Europe Turns Back to Coal, Raising Climate Fears," *The New York Times* (April 23, 2008), www.nytimes.com.

84. Organization for Economic Cooperation and Development/International Energy Agency, *Prospects for CO2 Capture and Storage* (OECD, 2004), quoted in Monbiot, *Heat,* p. 89.

85. Totten, "Honey I Shrunk the Planet's Footprint." February 14, 2007.

86. "NRC expects applications for 34 nuclear power plants by 2010," *EERE News,* July 16, 2008, www.eere.energy.gov.

87. House of Commons EAC, *Keeping the Lights On,* Vol. 1, Summary, para. 7.

88. Intergovernmental Panel on Climate Change. "About the IPCC," www.ipcc.ch/about/index.htm.

89. Stern, *Economics of Climate Change,* p. 454.

90. "Economics of Climate Change." *Bangkok Post,* www.bangkok post.com/130708_Perspective/13Jul2008_pers005.php (accessed April 16, 2009).

91. "Fact Sheet: Stepping Up International Action on Climate Change, The Road to Copenhagen," www.unfccc.int/files/press/backgrounders/application/pdf/the_road_to_copenhagen.pdf (accessed August 20, 2008).

92. Peter N. Spotts, "Bangkog talks to set timetable on global warming pact" *The Christian Science Monitor.* March 13, 2008, p. 4, www.csmonitor.com (accessed April 3, 2008).

93. Mark Lyons, "Climate change catastrophe by degrees," *Guardian* (August 7, 2008), www.guardian.co.uk.

94. Spotts, 3.

95. "The long-term perspective: scientific and socio-economic aspects relevant to adaptation and mitigation, consistent with the objectives and provisions of the Convention, and in the context of sustainable development." In *Climate Change 2007: Synthesis Report,* An Assessment of the Intergovernmental Panel on Climate Change, November 2007.

96. Daniel Bodansky and Elliot Diringer, "Towards an Integrated Multi-Track Climate Framework," prepared for the Pew Center on Global Climate Change, December 2007, www.pewclimate.org; and Elliot Diringer, "Statement of Elliot Diringer, Pew Center on Global Climate Change, January 24, 2008, regarding International Climate Change Negotiations, Bali and the Path Toward a Post–2012 Climate Treaty," submitted to the Committee on Foreign Relations, United States Senate.

97. Bodansky and Diringer, 23.

98. Yvo de Boer, "Address to the World Petroleum Congress Sustainability Luncheon," Madrid, July 3, 2008 (www.unfccc.int), 4.

99. Yvo de Boer, 3.

100. Anna Mudeva, "East Europeans Fear Climate Policy Pinch," *Reuters* (July 28, 2008).

101. United Nations Framework Convention on Climate Change. "Fact Sheet: Financing Climate Change. Investment and financial flows for a strengthened response to climate change," www.unfccc.int.

102. Herman E. Daly, "Climate Policy: from 'know how' to 'do now.'" presentation at the American Meteorological Society, November 13, 2007.

103. Ben Lowe, Outreach Director for A Rocha USA, e-mail to author on June 25, 2008.

104. As quoted in "UN chief say US must take lead on Climate Change," www.ccchina.gov.cn.

105. Herman Ott as quoted in *Curbing Climate Change* by Colin Woodard. CQ Public Affairs Collection, February 1, 2007, 18.

106. Herman E. Daly, "Science, Religion and Sustainable Development: Reflections on the 1900th Anniversary of the Book of Revelation for the Conference: Revelation and Environment," September, 1995, Isle of Patmos, www2.iath.virginia.edu/cecmpe/patmos.html.

Notes to Chapter 8, A New Creation

1. Stern, *Economics of Climate Change*, ch. 21, p. 450.

SUBJECT INDEX

Scripture Index